Also by Malcolm W. Browne

The New Face of War

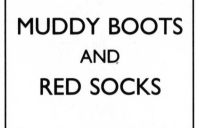

MUDDY BOOTS
AND
RED SOCKS

MUDDY BOOTS

AND

RED SOCKS

A REPORTER'S LIFE

Malcolm W. Browne

TIMES BOOKS

RANDOM HOUSE

Library of Congress Cataloging-in-Publication Data

Browne, Malcolm W.
    Muddy boots and red socks: a reporter's life / Malcolm W.
  Browne.—1st ed.
      p.   cm.
    Includes index.
    ISBN 0-8129-6352-0
    1. Browne, Malcolm W.   2. War correspondents—United
  States—Biography.   3. Foreign correspondents—United
  States—Biography.
  I. Title.
  PN4874.B783A3   1993
  070.4'333'092—dc20[B]   93-16418

Design: Timothy O'Keeffe
Manufactured in the United States of America
24689753
First Edition

To the dear dead whose sparks lighted my life

An Explanation

In Viet Nam it was said that there were two kinds of observers: those who heard about the war from others and those with muddy boots. I preferred the latter category.

As a GI in the fifties I came to loathe olive drab, and when the 8th Army PX in Korea had a sale on red socks I bought the lot. I've worn red socks ever since, which assures me of a match even when one disappears. And I still like red.

Contents

Introduction: An Apology

Memoirs are all very well for adulterous royalty, junk-bond convicts and the like, but for an ordinary person to expect his observations to interest strangers is probably foolish.

Still, a journalist has one claim to attention: during a working career, he or she witnesses a lot of things that other people merely read about or watch on the shadowbox. And in my experience, secondhand acquaintance with a news event is scarcely more faithful to reality than a reflection from a murky, rippling pond. That's an awkward confession for a journalist, but there it is. No secondhand news can touch the real thing.

As a journalist, I've had ringside seats at some historic spectacles during my sixty-odd years, and if I can't claim to have become wise, I've at least acquired a patina (or tarnish) of opinions.

As I sketch a checkered career I'll touch on the erratic personal lives of other journalists, and look at the interplay of journalism with governments and societies. Along the way, I hope to convey some advice on how to read newspapers or watch television while maintaining a firm grasp of reality.

A lot of Americans these days seem to regard journalists as subhuman "foul feeders," as one of Conan Doyle's press-hating characters called us. In our detractors' view, journalists derive their chief satisfaction from destroying the good names of good people.

I do not admit that view. Moreover, I believe that as an honest journalist gains experience in his trade he often becomes adept at observation and shrewd judgment, if only in the sense that a mature burglar finds it second nature to crack a safe as easily as a bread box. Most of us are not drunks, plagiarists or sybarites, and we do not sensationalize stories to "sell papers" (indeed, publishers survive by selling advertisements, not papers). Our "scoops" do not make us rich, and we take no particular pleasure from character assassination.

If we are sometimes less than reverent of the symbols other people cherish—flags, yellow ribbons, medals, hymns, wealth, motherhood, prizes, titles—it doesn't mean that we respect nothing. More than most people, we admire honesty and courage, because we know how rare those qualities are. If we sneer at the hyperbole and mawkish sentiment that permeate most forms of communication, it is because journalists, more than many other people, spend their lives boiling in the caustic bleach of reality.

We are eyes and ears, and our observations, however flawed and filtered, are the stuff of history: the archival mother lode that scholars mine when they cannot witness the show themselves—which, by the way, is usually the case. Critics accuse us of skewing our product to suit personal prejudices, but the fact is that most journalists in the 1990s are compelled by conscience and editorial policy to go out of their way to be fair. Indeed, "balance" in journalism can go to ridiculous extremes. Balance zealots today might insist that a reporter covering a Nazi concentration camp make his second paragraph read: "Mr. Himmler said, however, . . ."

Recognizing our manifold shortcomings, we journalists

press on as best we can. The results will never come up to the standards of even our most lenient critics, because the role of the journalist is to translate observation into news copy. Unfortunately, the Second Law of Thermodynamics—an immutable law of physics—decrees that information is always lost in such a transaction. No news report is any more reliable than the flawed observer who prepares it, and news will always be tainted by perspective and personal judgment, right or wrong. At root, journalism is subjective—never objective—and the best we practitioners can do is to try to be fair.

At various stages I've been a soldier, a laboratory worker and a journalist, and all three trades were instructive. As a journalist I worked for three newspapers (including the greatest of them all, *The New York Times*); three wire services (the Associated Press, United Press International and the defunct International News Service); a television network (ABC); several radio networks and a science magazine (*Discover*). I've also contributed to more magazines, journals and broadcasts than I like to remember.

I've covered a great assortment of twentieth-century endeavor and mayhem on every continent except Australia, I can understand a smattering of a half dozen languages, and I've met a lot of famous people. I've never been fired, and I've won some prizes. Best of all, I've savored a range of experiences granted to few people other than journalists.

A survivor by instinct, I've learned how to walk safely through minefields of both the literal and figurative kind, and since I can't take this skill with me, I'm seizing this chance accorded by Peter Osnos—friend, fellow correspondent and Random House editor—to set down some reflections. They are the bequest of a poor man to his beloved heirs.

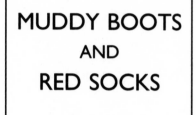

MUDDY BOOTS
AND
RED SOCKS

BLOOD, INK AND TEARS

I DON'T THINK MANY journalists take pleasure from human suffering, but since this is a personal chronicle, I have to admit to having sometimes profited from others' pain. It wasn't intentional, but that doesn't help. Journalists inadvertently influence events they cover, and although the effects are sometimes for the good, they can also be tragic. Either way, when death is the outcome, psychic scars remain.

After a while, the flood of death the average newsman witnesses begins to numb the senses and feelings. But some deaths continue to haunt newsmen throughout their lives, and for me, five of them stand out. One of my ghosts was an aged Buddhist monk. The other four were simple merchants who faced a firing squad for trying to profit from war. Many people, including journalists, profit from war; but some are unlucky enough to pay with their lives.

History treated the five deaths I'm speaking of in very different ways. The spectacular self-immolation of the Buddhist monk made headlines, helped to bring down a government, changed the course of a war and found a place in history books. The deaths of the four merchants, who died as victims of an anti-black-market campaign (that was generally applauded by the press) were mere footnotes in a day of news. They were forgotten by most people before their blood was dry, but I haven't forgotten them.

I get ahead of myself, however.

That Saigon should have been the scene of some of my most revolting memories seems strange, because Saigon is a beautiful place that enchanted me from the first moment I saw it. Its magic image began to form when I was a kid in New York City, catching my first whiff of a spice from the bark of a tree called Saigon cassia—a close relative of cinnamon. I'll always associate the name Saigon with that delicious smell.

The glory of Saigon for me was compounded from a thousand sights and sounds and odors, some delightful, some merely memorable. One of the most pervasive images I retain of that fascinating city, where I lived for about seven years, is of tamarind trees—arboreal patriarchs that arched over downtown streets, bearing sour, black, beanlike pods of fruit, and shading pedestrians and cyclists from the equatorial sun.

Saigon needed great trees, not just for shade, but to soften the ugliness of most of its architecture. The city's dwellings were mostly undistinguished two- or three-story cracker boxes faced with pastel stucco and barred, glassless windows, but the charm of Saigon was in its streets and people, not its buildings. The death that came to haunt those lovely streets seemed incongruous indeed.

Strollers loved Nguyen Hue, the wide boulevard leading from city hall to the Saigon River, where an annual Tet flower market exploded with color. The gingerbread facade of the city hall overlooking Nguyen Hue won no architectural prizes, but I fondly remember it as the place where Le Lieu and I were married in 1966, with François Nivolon, *Le Figaro*'s Saigon correspondent, acting as my best man. Thirteen years later when I beheld city hall adorned with a gigantic painting of Ho Chi Minh, it seemed that something had died.

The time of day in Saigon I loved best was dusk, which comes at around seven P.M. all year round. That was the time when office workers and shopkeepers headed home on their bikes, permeating the town with the tinkle of bells—a gentler sound than the blasts of our Western car horns and electronic sirens.

The stars of the show were Saigon's lovely girls and women, who serenely pedaled along in their conical palm-leaf hats, silk trousers and brilliantly colored *ao-dai* dresses, which billowed behind their bikes like the plumes of exotic birds. Alas, the new Asia, from Tokyo to Mandalay, is divesting itself of the poetry of traditional garb.

With evening came the lighting of gasoline lanterns and a symphony of food odors—the pungent smell of *nuoc-mam* fish sauce, the mouth-watering aroma of noodle soups, the reek of durian (sometimes called "jack fruit") and the scent of curry spiced with Saigon cassia.

There were special evening sounds, too—the tock-tock of noodle vendors' sticks, the croaking of satisfied geckos gorged on rich mosquito dinners, and the tuneless music of Vietnamese folk opera weeping from a million portable radios slung from the hammocks and mosquito nets of Saigon's street people.

But in the summer of 1963, Saigon was in turmoil, and events were moving toward a crisis that would change both the United States and Viet Nam (not to mention my personal life). The picturesque rush-hour crowds began to include clusters of angry monks, conspicuous in their saffron robes and carrying flags and banners instead of their traditional begging bowls.

Despite what President Kennedy and his advisers were saying, the war against the Viet Cong that summer was going badly, and far from "winning hearts and minds," the American war effort was alienating growing numbers of Vietnamese. An occupying army is never popular, and by 1963, American military men and civilian advisers with plentiful supplies of the dollars sought by local bar girls were becoming ubiquitous. Middle-class Vietnamese, including many who had initially welcomed the *co van my*—the American advisers—began to feel as Britons had during World War II: that the Americans were "overpaid, oversexed and over here."

Many Vietnamese held President Ngo Dinh Diem responsible for the American invasion, and his popular support, such as it was, eroded.

Diem, like President Kennedy, was a Catholic and the scion of a large and influential family. Shrewdly, the leaders of South Viet Nam's normally easygoing Buddhist community (as well as the Viet Cong) spotted a chance to exploit the unpopular American connection—including its Catholic associations—as a chink in the Ngo government's armor.

The crisis came because of a flag.

On May 8, the ceremonial birthday of the Buddha, marchers in the central Vietnamese city of Hue tried to display the five-colored Buddhist flag in defiance of a government order. Central Viet Nam, however, was ruled as a satrapy by one of President Diem's brothers, Ngo Dinh Can: an authoritarian Catholic hated by Buddhists, human-rights activists and a lot of other people, and he cracked down hard.

When the Hue marchers took to the streets with their Buddhist flags, police and troops attacked, and eight of the demonstrators were killed and several dozen injured. Overnight, the word of the Buddhist martyrdom spread by word of mouth, and the revolt soon reached Saigon.

Critics saw the Ngo family—and especially Can (who in 1965 faced a firing squad himself)—as guilty of making Roman Catholicism a state religion, and the Buddhists, who constituted the overwhelming majority of the population, were especially resentful. Only Catholics, it was widely believed, could hold the most important offices and jobs.

The significance of that summer's events is still hotly debated, especially by present or former American officials, journalists and military men. Some of these people were mere children in 1963, but so enduring are the issues brought to a head that summer that later generations have gone on debating them as vehemently as if they had actually been in Viet Nam in 1963.)

As an overworked, thirty-two-year-old bureau chief of the Associated Press, I regarded the Buddhist uprising merely as an important story, not a cause. Wire services do not tolerate agenda journalism, and I wholeheartedly embraced the depersonalized, factual approach of wireservice news coverage.

The office I took over in 1961 was a single ground-floor room (with a small bathroom) facing a courtyard that opened on Rue Pasteur—one of the loveliest and richest streets in the city. Our frosted-glass office window afforded no view, but a few steps from our door was the pleasantly landscaped park of Gia Long Palace, later to be occupied by President Ngo Dinh Diem, with his brother Nhu and Nhu's wife—the notorious Madam Nhu.

My Chinese-Vietnamese assistant, Ha Van Tran, and a capable office boy named Huan kept me from suffocating in the avalanche of red tape that beset all foreign correspondents, and the three of us maintained a tight ship, paying our bills and stoking the news wire night and day.

When events turned nasty I began to get reinforcements, including a tough young New Zealander named Peter Arnett, and a German photographer, Horst Faas, whose first taste of war had been as one of Germany's child soldiers in the suicidal 1945 defense of Berlin. Peter and Horst both went on to win Pulitzer prizes, and our paths have crossed frequently in the decades since then; in 1991 I was reporting for *The New York Times* from Saudi Arabia on the Persian Gulf war, while Peter was reporting the same war from the enemy capital, Baghdad, for Cable News Network.

The 1963 Buddhist story was mostly my personal beat, because I had already lived in Viet Nam for a couple of years and I knew something of the country's society and politics. Relying mainly on French to communicate, I could at least catch the drift of conversations in Vietnamese. I also had tremendous help from Le Lieu, my wife-to-be, who had been a senior official in the South Vietnamese Information Ministry and had an unerring sense of the subtleties of Vietnamese power politics.

My own feel for Viet Nam led me to believe that the Buddhist revolt would become a national revolution. But this feeling was not shared by other foreign newsmen at the time, so I was on my own when I interviewed monks at the pagodas where the foment centered. Many of the monks were barely literate sons of farming families, who had spent their entire lives in the cloistered pagodas, chanting, meditating and performing such routine ecclesiastical chores as begging for rice. But other monks had come to the pagodas as adults after leaving careers in business or the professions, and these holy men were politically sophisticated, despite their shaved heads and show of piety.

A fair number of the latter group had been educated abroad. An activist monk named Thich Quang Lien, for instance, who was particularly distrusted by American officials, had been a student at Yale.

In time, some of the monks at the four main pagodas I was watching came to trust me, although I made no pretense of sharing their religious or political beliefs. It was this trust that made me the sole foreign journalist to witness a fiery suicide that would shock the world.

All the newsmen in Saigon knew of the Buddhist threat to stage a protest suicide, but the monks themselves were in no hurry to allow anyone to die, because killing and suicide are anathema to Buddhist philosophy. Instead, the monks marched, gathered at street intersections and addressed the initially modest crowds of listeners with their battery-powered bullhorns. The Saigon police dispersed audiences but left the monks alone, aware that beating or arresting robed clerics would prompt the worst kind of publicity for a regime already under heavy criticism from liberals in the United States and Europe.

The men in saffron robes reiterated their suicide threat, which they promised to carry out if the government persisted in ignoring their demands for freedom from arbitrary arrest, for the right to public assembly, and for the right to fly the Buddhist flag in public. They also demanded an end to alleged Catholic bias in the appointment of government officials.

Early that summer, Thich Duc Nghiep, one of the monks' spokesmen, announced that two monks had volunteered for martyrs' deaths, one by disembowelment and the other by fire. I learned some gruesome details about their preparations only later, when monks told me about some experiments they had performed.

"We realized after a few trials," one said, "that although gasoline is easily ignited and burns with great heat, it is consumed too rapidly to complete the destruction of a human body and assure death. We found that by mixing equal parts of gasoline and diesel fuel we could produce a fire that was both intense and sufficiently long-lasting."

As I made the rounds of the pagodas I picked up a lot of interesting news, as well as some delicious vegetarian meals served to the monks. Despite the growing tension in the streets, the temples themselves, especially the Xa-Loi headquarters pagoda, were restful places; the monotonous chanting, the chiming of brass prayer gongs, the odor of burning joss and the stifling tropical heat could reduce even a visitor to an unwilling trance.

In the early stages of the uprising, Buddhist demonstrators had gathered by stealth, arriving at demonstration sites from separate directions in buses, cyclos (tricycle pedicabs) and blue-

and-cream Renault "Quatre Chevaux" taxis. The police were nearly always taken by surprise by such exercises, but eventually they ceased to care, convinced that the demonstrations were having no impact on the general populace. Foreign newsmen lost interest completely.

I was an exception, convinced that the monks would eventually make good their threat. And when Thich Duc Nghiep telephoned a few dozen foreign correspondents on the night of June 10 to say there would be an important event at a small pagoda the following morning, I alone took him at his word.

My Vietnamese colleague Ha Van Tran and I set out before dawn on June 11, but despite our early start, the pagoda was already packed with yellow-robed monks and gray-robed Buddhist nuns. One of the latter hastened to serve us tea, tears streaming down her face. The spokesman, Thich Duc Nghiep, spotted us and scurried over to whisper a warning that we should by no means leave until events had run their course.

The air in the little temple was suffocatingly hot and thick with joss smoke, but the atmosphere was charged with tension. The monks and nuns seemed to be pouring their souls into the chanting—a steady, monotonic drone whose cadence quickened a little every few repetitions. A half hour passed and then, at a signal from the leaders, the entire assembly fell silent and moved into the street to form a column of marchers. At their head was an old Austin sedan occupied by five monks.

As we walked along, a white police jeep approached, not to interfere, but to lead the way and clear traffic ahead of the marchers; so bored had the government become that Buddhist marches and gatherings at that point were treated as mere traffic nuisances.

But when we reached the intersection of two main streets, Phan Dinh Phung and Le Van Duyet, the car and march- ers halted and formed a circle blocking all approaches. Three monks emerged from the car, one of them old and feeble, the other two, both young, helping to support him as he walked to the center of the intersection. A horror show was at hand, I realized, and the sweat started from my brow as I cocked my camera.

The two young monks placed a square cushion on the pavement and helped the old man, Thich Quang Duc, to settle himself in the lotus position. The two assisting monks lugged a large plastic gasoline can from the car, and then, rather hastily, they sloshed the pink fluid over the seated monk, soaking his face, body, robes and cushion.

As they stepped away from him, I saw Thich Quang Duc strike a match in his lap and let it fall. Instantly, he was enveloped in a column of smoky, yellow flame.

As the breeze whipped the flames from his face I could see that although his eyes were closed his features were contorted with agony. But throughout his ordeal he never uttered a sound or changed his position, even as the smell of burning flash filled the air. A horrified moan rose from the crowd, and the ragged chanting of some of the monks was interrupted by screams and cries of anguish. Two monks unfurled a large cloth banner reading (in English) A BUDDHIST PRIEST BURNS FOR BUD-DHIST DEMANDS.

As the minutes passed, police vehicles converged on the awful scene and a fire truck pulled up to extinguish the pyre. But to prevent it from intervening, several monks prostrated themselves under its wheels and hung on, while the driver vainly blasted his horn and siren to get them to move.

Numb with shock I shot roll after roll of film, focusing and adjusting exposures mechanically and unconsciously, almost as an athlete chews gum to relieve stress. Trying hard not to perceive what I was witnessing I found myself thinking: "The sun is bright and the subject is self-illuminated, so f16 at 125th of a second should be right." But I couldn't close out the smell.

After about ten minutes the flames subsided and Thich Quang Duc pitched over, twitched convulsively and was still.

Concealed up to that moment, a wooden coffin materialized from somewhere and the monks tried to jam the body into it. But Thich Quang Duc's limbs had been roasted to rigidity, and he could not be bent enough to fit in the casket. As the procession moved off toward Xa-Loi Pagoda, his blackened arms protruded from the coffin, one of them still smoking.

A lot of things happened after that.

My photographs were published all over the world, and the Buddhist leaders displayed them to goad the Vietnamese masses to revolt. Even today in communist Saigon, one of my photographs remains affixed to the car that carried Thich Quang Duc to his death—a car now revered as a sacred relic.

Henry Cabot Lodge, who had just been named U.S. ambassador to Saigon, was in Washington at the time. When Lodge went to the Oval Office for his instructions, he told me later, he saw one of my immolation pictures on President Kennedy's desk. "We're going to have to do something about that regime," JFK remarked.

Soon afterward, Washington began reducing its assistance to Saigon, starting with a sharp reduction in donations of powdered milk. This stung, because the Saigon government earned money to pay its troops by selling U.S. agricultural surpluses to the Vietnamese people. Washington called the system "counterpart funding," and it was a vital economic prop of the Diem administration.

Partly because of the uproar my immolation photographs had caused, I became a target of various Saigon machinations that led to some hair-raising adventures.

One hot morning I was with a group of reporters that included my AP colleague Peter Arnett and David Halberstam of *The New York Times.* We arrived at a pagoda to cover a Buddhist march, only to discover that we ourselves were the center of attention. Outside the gate of the pagoda we were attacked by a dozen or so plainclothes Saigon police agents who had been instructed to rough us up and smash our cameras.

In the brief melee that followed, Peter Arnett tried to fight back but was seized by several of the goons, who hit hard, opening some cuts on Peter's face. Halberstam jumped in front of Arnett to fend off some blows, while I photographed the attack.

The fight ended as quickly as it began, but one of the cops, noticing that I had been taking pictures, approached me from behind and brought a brick crashing down on top of my camera, shattering its lens and parts but happily leaving the film intact.

We returned to our offices to lick our wounds and file stories about the incident, but before we could get any cables out, Arnett and I were arrested and told we would be charged with assaulting the plainclothes police.

The American Embassy, still in the hands of officials committed to supporting the Diem administration, declined to intervene. It was only through the prompt and effective diplomacy of New Zealand's consulate that we escaped serious consequences.

Although the Saigon government was blocking radio-photo transmissions as well as shipments of film and even cable communication, correspondents in Saigon had begun to make heavy use of "pigeons"—airline passengers who volunteered to carry news or film to news offices outside Viet Nam. Volunteering for "pigeon" service could be risky. A helpful traveler faced possible arrest by Saigon police in that summer of 1963, and the supply of pigeons fell to almost zero.

Hoping that the film in my shattered Canon camera had not been ruined, I was desperate to get it to New York and

Washington, where it would show what really happened during the pagoda fight and get Arnett and me off the hook. By a stroke of luck, Chester Bowles, the United States ambassador to India, was in Saigon on a visit, and when I talked to him, he instantly agreed to carry out my film.

A word about the late Ambassador Bowles: few politicians or diplomats I have known seemed to me as wise, right-headed, humane and free of doctrinaire bias as he. An Adlai Stevenson Democrat and civil rights leader, Bowles had been one of John Kennedy's earliest supporters, and yet, when President Kennedy surprised his early allies with his military operations in Cuba and Viet Nam, Ambassador Bowles had the courage to back away. He remained a member of the Kennedy circle, but he quietly sought to discourage American interventionism, particularly the kind that supported dictators like Diem in many parts of the world.

After Kennedy's colossal failure in the Bay of Pigs invasion of Cuba, Mr. Bowles wrote in his diary: "The Cuban fiasco demonstrates how far astray a man as brilliant and well-intentioned as Kennedy can go who lacks a basic moral reference point." I think he sized up Kennedy to a tee.

Thus, Ambassador Bowles was one of the few American friends on whom the beleaguered foreign press corps in Saigon could count, and with his help, my pictures reached the outer world—the White House as well as my AP editors. Realizing the political liability a martyred American press might mean for him, President Kennedy dispatched some of his best men to Saigon to lean on the Diem government. From then on, we newsmen had no further overt police harassment.

But the Saigon government had not settled its score with us. Rumors circulated among diplomats that several newsmen—Halberstam, Arnett, UPI's Neil Sheehan and myself, among others—were on an assassination hit list the secret police had supposedly prepared. I assumed the rumors were merely intended to scare us, and I ignored them.

There were other developments that did worry me, however. Le Lieu, my wife-to-be, had angered the Saigon government by quitting her job in the Information Ministry, leaving the government altogether, and joining the United States Information Service. This made her not only the fiancée of a hostile newsman but a defector from the Vietnamese government working for the hated Washington government, which at that point was no more popular with the Saigon government than Ho Chi Minh himself.

So the police were put on to Le Lieu.

One night at about two A.M. there came a hammering at my apartment door, and I could see through the frosted glass that the two visitors were wearing white uniforms—cops. I reached for a weapon.

In the 1960s Saigon was full of guns abandoned or sold by Special Forces alumni, mercenaries and spooks, and I had been given a Schmeisser submachine gun. This gun, manufactured by Nazi Germany, was one of thousands seized by U.S. forces at the end of World War II and shipped to warehouses in Virginia, from which they were ultimately distributed by the CIA to its partisans among the mountain tribes of Central Viet Nam.

With the machine gun slung over my arm, I opened the door and bade the cops good evening. They demanded to search the premises for Le Lieu, but glanced nervously at the Schmeisser as they fingered their pistol holsters. I politely told them that I was the only occupant of the apartment, and that it would be better for all of us not to insist on a search. After some whispered consultations between them they turned away and disappeared into the night.

Soon afterward the Diem government was overthrown,

but if it had lasted much longer I'm sure my apartment would have been visited by a better-prepared police delegation.

The summer became ever more violent; hundreds were arrested and some were killed. Finally, at JFK's command, American officials signaled to leaders of the South Vietnamese armed forces that a coup against the Ngo family would be acceptable to Washington.

On November 1, Diem was duly overthrown and slain, and an era of military rule began in South Viet Nam, which, aside from a brief interval of civilian administration, ended only when Hanoi's tanks smashed through the gate outside Saigon's Doc Lap Palace on May 1, 1975.

A few months after Thich Quang Duc's death I was called to The Hague to receive the 1963 World Press Photo Award from Prince Bernhard, and the following year, I shared a Pulitzer Prize (with Dave Halberstam), not for my photograph, but for general news coverage of Viet Nam. Partly on the strength of that prize, I began getting some tempting job offers, and I accepted the one from ABC-TV. A book I wrote about the war was selling briskly, and my career bloomed.

So I can hardly deny having profited from the horrible death of a harmless old monk, and I profited as well from the deaths of President Diem, his brother, Ngo Dinh Nhu, and probably many others.

For that matter, there are still critics who persist in blaming journalists like me for the fall of Viet Nam because of our alleged roles in overthrowing Diem.

Even during my coverage for *The New York Times* of the 1991 war in the Persian Gulf, some detractors, evidently not informed of what I had actually written, peppered me with letters accusing me of sabotaging the American war effort against Iraq as I allegedly had done in Viet Nam. This is just silly, of course. To the extent that American newsmen "took sides" in either Viet Nam or the Persian Gulf, it was on the side of the United States. That did not mean that we were necessarily supporters of the South Vietnamese or Saudi Arabian governments, however.

At any rate, I have sorrowed these many years for Thich Quang Duc, as well as others for whose deaths I may bear some responsibility, including four Chinese war profiteers.

Throughout the Viet Nam War one of the themes on which news agencies and reporters continuously harped was the pervasive corruption of the Saigon government and the black market it tolerated. Many of us believed that no government could "win the hearts and minds" of a people, if the people were constantly gouged by racketeers, profiteers and shakedowns.

Stung by such reporting, Air Vice Marshal Nguyen Cao Ky, the officer who seized power as the nation's premier in 1965, decided to crack down on profiteering by Saigon businessmen. Ky was not a man known for restraint; an avowed admirer of Hitler, the flamboyant pilot quickly drifted into a role as a despot. When he cracked the whip he wanted the world to know what he had done, and some horrifying photographs recorded the results.

One of these pictures was of a street-corner execution carried out in 1968 by Ky's police chief and interior minister, Colonel Nguyen Ngoc Loan. When an alleged Viet Cong prisoner was led up to him, he simply drew his revolver and blew the man's brains out. The AP's Eddie Adams was on hand, and his photograph of the atrocity won him a Pulitzer Prize.

But long before that incident, Ky had closed down all the Vietnamese-language newspapers and issued a series of harsh decrees that mandated the death penalty for anyone convicted of war profiteering.

Convictions were not slow in coming, and soldiers quickly erected sandbag walls and wooden stakes on the National Railway Building sidewalk facing Saigon's main market square. A few nights after the stakes went up I was roused from my bed to observe their use.

It was about three in the morning when I arrived, and although the night was almost spent, the muggy air seemed as oppressive as it had at sunset. In the darkness, the four stakes were brightly lighted by the headlights of several jeeps parked in front of them. The glare of the execution site contrasted starkly with the subdued and peaceful kerosene lamps marking hundreds of little market stalls. People were up early, but not to sell food.

On one side of the stakes a fire truck stood parked, and on the other, four wooden coffins were lined up. Behind a cordon facing this tableau were a few hundred gaping street vendors, soldiers, journalists and other spectators.

At the appointed hour an ambulance arrived, backed up to the stakes and unloaded the four condemned men. Since all the prisoners were ethnic Chinese, Ky and his advisers expected little popular objection, since many Vietnamese detested the wealthy Chinese businessmen living in their midst.

The four firing squads, each with five soldiers armed with American carbines, stepped into place, and the prisoners were tied to the stakes. Three were pinioned with their hands tied behind the stakes, but the fourth, a recent convert to Christianity, had asked that his hands be left free so that he could die with his palms together in prayer. The executioners obliged him.

The squad leader barked a command, the carbine bolts clattered, and in the brief silence that followed we could hear the Christian praying loudly, his blindfolded face raised toward heaven. Then came the command, and when the twenty carbines fired a ragged volley, three of the men instantly slumped from their bindings and were still. But the born-again Christian remained alive, horribly chanting a hymn. His hands, torn and shattered by bullets, had evidently deflected the volley, leaving his heart beating.

After an interminable pause the squad commander, his voice hoarse with annoyance, ordered his men to fire another volley. This time the prisoner slumped, but we could still hear him trying to sing as blood foamed from his mouth. Finally, the squad leader drew his .45 pistol, chambered a cartridge and shot the merchant through the head.

The executioners exchanged some whispered conversation and then their leader barked a command and marched them away. The ambulance crew cut down the bodies, heaved them into the coffins and carted them off. The fire truck began hosing away the blood and the crowd drifted away.

I had seen many people die, including some who were executed, but I experienced an unwonted wave of hatred that morning—hatred not only for Ky and his firing squads, but for all other cold-blooded executioners. There's something about the slaying of a helpless creature—a man at a stake or a bull in the Madrid ring—that brings me to a state of vengeful fury.

That morning I also hated the smooth American diplomats, the State Department and White House, and everyone else who had connived at placing Ky in power. And yes, I hated journalists, too—reporters, including myself, who had contributed to this bloodbath by goading a childish dictator into ordering a bloodbath.

Fortunately, rage passes. No journalist can indulge in rage at others or in self-hatred without losing the balance needed to ply his trade. But there are some deaths reporters cannot forget. The best that can be said is that such deaths season us and make us think twice before writing something that may leave blood on our hands.

NURTURE

I WAS BORN IN 1931 in the depths of the Great Depression, the year Wallace Carothers of DuPont invented nylon. Carothers and many other desperate Americans committed suicide, but it was fundamentally a time of hope and promise. I have been unbelievably lucky to have lived during the greatest turning point in human history, and if the chief value of life lies in its variety of experience, I have been uncommonly blessed. I have seen men land on the moon, but I have also stoked and emptied my mother's wooden icebox in the days before we had mechanical refrigerators.

The transition from old to new has not been an unalloyed pleasure for me. I feel some pangs of nostalgia for childhood summers long ago, when I read and studied by the soft light of kerosene lamps and imagined ghosts in the shadowed nooks of our old stone house. I miss lilac bushes and birch groves and maple trees that were cut down to build a road for the convenience of the trucking industry. I miss the wildernesses that became suburbs, losing forever the thrushes and whippoorwills that once sweetened eventide with song.

I also miss some New York City sounds. There was the clip-clop of horse-drawn carts at dawn, delivering milk in glass bottles with a couple of inches of golden cream floating at the top. I miss the deep-throated steam horns of great ocean liners departing for the seven seas, and the sad, lonely songs of the tugboats on foggy days. For me, one of the most evocative things about old movies like Hitchcock's *Rear Window* is their sound-tracks—slices of oral history that preserve those wonderful van-ished sounds of a once great port.

I don't feel old, and yet I am conscious of being a link to a past very different from the present.

My grandfather called on his Long Island patients in a horse-drawn buggy—something doctors don't do these days, even in their Cadillacs. Stricken with pneumonia himself, Harry Wilde was still making his rounds on a bitter winter morning up to the hour when he died of a pulmonary embolism. He was only thirty-five, and he perished partly because the pharmacopoeia of his day did not include antibiotics, medications we have taken for granted for a couple of generations.

My grandmother's youth was in an era that today seems inconceivably ancient. For instance, she had vivid childhood memories of Buffalo Bill's wild west shows, Sitting Bull—the victor of the Little Bighorn—and demonstrations by Annie Oak-ley of her legendary marksmanship.

I was born with wonderful advantages. My ancestors were a polyglot mix of Europeans that typified the American melting pot. My father, Douglas Browne, was born in a rural suburb of Detroit the year the Wright brothers first flew. His parents, of English and German stock, later moved to Los An-geles and raised him as a Roman Catholic, but like many in our family, he discarded religious faith on reaching majority, and set out eastward to seek his fortune in New York City.

Forced to abandon his studies in architecture when the Depression hit New York, he had saved just enough money to pay for lessons in commercial art, and the teacher he chose was my grandmother-to-be, Florence R. A. Wilde. The connection led to his meeting with her daughter Dorothy, a courtship and the marriage that brought me into the world.

My mother, Dorothy ("Buddy" to her friends), came of a blend of the Bohemian with the straitlaced. Her father, Dr. Harry Wilde, was the last of a nineteenth-century line of prosperous Dublin physicians who played a lot of chess when not ministering to the sick. But the clan also included a notorious black sheep—Oscar Wilde. Oscar was a cousin of my doctor grandfather's, and his ghost was something of an embarrassment to me as a kid until I began to appreciate his literary virtues. For a time, I even tried to conceal from school classmates that my middle initial stood for Wilde.

My grandmother Florence (we called her "Donna," for some long-forgotten reason) was of a different breed; her father, a Dutch-American businessman, became enormously rich, and for a time he had a seat on the New York Stock Exchange, a Long Island estate with a large staff of servants, a large stable and a keen taste for music and the arts. His many children were brought up to enjoy the fruits of educated leisure such as painting, composing music and reading poetry, none of which particularly prepared them to earn a living. The family, my grandmother reminisced, presided over a brilliant salon, whose guests often included such luminaries as Ignace Paderewski, the Polish statesman and pianist.

But around the turn of the century my great-grandfather did some injudicious speculating in the spice market, and when the wheel of fortune turned against him the family was ruined. Suddenly, there was no more money to pay the servants or buy fodder for the horses or even feed the household adequately. It's hard to imagine a family more ill-prepared to cope with practical problems of poverty.

But cope they did, with the help of a couple of servants,

who, with no place to go, stayed on as unpaid retainers. Some of the boys in the family sought adventure; my grand-uncle Ned worked as a gunslinging marshal in a Nevada frontier community for a time, and then joined the army to fight the Spanish in Cuba, where he died of influenza. Another grand-uncle, Bernard, schemed to become a pearl diver in the South Pacific, but illness interfered, and he earned a meager living giving students cello lessons.

My grandmother, an accomplished sketcher and water-color painter, did better than her brothers and sisters, becoming a successful art teacher. But life dealt her one financial blow after another. Her hardworking but impecunious physician husband, Harry Wilde, died at thirty-five, leaving her with two young daughters to support. By enlarging her art classes, however, she scraped through, and at least her family had free medical care from her late husband's professional colleagues.

Her classes in New York City went so well in the 1920s that my grandmother took out a mortgage and bought a house of her own in the Catskills, which she used as a summer school for her flock of art students. The stone house, as we always called it, was built around 1690 by the Wyncoops, one of the earliest Dutch families to farm the Catskill Valley. It stood on sixteen hilly acres, mostly wooded, with a delightful tree-shaded creek whose frigid pools have enticed swimmers for three centuries.

With the stock-market crash and the Depression came a new round of poverty. The bank nearly foreclosed Donna's mortgage on the stone house, but Franklin Delano Roosevelt stepped in with his banking moratorium just in the nick of time—an action that transformed Donna into a lifelong Democrat. Walt Disney's movie *The Three Little Pigs* had just been released, and Donna sent the bank a partial mortgage payment and a note: "Who's Afraid of the Big Bad Wolf?"

The stone house was not merely a place where I spent

my childhood summer vacations—it was my tutor and my home, more than any I have had since. I was given a good formal education at Friends Seminary, a Quaker school in New York—and subsequently at Swarthmore College—was the stone house that taught me many of the things that shaped my career.

The old property lacked electricity and a gas stove, and for water, we drew up buckets from an ancient well or cranked up an ancient gasoline-powered pump once a day to fill a pressure tank with washing water from the creek. The open-air pump and its water tank, standing a quarter mile from the house, had an evil reputation that thoroughly daunted my female relatives.

The pump engine had to be started up by cranking a heavy iron flywheel, and it could backfire and break an arm. While the engine was running, its operator had to keep an eye on a pressure gauge. One day when I was very young my father fell asleep in the tall grass while he was supposed to be watching the pressure gauge, and the big tank exploded with a blast that was heard a mile away.

That was the kind of practical lesson that instructed our family in the arts of rural survival. My grandmother, raised in incompetent luxury, eventually learned something about practical plumbing and how safety valves can prevent accidental explosions.

Among the charms of the stone house were its fireplaces, and on cool nights we lighted crackling blazes that cast spooky shadows on the dimly lighted walls. The wind used to moan in the chimneys and around the corners of those thick stone walls, and it was easy to imagine the sounds as the lonely shades of former residents. Some of the stone house's early residents, according to tradition, were killed in an Indian massacre in the dining room. As children, my siblings and I hoped that their spirits had found peace in the graveyard up the hill, but on windy nights we were never sure.

Frank Klamroth, an old German handyman my grandmother employed every summer, claimed to be an authority on
ghosts; I remember as a young child listening spellbound to
adventures he claimed to have had as a seaman, including two
encounters with the dreaded phantom Flying Dutchman. Many
years later when the family had grown up and scattered we
learned that Frank, more drunk than usual, had died under the
wheels of a Madison Avenue bus.

My father, struggling to earn a living as an architect (or
a cabinetmaker, or an elevator operator, or whatever job he could
find in those difficult days) worked in New York City and took
the Hudson River Night Boat up to the Catskills on summer
weekends. My mother, who cherished hopes of becoming a concert pianist, a successful novelist—or both—spent her days in
drudgery, cooking and cleaning for her children (of whom I was
the oldest, followed by sister Miriam and brothers Timothy and
Christopher), as well as for her mother and the ever-present mob
of summer art students.

For those who have never tried it, cooking for twenty or
so people over a four-burner kerosene stove is no picnic. Filling
buckets from a muscle-powered pitcher pump (when the gasoline pump was broken), heating water over the stove for washing
dishes and clothing, scrubbing laundry on old-fashioned wash-
boards with harsh, yellow Octagon soap—such was my mother's
summertime existence.

There were times late at night when I could hear her
weeping, exhausted and depressed. Her lifelong bouts with depression, I suspect, had as much to do with her death at fifty-
seven as did her heavy smoking and genetically weak lungs—a
curse of our family.

But more often on those long summer nights I remember
hearing the cheerful two-fingered clatter of her rickety little
typewriter—the vehicle, she hoped, to a career as a writer of

detective and adventure novels. Sometimes I peeked through a crack in the floor of my bedroom, from which I could see the living room in which she worked, bathed in the golden glow of a Rayo kerosene lamp.

Our entertainments were rather simple. On many evenings my grandmother would heat up cocoa and treat us to a piano recital of Chopin études and waltzes, often concluded by her rousing rendition of a tune she had learned as a girl—Joplin's "Maple Leaf Rag."

We all worked hard. Even the students pitched in, when they were not mixing up the dried-out remnants of paint with which they sometimes had to make do while learning the rudiments of watercolor sketching. The well-meaning efforts of these city-bred youngsters, unfortunately, often misfired. One young man brought the wrath of the household upon his head by shooting a squirrel, which he had intended to donate to the community food larder. We Wildes and Brownes regarded squirrels as neighbors and friends, not food.

As a teenager I became the weekday man of the menage while my father was away in the city, where he worked at what was then called North Beach Airport (today's LaGuardia Airport). His nights in our sweltering Greenwich Village apartment were lonely and miserable. Most New Yorkers today, sheltered from the city's semitropical summers by air-conditioning, have little notion how uncomfortable and unhealthy the city used to be.

It became my job to fix the simple machinery and engines on which life in the stone house depended. I also painted walls, scythed high grass and mowed the lawns, hoed and weeded the gardens, polished the house's ancient oak beams with linseed oil, repaired what plumbing we had (and dug fresh trenches for the outhouse and garbage pit) and coped with all the other chores rural Americans used to take for granted. I loved the work.

Always short of money, we improvised constantly, although not always successfully. The odd nails and bits of string with which my grandmother held together some of our superannuated furniture would constantly give way. But her dietary innovations were more successful. She discovered, for instance, that stale bread could be toasted almost to charcoal, and when ground up and steeped in boiling water, it yielded a kind of ersatz coffee. This fluid, served hot and sweet, tasted vaguely like a popular Depression-era product called Postum, and as a kid I liked my grandmother's phony coffee better than the real thing. For me, if not for my parents, the Depression was fun.

Summers at the stone house brought never-ending discoveries in the shadows and crannies of musty attics and closets, and in the barns and cabins scattered over the property, some of which were inhabited by the students. In these ramshackle buildings we sometimes came upon caches of curiosities from centuries gone by, and the junk I discovered was often exciting.

In the main barn was a Model-T Ford engine, which, unlike modern engines, could be taken apart, comprehended and reassembled, even by a young boy. The barn also contained a pair of once-stylish old sleighs, their leather accessories crumbling and spattered with pigeon droppings, but trimmed with iron bells that still jingled. I sometimes sat in those sleighs, trying to imagine what a dash along a snow-encrusted lane must have been like in my grandfather's day at the turn of the century.

There were bushels of old magazines and newspaper rotogravure sections (printed in beautiful sepia ink), saved by someone as kindling for the fireplaces, but brimming over with contemporary history I found fascinating—the rise of Mussolini, the Lindbergh kidnapping, the bombing of Madrid by Franco's air force, national cat shows and other great events.

The stone house also held some wooden camp chests with the stenciled names and ranks of men who had fought in several conflicts, including the Civil War. One had belonged to none other than Grand-uncle Ned, the frontier marshal, and on receiving permission to open it, I found a folding silk opera hat, as glossy and black as the day it had been made. I regret never having had an opportunity to wear that hat in public. One of the many changes I've seen over the years has been the transition to a hatless society—a change that may be about to be reversed as people realize that ultraviolet radiation leaking through our devastated ozone layer is dangerous to scalps and skin.

Another abandoned chest, the property of a long dead geologist beau of my grandmother's, was locked, and it therefore consumed me with interest. One day my pleas persuaded my grandmother that the time had come for a peek inside, and we carefully forced the lock. To my delight, it contained some surveying instruments, laboratory glassware, rock specimens and mechanical gadgets. But best of all, it held a crumbling, toothless human skull, complete with two jawbones!

That old skull, the first I ever held in my hands, was a thing of wonder; it was a tangible embodiment of mortality—a condition of life that until then had seemed more or less an abstraction.

The skull in my room became a kind of *memento mori* that started trains of thought for me probably familiar to the medieval monks who also kept skulls in their cells. As I ran my fingers over the zygomatic arch and peered into the cranial cavity, I thought about the brain that had once dwelled there—a brain much like my own, no doubt, perceiving, feeling, thinking. Might this person, whoever he or she had been, also have experienced the strange sensation of holding another person's skull and thinking about death? I visualized an infinitely receding succession of people like myself, each holding a skull in his hands and looking backward in time through it—the kind of view one has sitting between facing mirrors in a barbershop.

Teenagers are prone to such thoughts.

The stone house demanded exertion, but it wasn't all work. In the heat of the day our family took to the creek, which, like the house, was a teacher. We discovered, for instance, that many of the rocks along its banks could be cracked apart to reveal fossils of fern leaves and other defunct organisms. My father showed us how to capture pollywogs and nurture them in buckets through their incredible metamorphoses to froghood; I learned from those buckets that ontogeny really does recapitulate phylogeny.

The creek also introduced us to some rudimentary hydrocarbon chemistry. We children used to hate stepping on a certain patch of soft muck under shallow water near the creek's edge, because when we did, clouds of foul-smelling bubbles would boil up. But by about the time my voice was changing I knew that rotting vegetation produces methane—a bit of knowledge I set out to prove. By inverting a water-filled fishing boot over the creek bottom I quickly collected enough gas to fill the boot, into which I tossed a lighted match. The ensuing explosion made me a hero in my brothers' eyes for a few days.

Lacking refrigeration, we had to buy our milk, eggs and butter almost daily, and since our family had no car, this meant an hour's bicycle trip for me. I usually pedaled fast on the way home, because the raw milk I bought from a dairy farm soured in a matter of hours, especially, according to folklore, when an electrical storm was brewing.

There being no television, no nearby neighbors, and only feeble radio reception, I spent a lot of time reading and studying. I got interested as a teenager in medieval romances like *Sir Gawain and the Green Knight,* and I liked to imagine the high green branches arching over our creek as the vaulted roof of the knight's Green Chapel. I read a lot of Russian novels and I got hooked on Goethe—so much so that I started studying German, just to be able to read *Faust* as it was written. German was one of many gifts from the stone house that made life easier for me when I eventually became a foreign correspondent.

In the spring of 1945 I turned fourteen and the following months were memorable for two reasons. One was my discovery of great music, and the other was the detonation of the atomic bomb.

By 1945 my grandmother's summer school had about run out of students and she was beginning to spend her winters in Florida, teaching art at Rollins College. The draft had swallowed up most of the young men who might have been art students, and although the war was nearly over, times were changing.

Perennially short of money, however, our family continued to fill our stone house cabins, not with students but with summer tenants—mostly young people who could barely afford the $150 my mother charged for a summer's rent. At that price the cabins were always rented, despite the lack of plumbing and electricity.

One of our tenants was a Latvian refugee named Maxim Shur, who, with his Swedish wife, wanted a summer to recover from World War II. This man, a concert pianist by profession and a soldier by necessity, had spent several desperate years in American uniform fighting the Germans, and had been wounded badly enough for an early discharge. Our cabin appealed to him because it was very cheap, and because its rental entitled him to practice each day on our old upright piano.

I had grown up with great music and loved it, but my mother, the best of the family pianists, was never more than a gifted amateur. Maxim Shur was the first professional I got to know.

Shur and I never became real friends, and we hardly ever talked about music or anything else. But his playing deeply affected me. Every day for six or eight hours he practiced the dozen Mozart piano concertos he had set out to master, and when I was working or reading within earshot, the music of Mozart—magnificent even without orchestral accompaniment—seeped into my soul. Shur also practiced Beethoven concertos and sonatas, some Brahms, and a fair sampling of the rest of the standard concert hall repertoire. In time, I came to know the piano scores for these compositions by heart, and that gift from Maxim Shur brightened the rest of my life. If he is still alive somewhere, I'd like him to know that.

Our placid existence at the stone house was abruptly changed on August 7, 1945, when a staticky radio broadcast told of the destruction of Hiroshima by an atomic bomb.

Like most Americans, I was nonplussed but excited. A year earlier my science teacher at Friends Seminary in New York City had described for our class the 1939 discovery by Otto Hahn and Fritz Strassmann of uranium fission, but nothing he said had prepared us for the spectacle of a city obliterated by a few pounds of nuclear fuel. I hung on the radio for more details.

They came swiftly, as did news of the second bomb at Nagasaki, and the end of the war. And then magazines and newspapers began disclosing details of the bomb and the magicians who had contributed to its birth: Oppenheimer, Seaborg, Conant, Urey, Bethe, Bush, Lawrence and the rest of that brilliant pantheon. Americans born since 1945 have little notion how deeply the nation admired (and perhaps feared) the scientists who brought World War II to an abrupt stop.

I never wanted to be a ball player or fireman, but during that summer of 1945 I wanted very much to become a nuclear physicist.

It pains me to admit that at the time I didn't think much about the 30,000 scorched bodies and 100,000 other casualties that the dawn of the nuclear age had left in Hiroshima. What I knew of the war was what I had gleaned from newspapers, newsreels and popular magazines—the sources which I now know can never be entirely trusted, especially in wartime. The Second World War was a time when we were urged to buy bonds, save tin cans, grow victory gardens, work in defense plants, eat within the limits imposed by our ration stamps, stifle all lights when the air raid sirens sounded, "Praise the Lord and pass the ammunition," and hate the "Japanazis," as our cheerleaders dubbed the collective enemy. In movie theaters, images of flaming enemy suicide planes and smoking enemy cities prompted applause, not horror.

This view of the war was tempered in my family by my Quaker mother's unflinching devotion to pacifism and nonviolence, but to me, that awesome mushroom cloud seemed a symbol of scientific genius and righteous victory over an evil foe.

When I returned to school in New York that autumn, it was with a new sense of purpose. I wanted to be part of the scientific community, and I plunged into the subjects that seemed appropriate. Later in my life, some of my friends told me they thought it strange that a boy raised in a Quaker home and attending a Quaker school should have been so interested in nuclear weapons—and who would later become a war correspondent—but to me, there seemed no real conflict. I didn't want to kill anyone, after all.

So I set to work with a vengeance on math, chemistry, physics and everything else that seemed to lie on the true path, and for the first time in my boyhood I became a straight-A student. I was still enchanted by music and literature, but even their appeal was eclipsed by the vistas revealed to me by my science teacher, Walter Hinman. A harsh but humane disciplinarian, he coaxed our little physics class to come to school early several days a week to study calculus. With that and an arsenal of pedagogical tricks, he first showed us the edifice of classical physics built by Newton and his followers. Then, having hooked us on the comfortable assumptions of Newtonian determinism, he knocked out the props with blasts of relativity and quantum theory, leaving us jolted but fascinated. It was heady stuff for school kids.

My mother's deep religious faith had always troubled me. I did not share it, and I can't remember a time when I thought of religion as anything more than ritual designed to celebrate some characters as manifestly implausible as Santa Claus and the tooth fairy. At the same time, I understood my mother's longing for the explanations she found in faith; as a child I lacked an equivalent cosmology of my own, but it seemed to me there must be some better explanation of things than religion. My high-school science teacher introduced me to the alternative I was looking for, and with all its shortcomings, science has supplied my spiritual needs ever since.

I even got close to some of the gods of my new faith. A year or so after the war, J. Robert Oppenheimer gave some symposiums and talks, and my science teacher arranged for his son and me to attend some of those sessions.

I remember Oppenheimer, the brilliant but politically doomed "father" of the atomic bomb, as very tall, stooped in posture, inclined to pace as he talked and smoking incessantly even while addressing large formal gatherings. He spoke eloquently of the power of nuclear weapons and the need for international control of them; he also vividly described the destruction and suffering his bomb had caused and could cause again if not placed under joint supervision by the world community, including the Soviet Union.

Dr. Oppenheimer's revulsion against mass slaughter was very moving for most listeners, but at the time, I'm afraid, I was really more interested in hearing how he and the other Los Alamos giants had actually made the bomb—a subject on which he had disappointingly little to say. Oppenheimer was naturally bound by national security rules to withhold the juicy details of isotope separation, critical mass, spherical shock-wave dynamics, neutron flux moderation and other matters of interest to boys like me, but I yearned to hear more.

In the late 1940s the specter of McCarthyism was already afoot, and Oppenheimer could ill afford accusations of security leaks to compound the problems created by his leftist political views. But he held me and his other listeners spellbound with his portrayal of physics as a golden key for solving the great universal riddles. Oppenheimer was a scientist who cared much more about the underlying mysteries of reality than about the nuts and bolts of nuclear weapons—an inclination he shared with the Soviet bombsmith Andrei Sakharov. Oppy, moreover, could infect listeners with his own passionate fascination with astrophysics and cosmology. I came away from one of his late-night meetings at New York's Cooper Union converted, basking in smug self-confidence like a young Saul on the road to Damascus.

My conversion was not purely intellectual; I'm afraid my enjoyment of explosions also attracted me to science. Freud suggests that all careers are chosen for hidden reasons: that the impulses of the ax murderer may underlie the skills of the surgeon, for example. An innate love of explosions may similarly inspire the careers of soldiers, quarrymen, demolition workers, miners, chemists, physicists, timpanists and war correspondents.

Explosions set off purely for fun have become unfashionable in the new America, which is obsessed with safety. Most states have outlawed the private possession of fireworks, and I think we have lost a powerful pedagogical tool in consequence.

A lot of journalists of my generation cut their teeth on explosives. David Belnap of the *Los Angeles Times*, for instance, an editor who for many years was one of the best correspondents covering Latin America, survived a childhood punctuated by playful blasts of the kind dynamite sticks make when ignited under inverted dairy milk cans.

When I was a child fireworks were still legal almost everywhere. Lady crackers, cannon crackers, ash cans, cherry bombs—I loved them all.

The high point of summer at the stone house for the children in our family was always the Fourth of July, for which my parents, my grandmother and even the art students always managed to buy some fireworks. We exploded our crackers frugally, stripping them away from their braided strings and setting them off one at a time. The best part came with night, when the pinwheels, sparklers, Roman candles and rockets were lighted up. Even the fireflies in the lilac bushes seemed to join in the displays, and I still feel twinges of nostalgia when I smell the pungent smoke of fireworks.

At school, my chemistry classes and my fondness for explosions converged in the study of rapid oxidation reactions. The science teacher, Mr. Hinman, whose lungs and vocal cords had been severely scarred by mustard gas during the closing months of World War I, was no stranger to explosions himself. Risking dismissal by the Quaker school management, he encouraged some of my louder experiments, a few of which had mildly destructive consequences. I discovered how to make (and detonate) nitroglycerine, mercuric fulminate and other noisemakers, and although one of my objects was to impress several pretty girls in our school, I also began learning chemistry.

And somehow I survived childhood, all the richer for its hazards.

TEST TUBES TO TYPEWRITERS

By twenty-one I was married to a delightful girl named Diana, and with a baby on the way, I badly needed a job.

Luckily, there was enough chemistry under my belt by then to land me something with a New York company that sold chemical advice to manufacturers. The science pursued at this lab never approached the lofty levels I had glimpsed as a student, but it was often fun and it paid adequately if not regally. After baby Wendy was born, Diana and I lived in a succession of rather grubby little apartments, and both of us worked while Wendy stayed with Diana's mother. Wendy turned out wonderfully, no thanks to her father, who never really knew her until she became a mother herself. She grew up, finished college, worked as a corporate spokesperson, married, raised a daughter and son of her own and became a teacher.

Many of my laboratory projects had to do with processed food, which I came to regard in a new and jaundiced light.

For example, a company that manufactured frozen blintzes was having trouble keeping its pastry shells from cracking during frozen storage, and it took me quite a time to solve this problem. (The reader is better off not knowing how; suffice it to say that some of the polymers we think of as constituents of plastics are edible.)

Another job I recall was commissioned by a manufacturer of chewing gum in France. High-quality chicle had become scarce as the result of an upheaval in Guatemala, in which the CIA managed to overthrow the elected president, Jácobo Arbenz Guzmán. My assignment was to develop chicle substitutes for French gum chewers. This job took me less time than I expected; bountiful nature provides the makers of both chewing gum and condoms with many polymers and plasticizers that can be blended to get the desired properties.

I became something of a virtuoso with food additives, curing many a rancid product with chemicals like butylated hydroxy anisole. This stuff is not as sinister as it sounds; many of the antioxidant preservatives used in food are believed these days to confer some protection against free radicals—major suspects as carcinogens. (My interest in food additives was not passed on to my daughter Wendy or son Timothy, who, although raised separately, both became vegetarians and additive-haters.)

Accidents at my company abounded, but those were the days before OSHA, EPA and investigative reporters on the make, so we were not unduly bothered. Ether, which we used as a solvent for extracting various oils and fats, catches fire if you wink at it, but despite the hazard, we constantly had great flasks of the stuff boiling away on electric heating mantles. Every now and then an arc of fire would sweep across the lab to an open flame from some imperfectly sealed ether distillation rig. Survival in the lab depended on lightning deployment of the fire extinguishers we kept within reach, and even so, we had our share of explosions and casualties.

It was during this period that I suffered a street accident that had a pivotal effect on my life.

While walking along Thirteenth Street with Diana one day I stepped on a steel subway-access hatch in the sidewalk at just the instant a worker underneath it chose to push it up. The hatch tripped me, I fell, and feeling my weight on the heavy steel plate, the man underneath let go. The plate came down on the first two fingers of my right hand.

The fingers were not severed but they took a long time to heal, and in the meantime I was unable to use a pencil, since I was right-handed. During my years in school and college, all my papers had been written by hand, and I was utterly dependent on the fingers of my right hand even to sign my name.

Since my laboratory job required voluminous production of laboratory reports, I realized that I would quickly have to write in some other way, so I had a typewriter moved to my bench.

At first my hunt-and-peck typing was wretchedly slow but with practice, I got faster. Eventually one of my injured right-hand fingers mended enough to join the two left-hand fingers I had been using, and a limping three-finger gait became my typing style for life. I never learned to touch-type, but I could at least pound out pages pretty fast.

Speed typing is one of the most essential skills of journalism, and although I didn't know it at the time, my accident was an important step toward a new way of life.

The Korean War began in 1950, and since I expected to be drafted anyway, I volunteered for Officer Candidate School in the hope of becoming an artillery or tank officer. (My mother, who favored conscientious objection, was grieved but accepted my decision.) My application and test scores were duly recorded and filed, and I waited for word. And waited.

To this day, I have no idea what happened to those papers; the months and years passed, with neither a response to my application nor a draft call. Something in me had wanted to get to the war and I was a little disappointed not to be called. But whatever the administrative foul-up may have been, it may have saved my life; the life expectancy of second lieutenants in Korea in 1951 and 1952 was appallingly short.

In 1955, Diana and I had saved about $2,000—enough for an extended vacation bumming around Europe—and I asked my draft board for permission to leave the country for a spell. Only then did officialdom seem to realize that I should have been in the army long since, and the board reluctantly agreed to our trip, provided I report for induction as soon as I got back.

We made the most of that vacation, spending nearly six months traveling until our money was gone. In the 1930s my mother and I had spent a summer visiting my English cousins and doing a little European traveling, but I was very young at the time and my impressions were mainly of toy automobiles, shrieking train whistles and intense boredom with castles. I saw the Europe of 1955 through different eyes; the continent was still partly in ruins left by World War II but it was mending fast, and it was vibrantly exciting.

Diana and I looked for adventure and found some. At one point we lived in a partly bombed-out Berlin town house, owned by the widow of a Wehrmacht general, where the plumbing was gold plated but produced no water. The radiators were also useless, and a briquet of charcoal to fire up our room's potbelly stove cost a whole precious mark, so we stayed warm in other ways.

It was winter when we sailed home on the great (and soon to be scrapped) *Ile-de-France,* and we drank the free wine, danced and gazed at the mountainous waves of the stormy Atlantic, trying to forget that our lives were facing a long stretch of precarious uncertainty.

In 1956 I was drafted.

A subway pass the draft board had thoughtfully provided got me to the downtown army induction station, where my fellow draftees and I were stripped, herded through our physicals and shots and loaded aboard a convoy of buses for Fort Dix.

During the two weeks I spent at that cheerless New

Jersey post my head was shaved and I was issued a barracks bag full of khaki and olive-drab clothing. I spent a large part of my time on KP duty (mostly cleaning out sink grease traps), but I also took a battery of tests. When I admitted knowing German and French, the army tested me in those languages, and I was classified (overgenerously) as a "linguist."

Moving to Fort Knox, Kentucky, for basic training, I found that I had been assigned to a unit with other "linguists," most of whom were merely citizens of other nations who, as American residents, had been caught up in the draft. One of our group, Boris Ivanovich Oblesov, was a Soviet citizen, of all things; when our group later went to Fort Hood, Texas, for tank training, a Soviet consular official actually tried to serve a draft notice on Boris for induction into the Red Army.

This did not strike us as funny at the time. The year 1956 saw a great uprising in Hungary, and we expected to be fighting the Russians in a matter of weeks. We took our training very seriously, even though we "linguists" were assigned to a very peculiar training unit. Our studies mainly focused on the new M-48 tank and its powerful 90-millimeter gun, but we were also familiarized with several types of Soviet tanks. The rumor spread that we were to be dropped into Budapest to steal Soviet T-34s and JS-2s, and turn them against the Russians.

As we maneuvered our own tanks across the Texas desert we often coordinated our movements by radio in German, to the annoyance of our nonlinguist sergeants. But we became good tankers; about half of our group were Germans, and perhaps Panzer warfare is in the Teutonic blood.

The army educated me in several useful ways. It taught me about weapons, of course, but more important, it showed me how soldiers think, speak and act. In a world more often shaped by the sword than the pen, firsthand familiarity with soldierly ways is useful for historians and journalists.

Ralph Waldo Emerson wrote that "war educates the senses, calls into action the will, perfects the physical constitution, brings men into such swift and close collision in critical moments that man measures man." That's all very well, but when I was a GI we were instructed in simple butchery.

Raised a Quaker and instructed to believe that the meek shall inherit the earth, I one day found myself lunging across a Fort Knox drill field, thrusting my bayonet into the straw vitals of a scarecrow foe and yelling "Kill!"

At the time, I doubt that any of us draftees regarded bayonet drill as a prelude to real carnage. I'm also quite sure that none of us ever actually thrust a knife into an enemy soldier; even in battles fought at close quarters, bayonet fights have been rare since the invention of repeating firearms.

But for those of us who went through the old draft, bayonet drill was something not to be forgotten. It was a rite of passage, a graduation from the constraints of civilization to sanctioned savagery. A catechism ran through basic training in endless repetition: "What's the spirit of the bayonet?" the sergeant would yell. "Kill! Kill! Kill!" we screamed. It was a kind of kindergarten game, and like five-year-olds, we thought it was delightfully silly. The army makes boys out of men.

But bayonet drill wasn't a game, of course. Its object was to thicken the psychic callus, so that when the time came, real slaughter would seem almost part of the natural order of things. Bayonet training was conditioning for face-to-face, remorseless killing, and that is the essence of war, even in this age of smart bombs and electronic guidance systems.

People who have spent some time playing the war game, willingly or as draftees, become interested in military matters, and I was no exception.

Always too awkward and ill-coordinated to be an athlete, I nevertheless held my own in training marches, on obstacle courses and in calisthenics. I could crawl under barbed wire, disarm mines and shoot well enough to win a marksmanship badge.

I also learned that brawny linebackers who look like John Wayne are not always the best people to be around in tense moments. New soldiers are trained in throwing live grenades, and more than once I had the bad luck to stand near some soldierly-looking recruit with a live grenade in his hand and terror in his eyes. One fledgling GI, after pulling his safety pin and releasing the firing handle, simply froze up and clutched his pineapple as the seconds before detonation ticked away. A sergeant grabbed the grenade and heaved it just in time. Another trainee pulled his pin and simply dropped the grenade at his feet. I did the honors that time, chucking the grenade over the parapet. But funk causes more casualties than the army likes to admit, in war as well as in training.

I don't believe American troops are ever adequately trained for war. Even with a fully "professional" (nonconscripted) army in the Persian Gulf, more GIs were hurt or killed in accidents and by "friendly fire" than by Iraqi ground fire.

This has something to do with our national traditions. My experiences in the army and as a military writer convince me that Americans take a long time to get up to speed as soldiers. We are not a regimented people, and it takes time to learn reflexive behavior and obedience to orders, especially in combat.

Also, we have become an urban nation, and city kids grow up with virtually none of the skills and need for self-sufficiency our farmer forebears took for granted. American recruits today know little if anything about machinery, vehicles, electric circuits, plumbing, firearms or the many other things that are second nature to farmers. Manpower experts in the armed forces have told me that military instructors can no longer assume any useful knowledge or skill in a new recruit.

The army seems to have lost its enthusiasm for rifles as

it develops ever fancier technology, and I'm not sure the change makes for better soldiers. Infantrymen used to carry bolt-action Springfields or M-1 Garand rifles that were heavy and cumbersome. The M-1 could bite off a thumb if the user was careless in loading a clip. But they could shoot straight, and trainees were expected to riddle targets up to five hundred yards away. With today's jam-prone M-16s, soldiers are expected to fire satisfactory scores only up to three hundred yards.

Despite her Quaker ideals, my mother gave me my first rifle when I was fourteen, and I learned to shoot—never at animals or people, of course, since I had no more wish to kill anything than did my mother. But paradoxically, when I was drafted I already possessed a lot of the skills the army wanted. And I took to tanks like a duck to water.

Except in wartime, tanks are fun to operate, especially since Uncle Sam pays for their ravenous appetite for fuel. Modern tanks have real steering wheels rather than old-fashioned tractor levers, and they are quite easy to drive. The gearing has a few uncarlike features such as "neutral steer," which allows a tank to turn completely around without moving from its place, but the controls are easily mastered. A tank's brute power is staggering; when a driver steps on the gas his tank can rip through a dense forest as if the trees were matchsticks.

That kind of driving wonderfully stimulates any tendency to megalomania. Every now and then GIs used to go berserk and squash whole rows of parked cars under their 50-ton monsters. Tankers in my day also enjoyed blazing away with their 90-millimeter cannons at targets miles away, and watching the targets disappear in a smudge of gray smoke.

By the time I finished tank training the Hungarian crisis was over and the army had forgotten about linguists, so our group broke up and I was sent to Fort Devens, Massachusetts, to help instruct old soldiers in new gunnery techniques. Many of the "RAs" (regular army soldiers) there were alcoholics, and morale at Fort Devens was abysmal. When line companies like mine were mustered for reveille formation, half the men were drunk or badly hung over, weaving as they tried to stand at attention, often vomiting in ranks, and sometimes collapsing.

As a married soldier who had completed training, I was permitted to live off post with my wife. Housing in Ayer, Massachusetts, a village next to Fort Devens, was a lot less charming than our little Brooklyn Heights apartment, but Diana and I were happy to be together again. Our reunion was not to last more than a couple of months, however. My company commander received a requisition for two men to be sent to Korea, and since there were two draftee outsiders in the otherwise all-RA unit, we two were the inevitable choices.

It was a stunning turning point in my life. Korea was a place to which a soldier was forbidden to bring a wife even for a visit, and Diana and I faced a separation of at least one year, which our marriage was not destined to survive. My eyes were moist as the lights of Manhattan faded below my Seattle-bound plane.

The draft had its points, in that it democratized the army and salted it with educated men. But it was a cruel institution that sometimes broke more hearts with enforced separations than it did with bullets.

Fort Lewis, Washington, was the port of embarkation for troops going to the Far East, and its transient population was a peculiar blend of green kids frightened by horror stories and seasoned NCOs looking forward to another tour of duty wallowing in the fleshpots with their "mooses"—Japanese or Korean girls.

It took us thirty-two days to cross the Pacific in a decrepit troopship. On the troop deck, ten canvas bunks were slung between each of many pairs of poles, two on each side of the poles, and five levels high. Veterans had warned me to grab one of the upper bunks—good advice, as it turned out, for avoiding the cascading effluvia of seasick shipmates. (I've never been motion sick myself.)

We sailed north through the Gulf of Alaska, and the mountainous seas did not help the appetites or digestion of the GIs. Sanitary facilities were revolting. The urinals were steel troughs some twenty feet long, and in heavy seas, when their drains became plugged up, the accumulating fluid sloshed back and forth like an ocean wave. The day we put in for a stop at Okinawa and sighted our first Shinto tori arch was one of great relief.

At dawn a few days later we sailed into Inchon Harbor in central Korea, and my enchantment with Asia began. The tides in Inchon are among the highest in the world, and we rode at anchor for a few hours before boarding landing craft to take us ashore. Some fog and mist heightened the charm of a harbor filled with picturesque junks and fishing boats, beyond which the town itself rose steeply in an expanse of red-tiled roofs turned up at their corners in the ancient Asian style. The scene reminded me of a Chinese scroll.

We were confined to barracks at the 8th Army's Inchon replacement depot for a few days awaiting assignment to units, and I rather hoped to draw one close to the beautiful town. But no such luck; as a tanker, I was supposed to be a line soldier, and hence drew a post with the 24th Infantry Division north of the Imjin River a few hundred yards from the tense Demilitarized Zone dividing North and South Korea.

With twenty or thirty other new arrivals I heaved my barracks bag into the back of a deuce-and-a-half truck and climbed up after it. We jounced along a badly potholed road to Seoul, which we sped through without stopping. The view out the back of the canvas-covered truck body was obscured by the

dust cloud we raised, but I had an impression of a gigantic slum
with great piles of ruined masonry and bundles of long bamboo
poles leaning against broken walls. Once or twice I glimpsed
huge stone gates, and I burned with curiosity about the big city.

The road northward was unpaved and ascended through
mountains to hilly ground mostly covered by terraced rice fields.
Our truck speeded up as the road got rougher and the dust
denser, and with nothing to see through the dust cloud we were
all the more conscious of the bruising jolts. Pausing only briefly
at 24th Division headquarters in the war-shattered village of
Munsan-ni, we continued to the 19th Regiment north of the
Imjin River. As the truck bumped across Libby Bridge we left
civilian Korea behind and entered the American-occupied front
line, where three years of war had obliterated the rice fields and
villages, swept away the inhabitants and left a wasteland roamed
by packs of ferocious wild dogs; to some of us on that truck, the
broad, muddy Imjin seemed akin to the Styx.

The headquarters of the 19th, consisting of fifty or so
green quonset huts, some canvas tents, a motor pool and an
ammunition dump, sprawled over a valley hemmed in by high
hills and the barbed wire and minefields of the DMZ. I was to
stay there for a few days awaiting further assignment, so I
dumped my gear on a bunk in a "hooch" reserved for transients
and took a stroll.

As I sized up the place I discovered that its inhabitants
were friendly, helpful and casual—very unlike regular army
troops in domestic posts. It was then that I learned something
about fighting men in general: the closer they are to enemy guns,
the more they behave like human beings rather than cardboard
soldiers.

On my second or third day in camp I wandered into a
hooch with a sign that said "PIO," for Public Information Office,
in which a half dozen soldiers were producing a mimeographed

weekly newspaper for the regiment, as well as news stories and photographs for the GI newspaper *Pacific Stars and Stripes*. I struck up a conversation with some of them, in the course of which a PFC named Mike Poust said that one of the soldiers was about to end his tour and return home, and that there was an opening in the office, if I wanted it. Poust, who many years later became a New York City fire marshal, asked me whether I wouldn't rather work for Army PIO than pass my time in a tank.

"If you go out with an armored recon unit you'll spend your whole tour eating dust and seeing nothing but the DMZ," Mike said. "Join us, and you'll see the world—or at least the greater metropolitan Munsan-ni area." It took me less than a minute to decide.

Mike quickly made the necessary arrangements with the officer in charge, new orders were cut for me, and I moved my bag to a vacant bunk in the back of the PIO hooch.

On that day I became a journalist.

KOREA

KOREA INTRODUCED ME TO journalism and Asia, both of which dominated my life ever after. It was in Korea, moreover, that I learned the basic craft of journalism, at least in terms of its crude fundamentals.

Military journalism was more the kind of thing published in corporate house organs than real news. Much of it consisted of exhortations to the troops to buckle down harder, to "stand tall" during inspections and parades, to avoid accidents and venereal diseases and to fight for the team, be the game volleyball or war. The military press also carried a never-ending stream of achievement stories: the selection of the Soldier of the Month, the award of good-conduct medals, the winning of a boxing tournament.

Provided the cheerleading section of a GI newspaper was adequately filled, however, its editors were permitted to include some entertainment—comics, chaste cheesecake, jokes and anecdotes.

Stars and Stripes and the Armed Forces Network were closer than other military news outlets to real civilian media. They carried network feeds, syndicated columns and wire service news reports. But even *Stars and Stripes* and the Armed

Forces Network were not immune to military tampering or, on occasion, outright censorship.

Unit publications, on the other hand, made no pretense to being anything more than mouthpieces for unit commanders, and the troops generally discarded them without a glance after they were handed out. This was not for any lack of authentic news generated by the troops themselves; in fact, sensational events were frequent. For instance, our fellow soldiers of the 19th Regiment would have devoured a detailed news story when our commanding colonel blew his brains out one afternoon. But not a word of that (or any of the other dramatic happenings north of the Imjin while I was there) ever appeared in military print.

Our unit newspaper was subject to some interruptions not encountered in civilian life. Every now and then the North Koreans would start up their tanks and come charging south toward the barbed-wire boundary of the DMZ just over the hill from our compound. Their maneuvers were never more than feints, but our side could not be sure of this, and whenever the North Koreans practiced their assaults we were forced to brace ourselves for a real attack. We GI journalists would grab our shovels, sleeping bags and carbines, and dive into open trenches, where we sometimes remained for several days. During the frigid winter of 1957–58 the alerts were particularly uncomfortable, even though we wore heavy arctic clothing. Life in slit trenches was also excruciatingly dull; I managed at least to consume a Jane Austen novel during one protracted stint.

When the North Koreans were not acting warlike they often played soccer within view of several of our lookout posts. They played so enthusiastically that our own troops sometimes became fans of one enemy team or another, and I once suggested that we start reporting their games in the sports pages of our unit newspaper, if only to offer readers something new. My suggestion was not adopted.

There were also constant incidents at nearby Panmunjom, the cluster of buildings in the DMZ where United Nations
and North Korean commanders wrangled endlessly over alleged
truce violations. Some of the doings at Panmunjom would also
have made interesting reading for our troops if we could have
reported them, although the "incidents" were usually trivial in
themselves. On one visit to Panmunjom while I was looking at
a North Korean propaganda exhibit on alleged U.S. germ warfare, the pin securing my yellow observer armband came undone
and the armband fell to the ground. Two fierce-looking North
Korean MPs rushed over, yelled at me and scribbled something
on a clipboard. I learned later that they had charged me with a
truce violation for failure to wear the required armband, even
though it was off my arm for no more than thirty seconds.

Some of the brushes between North Koreans and Americans were far more dangerous. Fatal skirmishes between border
patrols occurred, and the accidental detonation of mines also
caused casualties.

There were casualties on our side of the wire, too, that
had nothing to do with the North Koreans. Whenever large
numbers of men carry loaded weapons around, accidents happen,
and helicopter ambulances often landed at our pads to pick up
the victims. Gunfire also sometimes claimed the lives of Korean
civilian intruders who occasionally sneaked across the river.
Most merely sought work as laundrymen and houseboys, but a
few were thieves ("slicky boys," in GI parlance) and a handful
were communist infiltrators. Once in a while a trigger-happy GI
on guard duty would open fire and kill one of these intruders.

Such shootings almost never resulted in trials or punishments; in fact, the shooters were sometimes rewarded with passes
or transfers to more comfortable units.

None of these incidents ever saw the light of print in the
military press or the outer world. Instead, our PIO staff filled a

dozen mimeographed pages each week with a vapid "commander's column," some glowing reportage of the latest training exercise, the movie schedules and some little stories about PFC so-and-so and his interesting hobby—raising Imjin River eels as pets, or whatever. Our best "stories," accompanied by photographs, were sent down to Munsan-ni for inclusion in a weekly division newspaper printed in Tokyo, and our products also turned up in *Stars and Stripes* and even (via the wire services) in civilian newspapers.

Considering how little we did to keep the soldiers informed about anything that really mattered, I found it hard to understand why the army tolerated our existence. We got to wear shoulder patches proclaiming us as "Official U.S. Army Correspondents," emblems that actually seemed to impress line officers. We were never required to stand in unit formations, pick up cigarette butts or even submit to regular inspections. Best of all, we had access to a jeep and could travel throughout the regimental sector, which extended quite a distance.

About halfway through my Korean tour of duty our little PIO group decided to abandon attempts at real reporting and brighten up our stories as entertainment rather than news. This campaign began with a series of bogus stories about space technology.

The Soviet Union had recently caused a sensation by launching its Sputnik satellite and frantic U.S. space scientists had yet to match the feat, so we of the Public Information Office of the 19th Infantry Regiment decided to advance America's cause on our own. After persuading a sergeant to cooperate in the hoax, we built a large and realistic dummy rocket out of cardboard, set it up on an improvised pad and photographed the sergeant gazing heavenward, with his hand proudly resting on the fake missile. An accompanying article reported that the enterprising infantryman was spending his off-duty hours building and testing advanced space vehicles on the banks of the Imjin, and would soon attempt an orbital launch.

The story made military readers chuckle, but when it reached Seoul, at least one civilian news organization took it seriously; International News Service (which later merged with United Press to become UPI) actually distributed a rewritten version of my account to subscribing newspapers in the States.

Our ease in fobbing off bogus stories on civilian news agencies came of the fact that civilian reporters rarely ventured north of the Imjin, so news bureaus in Seoul were reduced to using even suspect stories from official military sources. Besides, INS, already on its last legs, cared more about the entertainment value than the veracity of its stories. We wrote about Imjin River monsters, a Sumerian archaeological site discovered near Munsan-ni, ancient Korean flying machines and a lot of other nonsense. No one in or out of the army seemed to mind, probably because no sensible person would look for truthful reporting in a military publication in the first place.

Meanwhile, I bought a serviceable Japanese camera at the PX for $15, and my GI colleagues taught me the primitive darkroom techniques enforced by our frontier existence. Our hut was electrified but it lacked plumbing, and in winter it was warmed only during daytime hours by a cranky and dangerous kerosene heater. Our pans of developer and hypo froze at night, and our daily darkroom routine included thawing out the chemicals while we melted snow for shaving.

The lack of running water made life uncomfortable in other ways. A shower, fed by water trucked to the camp from the river, was turned on once a week and in temperate months we stayed fairly clean. But in midwinter the shower pipes often froze, depriving us of even this weekly respite from filth. We dusted ourselves with DDT powder, not only to discourage lice but to kill the mites that carried the dreaded Korean hemorrhagic fever. The army worried so much about these microscopic bugs that when we eventually returned to the United States, every stitch of our clothing was confiscated and burned.

One of the few strictly military duties PIO soldiers had to perform was guard duty, something I rather enjoyed, especially in winter. On cold, clear nights the Korean sky far from any town blazed with stars, and the silence and solitude of guard duty permitted some much needed meditation. I remember spending a Christmas Eve guarding our ammunition dump after a heavy snowfall, when the night was so cold that the loose flakes on the ground tinkled as I trudged through them. I looked up at the glowing Milky Way and felt rather happy.

The desolate hills around us had a certain austere beauty, but the river to the south and the DMZ to the north hemmed us in as virtual prisoners, and I seized every chance to get away for a few days. The invariable destination of GIs with weekend passes was Seoul, or one of its less savory suburbs like Yong-dongpo.

From our regiment the only means of getting to Seoul, some thirty-five miles to the south, was by hitchhiking on military vehicles. This was never difficult because traffic was incessant and drivers were instructed to stop for GI hitchhikers whenever they had room. But tearing along in dusty, bumping trucks was uncomfortable and caused a thick layer of khaki dust to be deposited on the freshly laundered and pressed fatigue uniforms we wore on pass. The trip was really noisome during the spring rice-planting season when the fields were fertilized with "night soil," human excrement, making the entire countryside smell like a latrine.

I explored Seoul mostly on foot, learning the complicated pattern of streets, visiting ancient palace gardens and admiring such glories as the fourteenth-century Great South Gate. Most of Seoul lay in ruins. The poverty was ubiquitous and obtrusive, and there was a constant danger of losing a wallet or camera to thieves. Shoeshine boys and street peddlers swarmed around lone Americans, endlessly pressing their solicitations to buy brass gimcracks made from the melted-down shell casings gathered up from battlefields, or mother-of-pearl lacquerware, wood carvings, paintings of tigers on black velvet, and often, "my cherry-girl sister." The street boys made strolling an ordeal.

I sometimes encountered cruelty as well. Once, on a winter day, on bustling Chungro Street, there appeared a mad-woman, stark naked, screaming and running aimlessly along the trolley tracks. While I was trying to decide what to do a crowd of youths began taunting the woman and throwing stones at her. Horrified, I ran toward her to try to shield her, but in a panic she dashed into an alleyway and shook off her persecutors. The boys howled with laughter and walked on.

But with the help of a GI friend from California, Isao Fujimoto, I began to meet educated Koreans. Like myself, Isao was a PIO soldier, but prior to being drafted he had been a probation officer and social worker, and he was deeply disturbed by the distress of Korean civilians. Among his interests was a large orphanage that he was helping, partly by enlisting his GI friends in a little black-market operation to help support it—an unlikely endeavor for a future Cornell University professor. Soldiers who visited Tokyo were asked to bring back large cans of Ajinomoto, the seasoning monosodium glutamate. The stuff could be sold in Seoul at a large profit, and the proceeds bought books and powdered milk for the orphans.

The Korean university students I met brought me a far wider perspective of the country than GIs ordinarily acquire. Not only did they instruct me in the nation's cultural traditions but in its politics, a subject American commanders wanted their troops to avoid. My circle of friends, mostly Koreans of both sexes but including some American GIs, would gather on weekends whenever we could. In warm weather the girls would pack picnic lunches for our hikes and climbs in the mountains just north of the capital, where we talked and sang each other's songs. (The Korean national anthem sounds a lot like the old Welsh tune "Men of Harlech.") On cold winter days we met in coffee shops, where one could sit all afternoon listening to classical music and nursing a single coffee and a glass of *mool*, hot water infused with roasted barley and garnished with a pine nut.

My student friends were painfully aware of the differences between Western democracy and their own government, headed by Syngman Rhee, an autocratic old Methodist who brooked no dissent from any quarter. South Korea's nightly curfew, its controlled press, and the ruthless arrest and punishment of critics had embittered young people deeply, and by the time I left Korea I knew that Rhee faced a coming insurrection.

During my year in Korea I could see the seeds of rebellion sprouting, as my student friends grew ever more angry at the repressions they suffered at the hands of the police, university administrators and military authorities. They also resented demeaning aspects of the American military occupation, despite the friendships many of them had with individual Americans. Nothing enrages a female university student (or her family and friends) more than being treated like a whore by foreign soldiers.

It did not surprise me that two years after I returned to the United States my friends and thousands of young Koreans like them took to the streets in bloody revolution. Many were killed in the fighting, but the young rebels ended by ousting Rhee and convincing themselves that they had at last brought Western democracy to the Land of the Morning Calm. Alas, my student friends, now grown old, have been disillusioned many times over. Korea's system of rule has lapsed repeatedly into tyranny over the years, despite the country's new skyscrapers, shiny cars, booming industries and general prosperity.

At the time the revolution was brewing I had a pretty fair notion of what was in the wind—better, perhaps, than some State Department and CIA analysts. But as a military journalist I could not report any hint of what I saw and heard, and it disturbed me that as a GI, I was just as tightly muzzled as any Korean newsman.

I was not used to the corruption that war inevitably begets, and something turned up by a Swarthmore College classmate of mine, Ted Conant, came as a nasty surprise. Ted, the son of James Bryant Conant (the Harvard University president who led development of the atomic bomb) was making documentary films about Korea for the UN while I was stationed there. In the course of his work he discovered that CARE packages sent to Korea by generous American donors were ending up in black-market warehouses for sale by big-time racketeers. Such a revelation wouldn't faze me today, but at the time, I was shocked.

Sometimes when I got weekend passes to visit Seoul I stayed outside town with the families of Korean friends, enjoying the warmth of a mattress pallet spread on the tiled floor. The charcoal heaters used in traditional Korean houses are ducted under the floors to warm rooms efficiently and make for cozy sleeping, but a drawback is that the ducts sometimes leak, causing the deaths of entire families by carbon monoxide asphyxiation.

The poverty of the students extended to their classrooms, and science and medical students made do with ridiculously primitive equipment. In the dissection room of a medical school I was shown the institution's supply of human cadavers, which had been chopped up, pickled in formaldehyde, and stored in *tokis,* the big ceramic pots in which Koreans ferment cabbage kimchi, a staple of the national diet. American educators who incessantly complain about their lack of computers, laboratory equipment and other amenities would have been surprised by the achievements of those Korean students, many of whom began distinguished medical careers poking around in those dreadful *toki* pots.

I also spent a lot of time in Japan, because brochures and other odds and ends our unit commanders thought they needed could be adequately printed only in Tokyo. I made friends and began studying Japanese partly because of the beauty of the language, which slips from the tongue as gracefully as Italian.

Japan was a good deal more picturesque in the 1950s than it is now. Kimonos and zori shoes were still standard streetware for women, and nighttime ferryboat rides along the Sumida River and its canals ran past thickets of paper lanterns lovely enough for a stage set of *Madama Butterfly*. Since then, alas, Japan has greatly changed, and a decade after my first visit, industrial pollution of the river had made it smell too foul to attract boaters. Tokyo, Taipei, Hong Kong and other great cities I loved in those days have also lost their luster, and everywhere in Asia, traditional garb has almost disappeared, except on holidays.

But in the 1950s I fell in love with Asia at the same time that I was becoming hooked on journalism—even the wretched version the army had taught me.

A few months before I was due to return to the States (and leave the army) I learned that my marriage was finished, and I spent an afternoon by myself in a Tokyo coffee shop, pondering the future. The next day I started hunting for a job that would keep me in Japan.

Some Americans I later knew achieved highly successful careers in Japan. Linda Beech, for example, the wife of the late war correspondent Keyes Beech of the *Chicago Daily News,* was a beautiful blonde who spoke flawless Japanese and was in great demand doing commercials for Tokyo television.

In the fifties a small army of Americans worked for news bureaus in Tokyo, and I got to know some of them as they swapped war stories and bought drinks at the old Tokyo Press Club. But I was a raw kid and none of them offered me work.

Next I tried the Japanese. I could barely speak the language, however, and my opportunities in Japanese journalism were decidedly limited. The English-language edition of one of the mass-circulation newspaper chains did offer me a temporary job in Osaka with a salary of $40 a month (before taxes). But that would have meant poverty even by Japanese standards, so I decided to return to America to start on a more conventional path into journalism.

CUB TO CORRESPONDENT

I PACKED AWAY MY discharge uniform, and after dividing up the books, records and other things Diana and I had accumulated in seven years of marriage—and finding a home for our cat—I looked in at the laboratory where I had worked before being drafted. I declined (with thanks) an invitation to return to work, and having thus bidden goodbye to chemistry, I began looking for work as a reporter.

My first tries were with *The New York Times*, the *Daily News* and some other New York City dailies. No one wanted me, so I tried the wire services, also without luck. After several weeks of fruitless efforts, I consulted a friend on the *Daily Mirror* who gave me two suggestions: abandon New York City, and get help from an employment agency. There really was an employment agency for journalists, with a name something like Ace Headline Agency. With no great expectations, I called on them.

That very afternoon, to my surprise, I was dispatched to a newspaper published in Middletown, New York, about fifty miles north of New York City in agricultural Orange County. *The Middletown Daily Record* had been founded only a year earlier by the J. M. Kaplan Fund, which seeded it with plenty of starting capital and the technology to make it the first daily newspaper in the United States published by the offset method.

The Record boasted better typography and printing quality than its Middletown competitor, and it had a staff of young men and women recruited in various parts of the nation, all eager to win their spurs. *The Record's* circulation of about twenty thousand was rising fast.

The editor, Al Romm, subjected all job applicants to a little quiz designed to test their general knowledge and vocabulary rather than journalistic experience, which he assumed to be practically nil. One of his questions asked for the gestation period of an elephant, and my guess of two years was evidently close enough, for I was hired on the spot.

Later that day the reporter I was replacing sold me his old but serviceable Pontiac for $50. The paper installed me in a cheap but comfortable apartment I was to share with two other reporters. Exuberant, I felt that I had at last secured a toehold in journalism.

The Record staff was a family of happy zealots, most of whom worked twelve-hour stints and produced more good copy per day than any comparable bunch I've known since. We had no union and the pay was modest compared to big city rates, but *The Record* gave a cub reporter the best education in the craft he or she could want. The paper's leaders, especially publisher David Bernstein, were pros, of course. Each week they assembled the junior staff for a workshop, at which our successes were lauded and our shortcomings gently pointed out. We were lectured on libel law, narrative prose, page makeup and many other useful subjects.

All of us, like hospital residents, were on call twenty-four hours a day, and phone calls at four A.M. were routine. Reporters were not only required to meet their copy deadlines by writing at lightning speed, but were expected to bring back publishable photographs taken with the cameras we always carried.

It would be many years before computers invaded newsrooms, and in the fifties we worked on large, noisy typewriters. Reporters really did yell "Copy!" when they needed someone to bring a fresh take to the copy desk, and with a score of people shouting into their phones as they typed notes, the cacophony could overwhelm a newcomer.

News copy of the precomputer age had a certain humane untidiness, which, like newsroom noise, I sometimes miss. We typed our stories on cheap newsprint paper, and we edited using scissors, paste and pencils with the softest, dirtiest lead available. Reporters and editors were issued spikes—long, vertical nails with heavy green bases—on which newspapermen impaled unused copy and stories that had been killed.

The spikes of celebrities were revered as sacred memorabilia. A copy spike used for many years by H. L. Mencken, *The Baltimore Sun*'s immortal curmudgeon, was melted out of shape by a fire that demolished the *Sun*'s newsroom, but that spike was enshrined for many years in memory of the Sage of Baltimore. (In 1960 I asked a young *Sun* reporter what had happened to Mencken's spike, and he replied, "Mencken? Who was Mencken?" *Sic transit gloria mundi.*)

Some of us on *The Record* had regular beats, covering the contentious politics of village school boards, town meetings and election campaigns. But everyone was expected to pitch in on murders, fatal accidents, fires and other crises, and I found that big cities have no monopoly on mayhem. The bucolic settings of Orange, Rockland and Sullivan counties, with their rolling pastures, wooded lakes and cozy villages, did not encourage domestic bliss, and when farmers murdered someone or committed suicide, the remains were often as sickening as any produced by war. Rural life also seemed to include plenty of incest, rape, child abuse and other crimes we tend to associate with crowded cities.

For me, *The Record* was a breath of freedom after having worked for military newspapers. There were few sacred cows or taboos at our little paper, and reporters were encouraged to hit hard when stories warranted it. We also got to try our hands at many different aspects of newspaper publishing; I got to do everything from interviewing beauty queens to laying out the paper, and I acquired a lot of out-of-the-way knowledge.

In the late 1950s *The Record* was doing so well financially that its owners bought out the competition and merged the two papers. Most of our original staff scattered to the four winds, some moving to other publications but others becoming successful free-lance writers. One of our alumni, Hunter Thompson, really hit his stride after *The Record* fired him, and his books about Hell's Angels and other notorious types made him a celebrity.

Hunter Thompson's problems at *The Record* were consequences of his volatile temper, not his writing. One day, when the office Coke machine failed to deliver him either a bottle or a refund, he demolished the machine with kicks and blows. Editor Romm tolerated many things but never shows of violence, and he dismissed Hunter on the spot.

Journalists keep running into each other and the next time I met Hunter was in Saigon, where he was working up an article by haranguing the Viet Cong delegation at Saigon airport. For once, the unflappable communists seemed nonplussed.

After a while *The Record* made me an editor, which increased my salary but was not nearly as much fun as scouting for news in my 1940 Hudson. (My fifty-dollar Pontiac had given up the ghost by then.) I hadn't become a journalist to sit behind a desk, after all; what I wanted above all else was something the late Paul Gallico, a role model of mine, called "the Feel."

Gallico wrote memorable magazine fiction back when magazines published the best stuff around, but he was also a sportswriter and editor of the New York *Daily News*. He believed deeply in the need for direct, personal experience as a prerequisite to rounded reporting. As a cub reporter, Gallico once asked the heavyweight boxing champion Jack Dempsey to fight a round with him, just to see what it was like. Dempsey knocked him flat, but Gallico counted himself the winner: he had acquired the Feel of being knocked down by a champion. For the sake of getting the same kind of Feel, Gallico played golf against champion Bobby Jones, swam with Johnny Weismuller and tried to get a hit off pitcher Dizzy Dean.

Gallico saw life itself as a vehicle for attaining the Feel, and so do I. Life to him was a quest for the greatest possible range and depth of experience, including physical sensations, of course, but much more. The Feel can come from a brush with quantum theory or a Bach fugue or a Blake sonnet, as well as a bullet wound or the caress of a loved one. The Feel arises from exultation, despair, agony, pleasure and revelation, not from a TV screen or a printed page. For people who truly crave the Feel—the full palette—there's simply no substitute for being there.

That's why journalism beckons so seductively to people like Gallico and me; no other pursuit offers a practitioner such richness of experience.

The big news of 1959 was Fidel Castro's triumphant entry into Havana on New Year's Day. Castro's guerrilla campaign had caused a sensation from its inception in 1956, and even in Korea I had caught a whiff of the excitement his 26th of July Movement aroused.

In the summer of 1959 *The Record* agreed to let me go to Havana, giving me some time off for the trip and paying part of my expenses in exchange for a series of reports. The assignment wasn't lucrative, but for me it was pure gold. Barely a year out of uniform, I had won a modest posting as a real foreign correspondent, and although I wasn't representing any big-name publication, I was at least going. The prospect thrilled.

CUBA LIBRE

H
OWEVER ONE MAY FEEL
 about Cuban communism, Castro's re-
gime during the past third of a century has treated the world to
plenty of life-and-death drama. Against a backdrop of arbitrary
despotism and occasional spurts of bloodshed, Cuba has managed to drag the superpowers through some nearly fatal crises,
and the poverty-ridden island has constantly kept onlookers on
the edges of their chairs.

My brief airplane hop from Miami to Havana's José
Martí Airport spanned two worlds as simultaneously similar and
different as the two sides of the old Berlin Wall. Both Miami and
Havana had palm-lined boulevards on waterfronts facing modern hotels and office buildings, and the weather in both cities was
appallingly hot. The midday air shimmered, casting a stupefying
pall over every living creature.

But in Havana one noticed police who looked very different from their Miami counterparts. Fear mingled with joy in
the Cuban capital, and there was a smell of incipient violence.

Lacking any knowledge of Havana (and with a still rather
shaky command of Spanish) I asked a taxi driver to suggest a
cheap hotel, and he dropped me at a four-story walk-up establishment on the Prado near the center of town. My airy room had

whitewashed walls, a comfortable bed with a crucifix over it and French windows with green louvered shutters, through which I could step out onto a little balcony.

The Prado was noisy. Radios blasted at full volume, and I got heartily sick of a song called "*Cállate, Corazón, Cállate.*" Day and night the sirens of police vehicles echoed through the streets as cops trawled for troublemakers, dissidents, suspected spies, former employees of the ousted Batista government, ordinary criminals and ordinary people, some of whom would end up as fodder for the firing squads.

The revolution's signs were everywhere: little chalked marks over doorways reading GRACIAS FIDEL, billboards proclaiming AÑO DE LA LIBERTAD, red-white-and-black badges of the 26th of July Movement, flags and heroically posed pictures of the leaders: Fidel, of course, but also an Argentine hero of the movement whose nickname meant little to me at the time—"Che." I little dreamed how much copy Che would provide me in the decades ahead.

A fiesta atmosphere prevailed, with crowds of boisterous strollers in the plazas and streets at all hours, packing coffee stands and bars, and seeking entertainment. Everywhere there were *barbudos,* men in green U.S. Army–style fatigues, whose beards proclaimed them as veterans of the Sierra Maestra guerrilla campaign against the hated forces of the ousted Fulgencio Batista.

Guerrillas the *barbudos* may have been, but their uniforms that summer were crisply starched and looked brand new, as did their polished leather boots and pistol holsters. With the nation groveling before them, the *barbudos* strutted Havana like cocks, accepting food from bodega owners and picking up every pretty girl they could get.

I wanted to meet people in the new government and my first point of contact was Juan Ossorio of Castro's press office. As

I walked into his cramped office, a staff member arrived with a stack of press releases in English, one of which was handed to me. It read: "Haven't you heard that Castro is drifting into the Red orbit, that Communists control Cuba, and that the island is bankrupt under Castro? Big lies put out by big fools. Their stolen millions are adroitly spent to influence American writers and journalists. Give a man a fortune and he will see red in his father's moustache." Ossorio assured me with many protestations that Cuba had no connections with communists.

But another official I met, Maria Witoska, was less reassuring.

I had been told that Miss Witoska, a private secretary and administrative assistant to Castro, exercised considerable power. She had been appointed by no less a luminary than Celia Sánchez, Castro's right-hand woman and an éminence grise of the regime.

One of the strangest of Latin American paradoxes is the ambivalence in attitudes toward women in politics. On the one hand, women are expected to be be God-fearing homemakers who whelp steady streams of children and leave management of the important things to men. But on the other hand, women occasionally achieve the status that elevates them to political sainthood, in the tradition of Joan of Arc and Evita Perón. Castro's friend Celia was among the Latin women who had achieved this status.

There was never a hint of any romantic connection between Castro and any of his female lieutenants. Celia Sánchez herself was a wiry, intense woman who chain-smoked and riveted interviewers with her piercing, almost fanatical dark eyes. There were some intriguing parallels between communism and the Roman Catholic church, and I've always thought of Celia Sánchez as a Castroite Virgin Mary.

Celia Sánchez died in 1980, and Haydée Santamaría, another of Castro's vestal virgins, committed suicide a few months later. But at the time I was in Cuba, Castro's women were national figures who could be ignored only at one's peril.

Maria Witoska was more an apparatchik than a leader, but although she was relatively inconspicuous, she wielded power deriving from the Kremlin itself. Unlike Sánchez and Santamaría, native Cubans, Witoska was a Pole who had lived in Cuba for only a few months. Her Spanish was halting, and next to her desk was a phonograph and a stack of Berlitz Spanish-language records. She told me, in German, that she had been assigned to Cuba by her own government, that of communist Poland, to advise and assist the Castro regime in the organization of its administrative structure. When I asked whether she herself was a communist, she merely smiled.

And so, on my second day in Cuba, I had already begun to look askance at Castro's claims to having no links with communism. Not that I cared myself, but at the time, debates over his alleged communist leanings were consuming mountains of newsprint in the United States. At one paper alone, *The New York Times,* two leading Cuba correspondents daily offered their readers startlingly contradictory interpretations of the Castro government. In the same edition, a reader could encounter both Herbert L. Matthews, a supporter of Castro, and Ruby Hart Phillips, who despised Castro, as they traded journalistic punches.

I went to see Osvaldo Dorticós Torrado, Castro's minister of revolutionary law and minister of agriculture (who later became Cuba's president and figurehead chief of state). Dorticós was a star of the guerrilla insurrection, and his assignment in the new government reflected the respect he enjoyed. He was in charge of collectivizing Cuba's farms and throwing out American landowners.

One day while waiting to see Dorticós I met another American in the outer office. As we chatted, he told me that for many years he had owned and managed a large tomato farm east of Havana, which he wanted to present to the new Cuban government.

"Batista was a bum and Cuba was the most corrupt country in the hemisphere," he told me. "Castro has done a great thing, and Americans who made money in Cuba owe him some help, now that he needs it."

The American's proposal, he said, was to reorganize his farm as a cooperative that would be owned and administered by the Cuban workers themselves. But he had been frustrated. Each time he had tried to discuss his idea with the *barbudo* bureaucracy, he had been rebuffed; indeed, he had been cooling his heels in Dorticós's outer office for two weeks.

That day, as usual, he had been waiting for nearly an hour when I arrived, but I was nevertheless received first. Those were the days before Havana began the mass expulsion of American journalists, and we were generally treated with kid gloves.

Dorticós, a short man with a prim and cruel-looking mouth, waved me to a chair and asked what I wanted. I had originally intended to ask about his plans for Cuban agriculture, but instead, I started the interview by mentioning that an American tomato grower who had been trying to give Cuba his farm was also hoping to see him.

"We have no need of gifts from the imperialist planters," Dorticós said. "We shall expropriate the land for ourselves at our own pace, and reorganize it according to socialist norms, not the wishes of its former Yankee owners." Whereupon Dorticós changed the subject to sugar production, plans for agricultural diversification and economic cooperation with Cuba's socialist allies.

My early contacts with Cuban officials had been polite and even friendly, but I soon got a taste of the sterner side of the revolution. One day I attended a large rally, at which several thousand sugar workers bused in from the countryside were treated to one of Fidel's spellbinding harangues.

At one point the speech drew a jubilant cheer from the crowd, and the *macheteros* raised a salute to the leader, their right fists clenched in the classic communist style. I raised my camera and shot several exposures, but suddenly there was a strong hand yanking my shoulder as another hand grabbed my camera. I was a prisoner of the cops.

A couple of hours later, having convinced my captors that I intended no harm, I was allowed to leave the police station with my camera. But my film had been ripped from the camera and ruined. "You'll understand," the chief told me, "that your readers might get an erroneous impression seeing pictures of our people saluting that way."

The chief of the Havana bureau of United Press International, Francis McCarthy, warned me that trouble was brewing for the foreign press corps in Havana and that the country was about to undergo a sea change.

Newsmen packed UPI's stuffy radio room whenever Castro broadcast a speech, listening to his high-pitched voice for hours at a time and filing their stories even while he was still speaking. Castro was no respecter of deadlines.

It was at one of these late-night sessions that I met a pretty, free-lance reporter named Jean Secon, who had a taste for adventure. Over a late dinner she told me of her staunchly respectable upbringing in Syracuse, New York, and her childhood as a highly respectable Rainbow Girl (the Order of Rainbow Girls is an affiliate of the Masons)—a background she had thrown off with a vengeance. I doubt that Jean realized how dangerous and tempestuous her life was about to become.

As I roamed Havana I learned that quite a number of Americans had fought shoulder to shoulder with Castro's guerrillas. A few of them had been rewarded with important positions in the Cuban government.

I met one, a twenty-three-year-old Marine Corps de-
serter, at a Havana soda fountain that had once been a hangout
of American tourists. Ex–Marine Sergeant Gerry C. Holthaus
from Illinois had been based at Guantánamo, the big U.S. naval
base, when he decided to throw in his lot with Castro's rebel
forces.

Holthaus told me that in the previous year he and some
Marine Corps companions had been riding a bus that was ambushed by the guerrillas, and the passengers were briefly taken
captive. The rebels released their American guests after a day or
so, but asked them to consider joining the cause and helping the
revolution. The invitation appealed to Holthaus, and after returning to his unit at Guantánamo, he remained in contact with the
Cubans. Eventually he deserted the base and joined them.

The young Marine had been a specialist in heavy weapons, and the rebels put him to work as an ordnance expert. After
the crash of a government fighter, the guerrillas salvaged one of
the plane's electrically operated 20-millimeter cannons, and with
Holthaus's expert guidance, mounted it on a jeep and put it in
firing condition. "We used the gun against a Batista blockhouse
that had been holding out for days," he said. "It jammed after a
few rounds, but it did the job. Once the *batistianos* knew they
were under cannon fire they quit."

Holthaus was appointed a lieutenant in the Cuban forces
(in which the highest rank was major), and after the rebel victory
was given a sinecure as chief of Havana's tourist police. The
duties were negligible and he found little to do but hang around
the coffee shops and soda fountains, hoping to run into Americans. Homesick, repentant and with little knowledge of Spanish,
he wanted to return to the States but feared the harsh sentence
he would certainly draw from a Marine court martial.

Holthaus's predicament came to the attention of Dickie
Chapelle, a woman journalist regarded by many Marines as one
of their own, and certainly one of the most sympathetic reporters

the Corps ever had. The friend of privates as well as the commandant himself, Dickie had covered the Marine Corps for the *Reader's Digest* in every campaign from World War II on.

Using her influence with Marine commanders, Miss Chapelle worked out a deal by which young Holthaus could return to the United States and face reduced charges that would send him to prison for a relatively short term. He made it home. "Marines kind of think of me as a guardian angel," the gravel-voiced Chapelle told me. "I can't let them down."

For all the support she gave them over the years, her leatherneck friends could not save Dickie from the Viet Cong land mine that ended her life in 1965.

Some other Americans played a deadlier game in Cuba.

One of them, William A. Morgan, was a skilled lieutenant and confidant of Castro during the Sierra Maestra campaign, and rose to the rank of major, equal in grade to Castro himself. After the rebel victory, however, the gringo soldiers of fortune were faced with the prospect of holding ordinary office jobs that offered little appeal to men of action. Bored, Morgan became a plotter of coups.

At first, his plots were aimed at overthrowing or embarrassing some of the Caribbean governments hostile to Havana—especially the Trujillo regime in the Dominican Republic. But later Morgan turned against his Cuban bosses, set up an anti-Castro rebel base in the Dominican Republic, and began organizing a quixotic anti-Castro insurrection.

Naively assuming that the secret police were ignorant of his machinations, Morgan and some confederates flew back to Cuba in a light plane and landed on a highway near Havana. The police were waiting for him, of course, and the traitor Morgan was executed a few days later.

Another American, Captain Herman F. Marks, became one of the most hated men in the Castro regime, and not incidentally, a star of the international press. He also had an impact on my personal life.

Marks was nicknamed "the Yankee Butcher" for good reason: he commanded Castro's firing squads during the bloodiest period of the Cuban terror.

A renegade merchant seaman from Waukesha, Wisconsin, he had acquired an American police record that included thirty-two convictions for crimes ranging from armed robbery to rape. But he was a formidable fighter and gang leader—a man with talents the *barbudos* needed.

Marks had found prerevolutionary Havana very much to his taste. It was a town in which anything was available for a price. The sexual extravaganzas staged by "Popeye" and his troop of pornographic players were famous among lowlifes all over the world, and Havana's murderers, like its whores, were good at their jobs and came cheap. After the revolution Havana's demimonde took some time to fade away. The girls were still plying the bars in 1959, and an underemployed hit man promised to reduce his usual $1,000 rate by half if I would get him a decent contract.

Marks swam like a fish in this environment, and when Castro's guerrilla agents began scouting the city for potentially useful recruits, Marks came to their attention. He joined the rebels in the mountains of Oriente Province early in their campaign, and fought so well that he was befriended by Che Guevara himself.

With the rebel victory, Guevara found himself in charge of La Cabaña, Havana's largest fort, where thousands of Castro's real or suspected enemies would be incarcerated or shot. But Guevara had other fish to fry as president of the National Bank and tsar of the new Cuba's economy. So Guevara turned over La Cabaña to Herman Marks—a post that made Marks Cuba's lord high executioner.

No one knows exactly how many political prisoners were executed by the regime during that bloody year of 1959, but the best guess is around seven hundred. At La Cabaña alone, some two hundred were shot. Marks took to the work with gusto, presiding over a six-member firing squad that sometimes dispatched as many as eleven prisoners a night. During the day, he often attended the *pro forma* military trials that processed the victims, his eyes glittering with anticipation.

One of Marks's former prisoners told me of an execution he had witnessed.

"The convict was a seventeen-year-old kid the tribunal had convicted of collaborating with the Batista forces," my acquaintance said. "As he was tied to the stake he asked Marks not to give him the *coup de grace,* because he wanted his face and head to remain presentable when his body was returned to his family.

"Marks agreed," my acquaintance continued, "the firing squad shot the boy, and then Marks walked over to the body and emptied his .45, shooting the kid's head from every angle. It looked like a smashed watermelon when he was through."

Up to the time I arrived in Havana, Marks had not been interviewed by newsmen, and he looked like a good target for me.

Built across the harbor from downtown Havana in 1774, La Cabaña fortress casts a shadow over the city as sinister as that of Dracula's castle, and in 1959, it was not a place that people visited by choice. However, a small ferry carried the fortress's guards back and forth, and I rode over on it. A steep walk up a dusty, winding road carried me to the top of the hill and the prison gate.

I asked to see "El Capitán Herman" and a scowling sentry ordered me to wait. The waiting room proved to be a cell with a straw mat, and two hours later I was still waiting—and yelling. I had begun to lose hope for an interview (or even of getting back to downtown Havana) when a guard threw open the cell door and ordered me to follow him—right out the front gate. I assumed that I was being ejected, but just as I turned to leave, Marks himself strolled out and asked me, "How about a beer? There's a decent bar down the street."

The sentries gave him a halfhearted salute, and as we walked to the cafe I studied the infamous "Butcher." He wore the usual fatigue uniform, and from his belt hung the .45 automatic with which he had shot many a dying prisoner. Clean-shaven and superficially good-natured, Marks at thirty-seven presented the impression of a U.S. Army noncommissioned officer. His slangy conversation focused mainly on "beer and broads," and he professed to be ignorant and distrustful of politics and ideology.

Far from exhibiting shame or embarrassment, Marks plainly enjoyed the publicity his gruesome job had begun to attract. "They even wrote me up in *Newsweek*," he said, "although they got a lot of things wrong. They said I did three years for rape, when it was just statutory rape." As for his firing squad, "Well, someone has to do the job," he said. "I don't mind it."

UPI carried a long story I filed about my meeting with Marks, which portrayed him as an outwardly mild-mannered sociopath and sadist. A few days later I ran into Marks on a downtown street and introduced him to Jean Secon, the UPI stringer with whom I'd been flirting for a week or so. I should have bitten my tongue and ignored the man.

Somehow or other, Jean took up with Marks, much to my chagrin.

But Marks's star had begun to set. Not long after I left Cuba the regime became fed up with his bloody spectacles and notoriety, which were beginning to tarnish the world image of the revolution itself. He was reassigned to another army post very much less exposed to public attention than La Cabaña.

But he and Jean stayed in touch.

Marks was soon bored by his new post and he began plotting—this time against not only the communists in government but against Castro himself. The watchful Cuban intelligence service soon got wind of Marks's half-baked scheming and moved to snuff out the traitors. In May 1960, about nine months after I had left Cuba, Marks learned that arrest warrants had been issued for both himself and his friend Jean Secon. Both faced virtually certain execution.

Marks and Jean fled in the dead of night to the Isle of Pines, where they found a fishing boat, subdued its crew at the point of a submachine gun, and set sail. Marks had fought in a foreign army and thereby forfeited his American citizenship, so the pair made for Mexico.

About midway through the ordeal, Jean later told me, the boat ran out of diesel fuel and the fugitives and their crew had to hoist sail. When they eventually reached Yucatán, Marks released his Cuban captives and he and Jean struck out through Mexico, finally crossing the Rio Grande and entering the United States as wetbacks. They made their way to New York City and Jean's East Seventy-eighth Street apartment.

Marks stayed out of sight, but Robert Kennedy, brother of President Kennedy and U.S. attorney general, had resolved to track the Butcher of La Cabaña to his lair and nail him. Agents of the Immigration and Naturalization Service pressed the search and in January 1961 arrested Marks at Jean's apartment. Kennedy issued a congratulatory statement.

Once again, Capitán Herman began making page-one headlines, but this time he was portrayed as the victim of political persecution. Among his defenders was the American Civil Liberties Union, which argued that no precedent existed for deporting any native-born American. Moreover, there were only two nations to which Marks could in principle be deported, Mexico and Cuba. Mexico, however, wanted no part of Herman

Marks, and sending him back to Cuba, it was argued, would be tantamount to a death sentence.

In the end, the Justice Department gave up, and Marks disappeared from public scrutiny. But he was still around. In 1961 I left the United States as the AP's new bureau chief in Saigon. By 1964 I had all but forgotten Marks, when I began getting letters about him from my mother. Jean Secon, it seems, had looked up my mother and told her that Marks had been beating her up. In desperation, Jean sought refuge at my mother's Greenwich Village apartment, where she had a brief respite from the Butcher. Later that year, on a complaint by Jean, Marks was arrested and charged with threatening her life.

The last news I got of Marks was from a brief newspaper story in 1965, which reported that he had broken his leg in a New York City courtyard after falling out of a tree. According to the police report, he had been perched in the tree with a pair of binoculars peeping through a window at a female neighbor.

Despite La Cabaña, postrevolutionary Cuba was an exciting country that touched my life for many years, although my requests for visas were always turned down.

Cuba taught me that however bright a revolution's flags and rhetoric may seem, they are often pretexts for cruelty, injustice and tragedy. Luckily, all revolutions run out of steam after a while, but their victims remain dead.

BALTIMORE

AFTER GETTING BACK FROM Cuba I returned to covering Orange County and editing *The Record,* but I had tasted the nectar of foreign correspondence and realized I couldn't do without it. In the summer of 1960 I drove down to New York to try my luck at the AP, which, I knew, was the world's largest employer of foreign correspondents.

The Associated Press building at 50 Rockefeller Plaza seemed like a temple to me—dwarfed by the neighboring RCA Building (or GE Building, as its new owners call it), but with charm of its own. The entrance is surmounted by a striking cubist relief sculpture depicting news coverage as it was in the 1930s, and it looked good to me. The AP is the oldest news agency in America, and its first battle casualty was Mark Kellogg, a correspondent who died with Custer at the Little Bighorn. I wanted badly to join the outfit.

I took the elevator to the fourth floor, where a surprisingly friendly receptionist showed me into the vast newsroom. A personnel executive and some editors asked me a few questions and then asked me to take a little test, in which I was asked to read through a list of imaginary happenings and then write an imaginary news story about them.

A month later the AP phoned me in Middletown to offer me a job, on condition that I move to Baltimore. I'd never been to Baltimore, but I jumped at the chance.

As part of my initiation I had to write a letter to the personnel manager, Wes Gallagher, describing my goals with the AP. It seemed to me that such an august personage probably had better things to do than read such letters, but I put my heart into it and said I wanted a foreign post, preferably in a third-world country, Viet Nam if possible. The fall of the French fortress at Dien Bien Phu and my own experience in Asia had convinced me that Indochina was likely to be a fulcrum of news and history in the years to come. I also mentioned that I could speak French, German and Spanish.

That letter was to do more for me than I could have dreamed.

I found a cheap apartment on Baltimore's North Charles Street, and Max Fullerton and his staff at the AP bureau plunged me into the hectic work of filing the wires, an occupation almost as nerve-racking as controlling air traffic.

The AP bureau was in the heart of the city, next to Baltimore's famous "Block," a string of waterfront striptease bars that have since been replaced by a fashionable shopping district. One of the very few stories I actually got to cover on site during my stay in Baltimore was a fire that gutted one of those seedy bars. It was close enough to the office that I could run over, interview the girls and dash back in time to file a story on the wire.

The newsmen (a job classification that includes women) typed out their stories and turned them over to desk editors, who passed them on to "punchers," communications craftsmen who retyped news copy on machines that converted the letters and numbers into holes in paper tape. This tape could then be read by a device that translated the holes into electrical impulses sent over the teletype wires. Compared with today's computer operations, it was somewhat primitive.

The quantity of rewriting an agency employee must get through on any day is staggering. Any story that breaks in the afternoon and is distributed to evening newspapers, for example, must be rewritten (and, if possible, updated) as a "night lead" for morning newspapers, and there were scores of night leads to write each day.

My biggest lesson that year in Baltimore was that news is a kind of all-pervading ether, in which no one's story is exclusive for more than a few minutes (unless, of course, the story is false). News agencies are like bacterial culture dishes, in which a single newsbreak propagates at lightning speed and fills the dish, obliterating all traces of the reporter who fathered it. No one outside the news fraternity knows or cares what journalist broke the story of, say, the end of World War II, or the sinking of the *Lusitania,* but to journalists, scoops still matter.

Editors demand that their reporters stay ahead of the pack, and speed is the primary concern of the news business. In the brutal contest to win customers and keep them happy, news organizations go to elaborate lengths to beat competitors on every story, even if only by a few minutes. Accuracy is important, too, but newsmen can't afford to spend so much time checking something that they end up beaten.

The agency reporter's bugaboo was the dreaded "rocket," a cable or teletype message from the home office (often arriving at four A.M.) informing him that some competitor was out with a major story that he would have to match instantly.

All press messages were supposed to be composed in a highly truncated language called "cablese," which developed to avoid paying cable companies for unnecessary words and punctuation. Evelyn Waugh satirized cablese magnificently in *Scoop,* his great novel about foreign correspondents, but the art of rocket writing rose to still greater heights after World War II.

Typical of cablese was the phrase "harp sharply," meaning to write concisely and briefly; a desk would order a reporter to "Harp sharply," and the reporter might reply, "Harping sharpest but need leastly 400 propoxviews etcolor," meaning "I'm writing as concisely as possible, but I need at least 400 words to include the police account and some color."

The point of such compression came home to me in places like Afghanistan, where my press cables cost my employers a dollar a word.

My year in Baltimore was a low point in my life for several reasons, including an unwanted marriage with a young woman I had inadvertently impregnated. The prospect of supporting her family for the next twenty-one years did not unduly disturb me (although in later years the burden was substantial), but my real anguish in 1961 was the fear that my wings would be clipped forever, and that I would spend the rest of my career rewriting weekend sports stories in Baltimore. For the first time in my life I experienced real despair.

People of my age, I strongly believe, enjoyed richer and more exciting lives than those of most of today's kids. But we had some monstrous problems they do not share. Today there are birth-control pills, legal abortions and single parents, but in my day, the choice was often between a ruined life and bitter resignation, or suicide. My generation could still weep over Dreiser's *An American Tragedy*.

But one autumn day as I was staring gloomily out the window of my Baltimore apartment, the phone rang. Bureau chief Fullerton was on the other end, and his message was brief: "You have three days to get up to New York for a week of indoctrination. The AP wants you in Saigon. Congratulations, and get going."

Cable desk veterans instructed me not to send them anything that smacked of travelogue prose. "We've seen enough copy on Cambodia's Angkor Wat to last a lifetime," I was told. "When you get to Indochina we want news, not art reviews."

This was some of the worst advice I ever got. It's been my experience that readers and listeners care a great deal about the setting of a story, often more than the story itself. A coup in Katmandu may have some political impact, but ordinary readers are at least as interested in the sights and sounds of that exotic capital as they are in its politics. There's a lot more to news than "what-when-where-why-and-how"; a reader is entitled know something about the look, feel, smell of a scene, even if only through a few deft phrases.

Preparations for a trip to some exotic destination are a thrill in themselves—picking up a ticket, getting a passport and the necessary visas, buying maps, a flashlight and Band-Aids, saying goodbye to friends, signing a will. I've never gotten over the wonderful feeling imparted by such activities.

Before leaving the United States I strolled through the New York streets and parks in which I had grown up, and I looked at passersby in a new way. I was about to plunge into an existence as alien as Mars, and I wondered if I would ever see New Yorkers in their native habitat again.

Having abandoned most of my belongings to two ex-wives, I found that I could easily pack everything I owned, including my forlorn checkbook, in a single Samsonite suitcase. With that and a very light heart, I set out for Asia.

VIET NAM: THE EARLY DAYS

"WELCOME TO VIET NAM, Mal," said the AP's Ha Van Tran, as he guided me across the field to the immigration counter. Two photographers snapped pictures of me as we walked. One, Tran told me, was from *The Times of Viet Nam,* the local English-language paper. The other worked for the secret police.

As our taxi drove out the airport entrance we passed a small, neatly landscaped park with a sign in Vietnamese and French marking it as a model airplane club. A couple of young men were flying a noisy little gas-powered model, and some others were fiddling with the engines of their planes or enjoying picnic lunches. It struck to me that Saigon must be enjoying a respite from its famous guerrilla war.

In fact, however, that peaceful scene was more than just a respite from war. It was normality. Riding through the crowded streets and markets, I encountered an important insight into the war news that was reaching American consumers from Viet Nam: the news, as transmitted, conveyed a radically different impression from what someone actually on the scene saw.

From what I've known of various conflicts, especially Viet Nam's, war consists mostly of long, relatively peaceful periods and a lot of waiting, interrupted by occasional battles and violence. Wholesale bloodletting is fairly rare in war.

This is why war news may be factually correct but very unrealistic in context, and therefore misleading. (I could add that *all* news, not just war news, necessarily distorts objective reality to some degree.) The distorted impressions created by vignettes that fill up the news are nobody's fault, least of all the reporter's. They are a consequence of the demand by consumers for news that is unusual rather than routine. War news is mainly about death, even though most people actually experiencing the war go on living.

In *Open Letters: Selected Writings 1965–1990,* Václav Havel, the playwright who became the president of Czechoslovakia (and later, of the Czech Republic), wrote: "As long as humans can remember, death has been the point at which all the lines of every real story converge." That's certainly true of journalism, but it doesn't necessarily reflect reality.

And so, even after having read a lot of what passed for news, Viet Nam came as quite a surprise to me. I saw, in time, that Graham Greene's memorable novel *The Quiet American* had caught the flavor of Viet Nam's war better than any newspaper or magazine article I had read. The novel, unlike news accounts, sketched the setting of the war, including its everyday routine, its uneventful lulls and its all-important political undercurrents.

War reporting often falls short of the truth because it is too much like sports reporting. A daily budget of war stories from Viet Nam generally included a box score (towns taken or lost, body counts, matériel captured or destroyed), a wrap-up of the day's game, the coach's pep talk, and the locker-room sidebar (that is, an interview with the winning colonel, perhaps, or a heartwarming hospital interview with a wounded soldier).

War cuts a lot deeper than a football game, however.

The real sea changes in Viet Nam occurred not so much on battlefields as in village meetings organized by the Viet Cong and in conference rooms at the Pentagon and the White House.

Now that the war is long past, we paint it with broad brush-strokes and we tend to forget the skirmishes, not only the scraps between enemies on the battlefield, but quarrels between allied diplomats and generals as they endlessly sparred for political advantage. Many a career was made or ruined in Viet Nam.

The Byzantine twists of the Indochina War from 1961 to 1975 were part of a history that today seems almost as remote as the Crimean War of 1853–56, a war that Viet Nam resembled in some striking respects. Like Viet Nam, the Crimean War had no long-term effect on history, aside from the fact that its dead remained dead.

Another parallel between the Crimean and Viet Nam wars was the bitterness between newsmen and commanding officers.

The best known of the correspondents covering the Crimea (and one of the greatest in the history of journalism) was William Howard Russell of *The Times* of London—a role model for all of us who succeeded him. Russell's dispatches eulogized the bravery of the British "thin red line tipped with steel," but they also attacked the wanton neglect of the British troops by their government, the bungling of Lords Raglan and Lucan, the horror of the military hospitals and the lack of food and clothing for the troops.

Russell's news stories so infuriated the British general staff that the journalist was banned for a while from the army's positions and was deprived of quarters, food and transportation. Some officers even accused Russell of revealing military secrets to the enemy. (Prince Mikhail Dmitriyevich Gorchakov, the Russian commander and a regular reader of Russell's articles in *The Times,* wrote to Russell after the war that his forces never gleaned any useful intelligence from them, however.)

In the end, Russell's reporting was vindicated. The government in London fell, the Crimean commanders were replaced and Florence Nightingale, appalled by Russell's dispatches, organized a nursing corps that brought some relief to the hellish Crimean casualty wards.

When the war was over the British forces pulled out of the Crimea, and although there were some shifts in the web of Balkan power politics, the war did little to change history. How many Britons or Russians today have the least idea what their countries were fighting over when the Light Brigade charged to its glorious extermination?

Like Russell, newsmen in Viet Nam were often at bitter odds with the military high command, but as in the Crimea, they sometimes did some good. In any case, Viet Nam already seems destined to become as forgotten as the Crimea. A few years from now, how many Americans will remember where or why the battle of Khe Sanh was fought?

But these thoughts came to me only many years after I first set foot in Viet Nam.

John Griffin, the AP correspondent I was replacing, took me to a tailor who offered to make me a new wardrobe of tropical suits at about $30 each, including a tuxedo. The tuxedo, John said, was likely to see nearly as much use as my field pants and shirt.

I found a cheap, windowless room at the Hotel Catinat (whose only attraction was a crowded rooftop swimming pool), and I set forth to meet some of my new neighbors.

The Saigon upper crust in those days was still dominated by the French—planters, businessmen and diplomats—who liked to show off their bronzed French and Vietnamese women at favorite haunts: the Hotel Caravelle's rooftop bar, the Cercle Sportif's tennis courts and swimming pool, the palatial villas where *le tout Saigon* entertained.

The ruling Ngo family—President Ngo Dinh Diem, his brother and political mentor, Ngo Dinh Nhu, and Nhu's

"Dragon Lady" wife, Madame Nhu—rarely condescended to attend any but official celebrations, but other key Vietnamese officials were always in evidence. One was the avuncular Ngo Trong Hieu, the minister of civic action and a world-class bon vivant, who roasted whole sheep and pigs for his dinner guests. He was mistrusted by some Vietnamese generals, who whispered that he had not entirely renounced his onetime Viet Minh affiliations, but such rumors merely added to his social luster.

Another frequent guest on exclusive invitation lists was Dr. Tran Kim Tuyen, a medical doctor who headed the Bureau for Political Research at the Presidency—an agency more or less equivalent to the Secret Service, FBI and CIA rolled into one. Dr. Tuyen was a short man who played the violin, read Proust and beamed gently upon fellow concertgoers and party guests. But he was dreaded by Vietnamese politicians on the outs with the regime, who spoke of him as a latter-day Heinrich Himmler. The Vietnamese generals, on the other hand, believed he was working for the American CIA as well as for Diem.

The diplomatic set included such Americans as Frederick Nolting, the courtly southerner serving as United States ambassador, Lieutenant General Charles Timmes, the commander of the Military Advisory Assistance Group (later supplanted by the Military Assistance Command Viet Nam, or MACV), and William Colby, the CIA's Saigon station chief, who later became director of the intelligence agency.

Along with Americans and French, Saigon's plot-stewing diplomatic corps included Indians, Canadians and Poles serving on the International Control Commission. These were a motley mix of serious diplomats, drunks, spies and smugglers, who were nominally responsible for supervising the 1954 international agreement that ended the first Indochina War, but who often made scandalous news for other reasons.

There were also some authentic "Quiet American" types,

spooks who were out to undermine not only the communist guerrillas but all other political groups that might stand in the way of victory. These were the knights of the Kennedy Camelot, the brave spies supposed to be as adept at silently strangling Viet Cong officials in their beds as at winning the hearts and minds of the people.

Some of these mostly young intelligence officers were former high-school basketball stars inspired by both Peace Corps idealism and James Bond mayhem. Others were case-hardened veterans like the CIA's Lou Conein, legendary for his OSS exploits during World War II and his later intelligence coups in Asia. (Conein was the last American to leave Hanoi when it fell to Ho Chi Minh in 1954, and he was the CIA's point man in the 1963 coup that overthrew Diem.)

The leading American spies in the 1960s made little effort to conceal their identities, even though most of them posed as diplomats or military officers. They held jobs in USOM (the United States Operations Mission, later renamed USAID— U.S. Agency for International Development), in the Embassy political section, in the U.S. Information Agency, in the Special Forces, and so on.

There was also a gang of American "illegals," spies in deep cover without diplomatic umbrellas. Some of them, authentic scholars, had been recruited from universities to reform Vietnamese agriculture, village politics and other institutions involved in the war effort. For them, the war offered an exciting opportunity to mix scholarship with derring-do.

Some of the spooks were Catholic academics recruited in the pro-Diem crusade preached by New York's Francis Cardinal Spellman. Others were agronomists from Michigan State University temporarily working with the CIA. Some were sociologists and political scientists from the RAND Corporation, and some were historians recruited to the cause by Brigadier General

Edward Lansdale, the spy-master model for Green's Quiet American.

When the war eventually went sour, many of these scholars came to regret their CIA associations, finding that as tainted ex-spies, they were no longer welcomed back by their former academic colleagues. Some of these poor souls haunted the Council on Foreign Relations in New York, which served as a kind of halfway house for former CIA analysts seeking to return to respectable society. I saw a good deal of them in 1966–67 during the year I spent as a press fellow of the Council.

And then there was the foreign press corps.

There weren't many of us around, back then. On November 11, 1961, the day I took up residence as the AP's bureau chief, the other staff correspondents living in Saigon were Merton Perry, the UPI bureau chief, Peter Smart of Reuters, Rakshat Puri of the *Hindustan Times,* John Stirling of *The Times* of London, and Simon Michau and Jean Burfin of Agence France Presse. The resident "stringers," free-lance correspondents working on retainers rather than salaries, were François Nivolon of *Le Figaro,* Jerry Rose of *Time* (a former teacher) and François Sully of *Newsweek* (a former coffee plantation manager in the Vietnamese highlands). Besides these, a few nonresident correspondents covered Viet Nam fairly regularly from bases in Hong Kong or elsewhere in Asia. Some of the best of them were Robert Trumbull of *The New York Times,* Peter Kalischer of CBS and Jim Robinson of NBC.

Both Rose and Sully were destined to die in crashes caused by Viet Cong gunfire, and Perry died of a heart attack. They were some of the early victims in a tragically long list of correspondent casualties.

On the whole, the Saigon press corps of the 1960s was conspicuously honest and fair-minded, but even in the early days there were a few infiltrators posing as journalists.

There was, for example, an American stringer named David Hudson, who did odd jobs for various news organizations, sometimes turning in unsolicited essays on such trivial matters (except to spies) as the number and types of bridges around Saigon. Hudson did not act like the average spook, but neither was he an authentic journalist. When the rest of us began reporting the flood of arbitrary arrests and other attacks on human rights by Diem's secret police, Hudson turned against his colleagues, and when some correspondents were actually expelled, he declined to join our protests.

In the mid-1960s Hudson abandoned his journalism cover and surfaced as an assistant to General Lansdale, thereby openly acknowledging his role as an intelligence agent. General Lansdale had earlier led the American intelligence operation that helped to destroy the communist Huk insurrection in the Philippines, and in 1965 he undertook a similar assignment in Viet Nam, with Hudson as one of his assistants.

Hudson, who later committed suicide, was merely the first of many who used press credentials as cover for conducting intelligence work and black propaganda. At one point, when the rolls of news representatives in Saigon approached one thousand, our ranks probably included at least a score of American agents with a variety of missions, none having to do with honest journalism. Some were keeping tabs on us, some were trying to organize us into a "Press Club" by which U.S. authorities could indirectly influence or even license our activities and some were busy drumming up disinformation.

This was often as embarrassing to high American officials as it was destructive to news coverage. Barry Zorthian, who headed the Joint U.S. Public Affairs Office (JUSPAO) in Viet Nam, recalled in an interview one of the incidents in which he and I played a part. Speaking of the ubiquitous CIA schemes in which every U.S. agency in Viet Nam was enmeshed, he told the interviewer:

> *Early in the game I had a somewhat down*
> *trip with [the CIA]. One of my people*
> *brought me one day a document from the*
> *captured materials showing that the VC*
> *were facing corruption in their ranks. I*
> *got that and I was frankly trying to*
> *establish myself with Malcolm Browne who*
> *was still with the AP there and had been*
> *a real critic of the war. I wanted to show*
> *Malcolm that my intentions were good and*
> *forthright and I fed him this thing, and he*
> *recognized it for what it was, which I had*
> *not. The sons of bitches had planted it and*
> *were kidding me. Malcolm worked me over*
> *on that thing and told, in print, how I*
> *tried to plant a story on him. And I*
> *blasted him publicly for that and then*
> *discovered I was very much wrong and*
> *promised myself I'd never be burned like*
> *that again.**

Nor did the Viet Cong side ignore the chance to infiltrate the foreign press corps by planting agents in their offices. All the foreign correspondents in Saigon were assisted by Vietnamese journalists working as reporters, photographers, office managers, red-tape fixers and interpreters, and many of them became famous in their own right. Huynh Cong ("Nick") Ut of the AP, for instance, was awarded a Pulitzer Prize for his heart-wrenching photograph of a screaming child running down a road after being burned by napalm.

*Kim Willenson with the correspondents of *Newsweek, The Bad War: An Oral History of the Viet Nam War* (New York: New American Library, 1987), pp. 218–20.

But the best-known Vietnamese reporter working for any news organization was Pham Xuan An of Reuters (and later, of *Time* magazine)—witty, articulate, well connected and almost incredibly well informed about Vietnamese politics. Besides furnishing his employers with a steady stream of valuable news tips, An helped any outside journalist who needed advice or a briefing, including scores of visiting nonresident correspondents.

After the fall of Saigon in 1975, An revealed that he had actually been working as a Viet Cong penetration agent all those years—not planting stories in the Western press, but using the press as a cover for digging up political intelligence to pass on to his Viet Cong superiors. At this writing, he lives in Saigon, where he holds the rank of brigadier general in the communist forces. He is still occasionally visited by his onetime American news colleagues.

Like all good spies, An had a superb eye for detail, and he could shrewdly interpret and accurately report everything he saw and heard. He happened to be with me one time when I visited a Mekong River Delta fortified hamlet that had been smashed and overrun by the Viet Cong, and his explanation and recapitulation of what had happened impressed me deeply. He pointed out all kinds of things I had not noticed—for example, how the guerrillas had not only destroyed the unpaved road to the hamlet, but had planted it with fast-growing bamboo to block relief efforts.

The intelligence communities in Viet Nam, Viet Cong as well as allied, were so pervasive that every journalist working in the country was bound to have at least tangential contacts with any number of spooks.

In 1961, Saigon was also a hotbed of public-relations lobbying, all of it aimed, at enormous expense, at the tiny foreign press corps.

I arrived in Saigon at a critical moment in the war. General Maxwell Taylor, Kennedy's personal military adviser, had just completed a trip to Viet Nam and concluded that more of every kind of American assistance was needed, not only to prosecute the war but to strengthen the Diem regime politically.

There never was a time when Diem's crown seemed entirely secure, and his position in 1961 seemed especially shaky because of the threat of a military coup. One year earlier, a group of Vietnamese parachute officers led by Colonel Nguyen Chanh Thi and supported by civilian opponents of the regime, had staged a half-baked coup that ended in failure. Thi escaped to exile in Cambodia, and the Diem government suspected that plots were still being hatched by the "Caravellists," the insurrectionists named for the Caravelle Hotel, where they had planned the coup.

And thus the Caravelle Hotel, the most modern and most luxurious hotel in Saigon at the time, became a permanent symbol of treason in the eyes of the Ngo family. Presidential suspicion of the hotel extended not only to Vietnamese who frequented the establishment, but to visiting American news correspondents as well.

The Ngo family used an American couple, Gene and Ann Gregory, to tar all unfriendly correspondents with the Caravelle brush as a symbol of betrayal of the war effort. The Gregorys, business partners who enjoyed the protection of the Ngo family, were proprietors of the English-language *Times of Viet Nam,* which was their vehicle for heaping scorn on American correspondents. The Gregory-painted image of American newsmen in Saigon depicted them as corrupted drunks who spent their days and nights at the Caravelle bar, picking up false rumors with which to defame the regime.

These allegations made life harder for resident correspondents like myself, who actually visited the Caravelle only rarely, and who had little time to waste at any bar. It might not have mattered if the smears had been confined to Saigon, but some influential American publications began to repeat them.

In 1963, Otto Fuerbringer, the managing editor of *Time*, embarked on a campaign to ridicule and discredit the American resident correspondents in Saigon, using whatever ammunition came to hand, regardless of its accuracy. The Gregorys and their allies supplied just what Fuerbringer wanted, and their cant, scarcely edited, repeatedly found its way into *Time*. *Time*'s own Viet Nam correspondent, Charlie Mohr, quit in protest, refusing to associate himself with the lies *Time*'s Fuerbringer was disseminating, but this did us little good at the time. Many an American official, believing what he had read in *Time*, arrived at his post in Viet Nam expecting to find a press corps made up entirely of enemy agents. It usually took a while to disabuse them of such nonsense.

During my several long sojourns in Viet Nam between 1961 and 1975, there were always rumors of coups in the air. Rumors and political gossip constantly bubbled at such hangouts as Givral, an ice-cream parlor that's still in business, Brodard, a cheap luncheon restaurant, La Pagode, a coffee-and-croissant breakfast nook, and the sidewalk café of the Continental Hotel. The talk at these places was known as "Radio Catinat," and although it was entertaining, it rarely did newsmen much good.

Writing political stories in the Viet Nam of the sixties could be risky. One of my AP predecessors, Rene Inagaki, had been summarily expelled from Viet Nam by Madame Nhu because of a story which that powerful lady had deemed offensive. The AP was not eager to have another correspondent kicked out on similar grounds, and my editors sent me to Saigon with the understanding that they wanted no political "gossip" in my reports.

In any case, I had come to Viet Nam mainly to cover the

war, so on my third day in the country I took a drive to Bien Hoa, a town about twenty miles from Saigon, where the Vietnamese Air Force had its headquarters base. I wanted to have a peek at the guerrilla-infested countryside, and I wanted to see how deeply Americans had become involved in the fighting. There was a U.S. Air Force contingent at Bien Hoa, I knew, so that was where I headed.

The official line then was that Americans in Viet Nam were serving purely as advisers and were only shooting at the Viet Cong in self-defense. To shoot first would have meant violating the 1954 Geneva agreement, which the United States did not want to be seen as doing. (The Geneva agreement had ended the war between colonial France and Ho Chi Minh's Viet Minh, leaving North and South Viet Nam as temporarily separate countries, with Ngo Dinh Diem in power in South Viet Nam.)

But there were reports that U.S. Air Force pilots newly arrived at Bien Hoa were not only flying missions against the Viet Cong, but were actually toggling the bomb-release triggers themselves—something mere advisers were not supposed to do. I felt that I should investigate, for after all, if the United States was really at war, Americans deserved to know it.

A word about my own attitudes: I did not go to Viet Nam harboring any opposition to America's role in the Vietnamese civil war. Since Washington had allied itself with the Saigon government, it seemed to me natural enough that American servicemen were joining in the fight, killing Vietnamese enemies and being killed. But what worried me was the unwillingness of the Kennedy administration to fight openly, preferring instead to wage a shadow war out of sight of the American public. If we Americans had nothing to be ashamed of, why not frankly acknowledge our role as belligerents?

I was to learn, however, that a major flaw of the Kennedy

administration was its passion for secrecy, a predilection that is really anathema to democratic leadership. It's my belief that Kennedy's love of back-alley military campaigns launched without the tempering influence of open criticism contributed strongly to his horrendous foreign-policy failures. The wounds inflicted by his Viet Nam adventure left scars on the United States that are still painful.

The spirit of those years was captured in a famous remark by Arthur Sylvester, the spokesman for the Pentagon, that every government is entitled to lie to protect its vital interests. (Sylvester's comment was a response to a reporter who complained about various Defense Department fabrications during the 1962 Cuban missile crisis.)

Whether or not Sylvester was right, it's a fact that governments do lie when they feel it is necessary, which is rather often. It is equally a fact that reporters in a free society are paid to penetrate and expose official lies.

As I drove to Bien Hoa along Viet Nam's only four-lane divided highway I thought how easy it would be for a Viet Cong ambuscade to pick off a lone car on the nearly deserted road; in fact, there had been two Viet Cong ambushes along that road the previous week. But it looked peaceful enough. The countryside, typical of the alluvial plains surrounding Saigon, was divided up into broad, rectangular rice fields bounded by high earthen dikes and groves of pineapple and banana trees. In some of the fields water buffaloes were grazing, often with small boys or birds riding on their backs.

I later learned an important survival lesson about such peaceful vistas, by the way: rice fields without little boys, farmers or water buffaloes were danger signals. Seemingly empty fields were places where ambushes were likely to await the unwary.

Arriving at the main gate of Bien Hoa air base, I was barred by a pair of Vietnamese MPs, and I could see that an

American with an MP armband was watching. But as I strolled outside the perimeter fence I could clearly see into the cockpits of some taxiing T-28 two-seaters with Vietnamese Air Force markings. The men in the front seats were Caucasians. I also got a good look at the pilot of a Vietnamese Air Force Skyraider, the wing racks of which were loaded with bombs. He, too, was an American.

Here, then, was visual proof that Americans were not simply placing themselves in harm's way; they were actively fighting, not just advising. I began taking pictures but in seconds the American and Vietnamese MPs rushed out the gate and pounced on me, seized my camera, ripped out the film and marched me off for a security check.

The air base authorities detained me only briefly and were extremely polite after ascertaining that I was an American and a news correspondent. But they ordered me away from the area and threatened to seize any more film I might expose.

The incident was a revealing prelude to my coverage of Viet Nam, and my first real brush with the Kennedy administration's love of stealth. My film would have disclosed no military secrets. The T-28 was an elderly, propeller-driven trainer modified to carry machine guns and some light bombs, and the propeller-driven Skyraider was known to pilots as the "Spad" (after the famous World War I fighter) because of its venerable propeller-powered technology. Nor could my vantage point outside the base have disclosed anything more than passersby (including Viet Cong agents) saw daily.

The point was that my photographs would have shown Americans back home that their fellow citizens were waging war, not merely training others. And that was intolerable to the administration at the time.

Even without photographs, my story was circulated by

the AP, but to my astonishment, it received little attention. I hadn't realized that most Americans neither knew nor cared about Viet Nam in those days.

To some extent, news agency bureau chiefs are chained to their offices, and up to the time of my arrival, this had been especially true in Saigon, where communications posed even bigger problems than gathering news. For nonofficial foreigners, the sending of news to the outer world had to be via the government-operated Post, Telegraph and Telephone office, and its officials did not make life easy for reporters. Two copies of each press cable had to be brought to the big PTT building facing Saigon Cathedral, and the text had to be counted, verified and accepted before the message was placed at the bottom of a stack of other press cables (from competitors), which were also awaiting transmission.

The time it took for a cablegram to reach the outer world was in proportion to its political sensitivity. Although not formally censored, each message or story was read by security officers before it was cleared for transmission. The most important dispatches were circulated not only among key Vietnamese officials, but also, secretly and illegally, among American officials, an arrangement I accidentally discovered during my first month in Viet Nam.

Since politically sensitive or critical news dispatches were simply mislaid by the PTT without transmission, *de facto* censorship prevailed in Viet Nam from the beginning of the war. Like so many other operations conducted by the Kennedy administration, even censorship was carried out in secret.

I remembered this thirty years later when Pentagon officials supervising news coverage of the war against Iraq insisted on censoring the dispatches of reporters. It was lack of censorship, some military officials contended, that had helped rob the United States of victory in Viet Nam, and this shortcoming was being rectified in the Persian Gulf.

Nonsense. Censorship in Viet Nam was usually unofficial, but it was no less pervasive. There were times when the Saigon government imposed what amounted to a complete news blackout, and at other times, behind-the-scenes censorship effectively pinched the flow of news. Of course, no American held the formal title of censor.

But senior American officials were informed of the contents of potentially sensitive cables submitted by correspondents to the Vietnamese telegraph office for transmission to the United States. When Vietnamese or American officials deemed a news cable to be prejudicial to political or military interests, the cable would either disappear permanently or encounter such a long delay as to make it worthless as news.

As for alleged breaches of military security by correspondents, Barry Zorthian, who for four years headed the U.S. information office in Saigon, testified at a Senate subcommittee hearing in 1992 that the problem was virtually nonexistent. With or without censorship, correspondents generally did not disclose military secrets in Viet Nam. The record is quite clear on that point, charges and innuendoes by various press-haters notwithstanding.

Since I was resolved to avoid becoming a slave to filing deadlines and the office, I took to traveling. Correspondents in Viet Nam were always free to travel wherever they chose, provided they could find the means—private car, bus, train, Air Viet Nam, boat or whatever. Covering operations sometimes required military transportation, but correspondents rarely missed stories for lack of access or transportation to the places they needed to visit. In this, the Viet Nam War differed enormously from the Persian Gulf in 1991, where American forces rigidly controlled correspondents' movements.

There were two ways to join military operations in Viet Nam in the early 1960s. If American advisers were involved, arrangements could be made through a civilian adviser of the

Vietnamese government named George Ortiz, a Madison Avenue publicist hired to present American military activity in a favorable (and not too revealing) light. The evasions Ortiz and his collaborators were forced to practice on the press often aroused the suspicions and mistrust of reporters, who redoubled their efforts to find out what was happening.

If a correspondent was interested in covering a purely Vietnamese military operation, however, he had only to bring his request to a government office on Le Loi Boulevard, where he was accorded the friendly help of a young woman named Huynh thi Le Lieu. Since she eventually became my wife, I'll digress for a moment to outline Le Lieu's background.

Le Lieu was the daughter of a Vietnamese provincial official in the French administration, who was abducted and murdered by the communists. Subsequently, her mother sent Le Lieu abroad to be educated in France and Britain, and this education steeped her in the quirks and characteristics of the Western press and endowed her with insights not shared by most Vietnamese officials. Since her credentials were impeccably nationalist and anticommunist, she was an obvious potential asset to South Viet Nam's government.

In 1959, recruiters from both Hanoi and Saigon had sought out Le Lieu in Paris, and diplomats from both sides invited her to join their respective governments. Naturally spurning the North Vietnamese, she returned to her native land and joined the Saigon government as an assistant to the information minister.

She made a lot of friends for the Saigon government, despite her work as chief censor of all English-language books brought into the country and as an official minder of the foreign press corps. Later, Le Lieu became disillusioned with the government because of its onerous mimicking of communist style: weekly self-criticism meetings for officials, blue Personalist Party uniforms, secret-police surveillance and harsh suppression of political criticism—all copied from Ho Chi Minh's style of rule, but without the Marxist-Leninist component.

A few days after my first visit to Le Lieu's office I was accredited to cover my first Vietnamese military operation. It was hard to buy field equipment in the Saigon flea market, but I found a pair of rubber-soled boots, a well-worn French Foreign Legion field pack, a canteen, a web belt, a hat and a few cans of food. I was as happy as a kid getting ready for a camping trip.

The journey southward into the Mekong Delta began with a fifty-mile automobile ride I shared with some Vietnamese officials. The car was a big black Citroën "Onze Chevaux," and we roared like conquerors through the wide boulevards of bustling Cholon, Saigon's ethnic-Chinese sister city. Outside the city gates we abruptly passed into verdant countryside where the war was more in evidence than it had been on the Bien Hoa superhighway. Every few miles we came to stockades, checkpoints with barbed-wire barriers, and stucco-faced buildings pocked with bullet impacts.

We passed a village named Go Den, a dozen miles from Saigon, guarded by a triangular fort with watchtowers at the corners. I saw a lot of Go Den over the years, because it kept getting overrun and looted by Viet Cong raids. Each time I visited the place I found a new team of defenders because the former ones had all been killed; they never seemed to realize the futility of their little fort.

The farther south we traveled the more tropical the countryside began to look. Tall flamboyante trees lined stretches of the road, their great boughs and flaming red blossoms forming a majestic archway. At My Tho, a provincial capital on the northernmost branch of the Mekong, travelers had to wait for a landing-craft ferry to continue southward, but they could rest at

thriving open-air cafés and enjoy fresh pineapples or *café sua*—
French coffee in little cups sweetened with an ounce or two of
condensed milk.

On the final stretch through Kien Hoa Province to Ben
Tre, the road was hemmed in on both sides with dense foliage,
and the driver speeded up, knowing that the roadsides often
concealed deadly Viet Cong ambuscades.

Ben Tre seemed to me more an overgrown village than
a city, but it was famous throughout the country for several
reasons. One was its tradition as a seat of learning in the arts of
guerrilla and counterguerrilla warfare. In the colonial era, Kien
Hoa Province had been ruled with an iron hand from Ben Tre
by a French province chief named Le Roi, who meted out
ruthless punishment to captured Viet Minh terrorists, but who
built swimming pools, amusement parks and theaters for loyal
citizens. Le Roi's style outlived the French colonial government
he represented, and his iron-hand-in-velvet-glove brand of administration was carried on by Colonel Pham Ngoc Thao, one
of the most enigmatic figures of the Viet Nam War.

Thao had a walleye that seemed always to be looking
over a visitor's shoulder, and people were never quite sure
whether his real intentions matched his statements. They were
right to be wary.

One of the reasons Colonel Thao became a star of the
Diem regime was that he knew more about the enemy's tricks
than any man in South Viet Nam. A onetime colleague of Ho
Chi Minh's, he had commanded the Viet Minh's intelligence
apparatus throughout the French Indochina War, playing a
major role in the Viet Minh victory in 1954. But after that Thao
had (supposedly) abandoned the communist side and joined the
new South Vietnamese government. Almost overnight, this
prodigal son became the darling of many American politicians,
military leaders and right-wing journalists such as Joseph Alsop.

I can't resist some observations about all the people who were suckered by Pham Ngoc Thao.

There is nothing dearer to the heart of an American than the redemption of a former sinner. The conversion of Whittaker Chambers from communist spy working under cover as a *Time* editor, to reformed anticommunist (hailed by *Time* as a latter-day Saint Paul) was enough to make Chambers a national hero (and some cynics sick).

And so it was with Thao, seen as a prophet by Alsop and other American boosters of the Diem regime. But Thao had a way of switching sides a little too readily to suit even his ardent admirers. In 1965 he led an attempted coup, and a few months later a government execution squad hunted him down and shot him. The execution team was commanded by an expert, by the way: Colonel Nguyen Ngoc Loan, the officer who achieved worldwide fame by blowing the head off a Viet Cong captive in front of Eddie Adams's camera.

Maybe Thao at one time was a genuine convert to the anticommunist cause, but I doubt it. He now lies buried just outside Ho Chi Minh City in a cemetery reserved for heroes who fell fighting for the Viet Cong side.

I had been in Viet Nam only two weeks the day I met him, and our conversation focused on the business of getting me out on an operation with his Civil Guard provincial militia. Thao was not going himself, he told me, but had assigned a key deputy as the operation's commander.

The night before, Thao took me to a Ben Tre theater where he had organized a kind of vaudeville show—folk dancing, juggling and the like. He said the show was part of his strategy for keeping the people happy and opposed to communism; bread and games, he called it.

At about three A.M. the next morning, I groped my way in darkness across a crowded river jetty to the deck of one of the three landing craft scheduled to carry our raiding party into enemy territory. The air was thick with clammy mist, the night was black as death and troopers hauling machine guns and mortar base plates clanked and cursed as they banged into each other in the darkness.

Switching off our running lights, the landing craft pilots opened up their diesel engines and we roared off in near-total darkness. Navigation through a complex web of waterways was virtually blind, and we barely avoided running aground several times. Scattered pinpoints of light on the river marked the moorings of sampans and other small boats.

It was too noisy to talk, and since most of us had been up all night, we tried to stretch out for a nap, with our heads propped against the piles of field gear and our bodies covered by ponchos.

The troops were dozing when a splintering crash and a sideways lurch shook us awake. People were screaming, and with a hastily lighted gasoline lantern we could see them in the water: a man, several women and a half dozen children were frantically flailing to stay afloat, their sampan smashed to matchwood by our craft.

The commander barked an order, the landing craft backed away from the wreckage, and we roared off at full speed. Horrified, I asked him if we couldn't try to help the people. whose boat we had destroyed, but he shook his head gloomily and muttered something about the importance of our mission.

The sun had just peeked over the eastern horizon as our three boats turned toward the shore and raced in. Ahead, I could see a cluster of thatched huts and a banana grove surrounded by a low mud dike, but no people.

Our bows crunched into the muddy bank, the landing doors went down, and we waded ashore in the best D-Day tradition. As we ran toward the hamlet several of the Civil Guard troopers fired automatic-rifle bursts, and we heard a woman scream.

The firing stopped and the troops began searching each of the banana-frond huts, most of which proved to be empty. Suddenly, however, a man in black peasant blouse and pants dashed from one of the huts and headed into a field of tall rice behind the village, where only his head and shoulders were visible. Almost reflexively, one of the soldiers fitted a machine-hine gun to its tripod mount and opened fire on the running man.

The farmer took a few steps, threw up his arms and fell, and I joined the soldiers who ran across the field for a look at the fugitive. The farmer lay on his back, blood streaming from his mouth into the muddy water where he lay. A wound in his chest made a gurgling sound as he attempted to breathe, and, undecided what to do, the soldiers stood around watching for a minute. Noticing a stout stick on the ground, one of them picked it up, jammed one end into the mud next to the wounded man's throat, and pressed the other end down, trying to strangle the dying man. I yelled and pushed the soldier, but his comrades pulled me back, and all I could do was photograph the atrocity. (My pictures were subsequently published by AP's subscriber newspapers.)

Just then, the wife of the wounded man ran up, screaming hatred at us as she dropped to the ground next to him. She cradled his head in her lap and chanted a kind of lullaby to him as tears streamed down her face, and the farmer gave her a faint smile just before he died. The soldiers turned away and laughed nervously.

In the subsequent search of the village, the Civil Guards found some paper Viet Cong flags and some anti-American propaganda in a little open-sided schoolhouse. But no one in the village offered any resistance, we found no weapons and there seemed little point in hanging around. By noon we were aboard the landing craft and on our way back to Ben Tre.

Back at the province chief's headquarters, I recounted the day's events to Colonel Thao, who looked grave but told me that accidental casualties are inevitable in war. As he spoke, however, his walleye seemed to be questioning the young officer standing behind me who had led our expedition. I wondered what Thao was really thinking.

In hindsight, knowing that Thao was probably a Viet Cong operative all along, I think he may have been pleased with the sickening performance of his Civil Guards. Their operation showed the government side in the worst possible light, an important Viet Cong objective, and there was even an American correspondent present to report the atrocity. After all, Thao knew, the Viet Nam War was a struggle for allegiances rather than real estate or dead bodies. If Thao as a Viet Cong agent could manage to turn some local farmers (and a lot of foreign newspaper readers) against the Saigon government, what matter that a poor farmer had died in the process?

Such thinking, I discovered, was the very fabric of the Viet Nam War. From start to finish, the war was a psychological conflict in which both sides were ever ready to throw away lives to tar the enemy with the atrocity brush.

Of course, I knew nothing about Thao's equivocal loyalties at the time, and it only seemed to me that the day's operation had been a disgusting fiasco. But I did understand for the first time that the Viet Nam War was something quite different from the crusade Washington depicted.

9

VIET NAM: THE QUICKENING PACE

ONE HOT DECEMBER MORNING in 1961 newsmen and other residents of Saigon awoke to find an aircraft carrier docked at the foot of downtown Tu Do Street, its deck jammed with olive-drab aircraft, mostly Sikorsky H-21 troop-carrying helicopters. The USNS *Core* was not a big ship as aircraft carriers go, but it loomed menacingly over the low waterfront buildings of the Saigon quay, and a crowd gathered to gape at the vessel as its American crew and technicians worked the cranes and machinery. Plainly, the Americans were arriving in force, and this time, it seemed, they had come to fight, not merely to advise.

In the company of a half dozen of my reporter competitors I tried to talk my way onto the *Core* or, failing that, to persuade a spokesman to come out and talk.

"There's nothing going on," an MP said, a twinkle in his eye. "Nothing to see here. If anyone wants to talk to you they'll be at USIS." We trooped over to the U.S. Information Service's downtown press office and were promptly shown into the director's office.

"What can you say about the aircraft carrier down at the foot of Tu Do?" we asked.

"Aircraft carrier? What aircraft carrier? I don't see any aircraft carrier," he replied with a smirk.

The newsmen groaned.

"Well, look," the press officer said, "you have to realize we can't discuss questions relating to military movements. As you are all aware by now, United States military personnel are in Viet Nam to advise and assist their Vietnamese allies, not to engage in combat. That's all I can tell you at present."

Annoyed, we returned to our offices to file reports of what we had seen of the *Core*, including its deck cargo, things any passerby could observe. But North Vietnam's spies roundly scooped us. Some forty-eight hours after the *Core* docked, Radio Hanoi broadcast not only the numbers and types of aircraft the ship had delivered, but even some of their serial numbers, details that the newsmen had neither seen nor reported. And still, U.S. officials in Saigon and Washington declined even to acknowledge the arrival of American combat helicopters in Viet Nam.

For newsmen, official refusal to admit the existence of the ship and its load was merely a nuisance; after all, there was nothing to prevent us from filing stories and photographs. But it struck us that real problems lay ahead—that the United States government had no intention of revealing any more than it could possibly avoid disclosing of its growing role in a real war.

Even as the Kennedy administration was trying to conceal the existence of a war in Indochina, Americans had begun fighting and dying. On December 22, U.S. Army Sp4 James T. Davis of Livingston, Tennessee, had become the war's first American combat fatality when the truck in which he was riding near Saigon was ambushed by a Viet Cong squad. Army officers held a press briefing at the USIS office and announced Davis's death promptly. In their anger, they let slip the interesting detail that the American had gone down fighting, emptying two carbine magazines at his foes before falling.

In the early days American newsmen had a lot of difficulty covering their compatriots in combat, but I had a little
more luck than some. After much cajoling and badgering, I
persuaded authorities to let me spend Christmas, 1961, with
some American field troops, a Special Forces team at a Vietnamese ranger training camp.

It was quite exciting. I climbed into a jeep and before we
had even left the Saigon city limits, my three Green Beret
companions rammed magazines into their Swedish "K" submachine guns and began looking warlike.

After leaving the outskirts of Saigon we turned onto a
rutted, unpaved road where our driver speeded up, spewing a red
plume of dust in our wake. "If Charlie tries to zap us we'll lay
down fire in all directions and go like hell," a lieutenant yelled
in my direction. "We probably won't hit him, but it usually
rattles him enough to get us through."

Our destination, the hamlet of Trung Lap (meaning
"neutrality"), was as close to being a frontline position as the Viet
Nam War ever had. The village was just a cluster of huts strewn
along the road, and I noticed that there were neither people nor
water buffaloes in sight—a bad sign.

But by and by we came to a broad cordon of barbed
wire, machine-gun emplacements and minefields, and after two
Asian soldiers opened a barricade for us, we entered a relaxed
and familiar world where it was Christmas Eve. Tinsel had
been draped over a bedraggled tree of some kind, and aluminum wash-basins filled with beer were passing from hand to
hand.

A welcoming basin was passed to me by a friendly American sergeant named Al Combs, a Special Forces veteran from
Brooklyn who had fought America's gray war in Laos and was
destined to serve five tours of duty in Viet Nam. For years, I kept
running into Combs at one embattled outpost or another, and I

came to regard him as a fixture of the country. But like many other fixtures, Combs was not destined to survive.

Toward the end of his last tour in 1965, he and his Vietnamese common-law wife, who was eight months pregnant, took their two children to the floating My Canh restaurant on the Saigon River for a night on the town. They were enjoying their soup when a pair of Viet Cong mines went off. Combs and his wife died in one of the blasts, and surgeons were unable to save her unborn baby. The Combses' children survived as orphans.

But that 1961 Christmas was a jolly one for Al Combs and his comrades. I asked how they liked the place.

"Trung Lap's OK," one said. "We're next door to a big VC base and training area, so we don't have far to go to get into a firefight. Our guys train on them, and they train on us. They have a bunch of tunnels around here and they're always popping up, popping at us, and disappearing. It's kind of a subway war."

The Trung Lap training staff consisted of a half dozen American officers and men. Special Forces troops in those days were not GIs, strictly speaking. They took their orders from a military cover organization that was really part of the CIA and was almost completely independent of the Defense Department. Many regular army officers hated the cocky Special Forces, but President Kennedy himself had been impressed by the shows they put on for him—parachute drops, Tarzan-style jungle traverses and frogman river assaults. While he lived, JFK kept his beloved Green Berets safe from their regular army foes.

With Kennedy's murder in 1963, however, the Special Forces lost their patron and their independence. From then on, they had to take orders and behave like real soldiers.

Somehow, the Asian rangers at Trung Lap, some three hundred of them, didn't look Vietnamese to me, and I soon found out why: although they were Vietnamese citizens, they were ethnic Cambodians.

"These guys are Khmer Krom," an American officer told me. "Ethnic Cambodians. Most of 'em speak English better than they do Vietnamese. They're larger and tougher than the Vietnamese, they're loyal—at least to us—and they're the best killers in Asia. They hate all Vietnamese, but we've got them pointed at the VC, so they're killing Charlie instead of ARVN. They're our kind of meanies." (ARVN, pronounced "arvin," stood for Army of the Republic of Viet Nam.)

The Vietnamese Khmers had somewhat the same status as that of the Sikhs in South Asia: they were scorned by many Vietnamese as *moi* (savages) but they were trusted to guard banks, jewelry stores, ammunition dumps, garrison gates and even the palace of the ruling Ngo family. President Diem relied not only on the fighting ferocity of the Cambodians but on their indifference to the political plotting that always threatened his regime.

There was some desultory shooting around Trung Lap while I was there, but nobody seemed very serious about it. Our Cambodian rangers had no interest in Christmas as a religious event, but they liked parties. I watched them prepare a Yuletide stew that included a boa constrictor they'd caught in a nearby rice field. Strips of its white flesh were still twitching as the grinning chef tossed them into his cooking bucket. The rangers had also contributed some tasty little crayfish, a basket of rats and some large blackbirds. As a journalist I'd often eaten figurative crow, but the real thing was a new experience for me.

There was a high, bright moon, the air was pleasantly cool, and by the time we had consumed the stew, a mountain of watermelons and an immoderate quantity of Vietnamese-brewed Larue beer, we were all singing drunk. Along toward midnight someone decided we should have a Christmas Star in the East, so Combs and two other Americans hauled a wooden crate of flare shells over to one of the mortars and began firing into the sky. Each dazzling flare ignited with a pop, hanging from its little parachute as other flares rose to complete the star.

The troops cheered, and at that moment, a Viet Cong guerrilla out in the darkness beyond the compound perimeter fired a long burst of red tracer bullets. But the slugs were not aimed at us. They rose into the patch of sky where our dazzling flares were descending, and the guerrilla seemed to be trying to embellish our Christmas star. It was rather touching.

Soon after my Trung Lap visit I began accompanying Vietnamese troops on operations carried into battle aboard American helicopters.

For me, those operations meant getting up at three in the morning while the geckos were still croaking and the city was asleep. At least, I had comfortable quarters by then; I had moved out of my sleazy hotel into a one-room apartment over the AP office on Rue Pasteur, and my new residence had a bottle-gas stove on which I could cook simple meals, a functioning air conditioner and an electric water heater.

Dressing for war in those early days took only a minute: khaki chino pants, a short-sleeved shirt, a canteen and belt (with a bottle of halizone water-sterilizing tablets) and a pair of sneakers. This garb was to change as the war grew hotter; we correspondents took to wearing inconspicuous olive-green fatigues and boots with steel plates in their soles. Some newsmen occasionally wore helmets and flak jackets—heavy armored vests lined with bullet-resistant nylon plates—but the cumbersome jackets were never popular.

Operations began with taxi rides to the military gate at Saigon's Tan Son Nhut airport, where a liaison officer would pick up the two or three newsmen accredited for the day's activities.

Operation officers would generally let us listen as they briefed their crews and the commanders of the Vietnamese units we were carrying into battle. Over the years I sat in on hundreds of those preoperation briefings, most of them tedious, some of them uncomfortable and many of them wildly unrealistic in their assessments of enemy positions and strengths. But there was another reason I hated those predawn briefings: a hissing gasoline lantern was always used to illuminate the battle map, and the lamp attracted maddeningly dense clouds of mosquitoes.

Morning helicopter sorties were often delayed for many hours or canceled altogether because of fog, which exacerbated problems caused by the mechanical shortcomings of the choppers themselves. The banana-shaped H-21, with twin rotors fore and aft, was underpowered for the jobs it was expected to do. To carry a squad of troops armed with machine guns and light mortars, an H-21 had to make an airplane-type takeoff, charging down the runway until its forward speed was sufficient to get it off the ground. Hovering for more than a few seconds overloaded the engine and was never done on takeoff with a heavy load. Pilots avoided long takeoff runs in fog, and fog often stopped helicopter operations before they could get off the ground.

But I have vivid memories of the days when we did get away on schedule. A long line of H-21s on the ramp looked in the darkness like a parade of carnival floats, their red and white running lights blinking festively, and their cranky gasoline engines barking blue and yellow flame.

The H-21 had just one door for its passengers, which was on the helicopter's left side toward its tail. Pilots would land with their left sides facing Viet Cong positions, so that their loads of troops faced the enemy the moment they jumped out, and could open fire without having to run around the helicopter.

But the Viet Cong discovered that the H-21 was not very ambidextrous and that it generally approached from the guerrillas' right front. This knowledge helped the Viet Cong to set up and aim their heavy machine guns in preparation for helicopterborne assaults, and their accuracy improved appallingly.

The helicopter of 1962 had a short range and had to

refuel often, mostly at makeshift pads the Americans set up all over the Mekong Delta. But there were also some excellent airports with long, paved runways, left by the Japanese forces that occupied Indochina during World War II. One of these was at Soc Trang, and whenever I landed there I was struck by the irony that this very base had served the Japanese bombers that destroyed Britain's two mightiest battleships off Malaya in 1941.

It also seemed strange to me as an American that some of my Vietnamese friends remembered the Japanese occupation troops as benefactors. The invading Japanese had jailed the French colonialist rulers of Indochina and occupied the region under the banner "Asia for Asians," offering peace and prosperity for all.

My wife remembers Japanese troops sharing picnic food with her family during a river outing when she was a little girl. Many Vietnamese children had similar experiences. Brutal as the Japanese troops were in other occupied countries, they apparently tried hard to win over the Vietnamese.

To curb crimes by Japanese troops against Vietnamese, the occupying army meted out swift and ruthless punishment. One of my friends saw Japanese military policemen catch a Japanese soldier in the act of stealing fruit from a Saigon pushcart, and they cut off the soldier's right hand on the spot.

At any rate, the U.S. Army made good use of those old Japanese airfields. With the end of the war in 1975, Viet Nam inherited a lot of other military real estate, including the huge American-built naval base at Cam Ranh Bay. The Soviet navy used it before the Soviet Union collapsed.

Looking back over the early 1960s I can scarcely distinguish one helicopter-borne operation from another, although I retain vivid images of what they were like in general.

Sometimes the government assaults I covered ran into heavy opposition, but more often they charged into villages seemingly inhabited only by women and children. The object of each of these missions was to catch Viet Cong forces by surprise, quickly landing a battalion or more of ARVN troops on top of the enemy. But one way or another, the Viet Cong usually knew we were coming and cleared out in time.

I remember that during one operation my friend and competitor Merton Perry, the UPI bureau manager, rested his great bulk in the shade of a parked helicopter, took a swig of warm Kool-Aid from his canteen, and grumbled, "What the hell can I do with this? A few dead, but no news. Color? We've filed enough of it to outlast the war."

But we went on covering every operation we could, and despite their sameness, a few images remain in my mind's eye even today. Some of those sights were even quite beautiful.

One morning I was aboard an H-21 a thousand feet higher than the main helicopter group, and as the rising sun peeped over the horizon it suddenly lighted up the formation below us, which was skimming at treetop altitude over a vast plain of flooded paddies. The helicopters' spinning rotors looked pure white as the sun caught them. Mirrored by the flooded paddies just below them, the choppers looked like a flight of cranes in a Chinese scroll.

But most of my memories are ugly.

One morning I accompanied a Vietnamese infantry unit as it landed in a rice field adjoining a strongly defended Viet Cong hamlet. The H-21s didn't actually touch the ground because their pilots were wary of getting stuck in paddy mire. The ungainly choppers merely descended to about four feet above the mud and slowed their forward speed to a walk.

The jump looked easy enough, but as usual, I faced a dilemma. I had to choose instantly between a return flight to Saigon to file a story, or jumping with the troops. If I chose to stay with the operation I risked being beaten by some competitor back in Saigon. But if I went back to Saigon, I might miss the operation story altogether.

On that day we were drawing fire even before arriving at the LZ (landing zone), and a heavy slug opened a hole the size of a half dollar in the skin of our chopper with a sound like the crash of a kettledrum. The engagement looked too interesting to miss, so I jumped with the troops.

Wading through hip-deep mud and water, the Vietnamese soldiers were scarcely more mobile than ants in molasses, and progress across the paddy toward our tree-line objective was glacial. Fortunately, the green rice plants were two or three feet high at that time of year, giving us some cover from the Viet Cong machine guns in the tree line that were spraying tracers at us.

Near me was a young Vietnamese ensign on his first combat operation, trying desperately to organize the platoon under his command and get it to move forward. He yelled and gestured as he exhorted his men to advance, but no one heeded him, and he fairly screamed with fury. Finally, exasperated beyond control, the ensign jumped up and began running toward the enemy position.

It was a very brave but very foolish act. He ran only a few yards before I heard the sharp snapping noise of bullets passing close to me, and I saw the ensign's head explode. I hugged the ground and compulsively dug my fingers into the mud as I watched rice stalks near me dance in the rain of machine-gun slugs.

All day we huddled in that field under sporadic machine-gun and mortar fire waiting for the air force to flatten the hamlet, which it eventually did with devastating verve. But the Skyraiders took all day at the job, returning with load after load of bombs and rockets, and by the time the enemy guns fell silent it was nearly nightfall. The ARVN commander decided to give up the operation as a bad job, and we all headed home.

At the time we left that wretched hamlet, our force had not advanced more than one hundred yards from our morning landing site, and none of our troops ever entered the hamlet, because the officers believed it was booby-trapped. All we could show for our trouble was a list of our own casualties, a dozen dead and a score wounded, and we lacked the least idea how many the enemy might have suffered.

But in Saigon the operation was reported as a victory.

The nightmare image of the young ensign's head stayed with me as we flew home. I jotted some thoughts in my mud-encrusted notebook, and when I looked up I noticed the American crew chief watching me. "Have a nice day?" he asked with an innocent smile.

Winnie the Pooh considered the anticipation of honey even more delightful than eating it. The expectation of death is also intense. On about my tenth helicopter outing, I experienced the excruciating anticipation of death a passenger feels while hurtling toward the ground in a stricken aircraft.

I had joined a Vietnamese task force for a large assault on a string of Viet Cong–controlled "combat hamlets" in paddy-field country in An Xuyen Province, near the southern tip of Viet Nam. The land was much the same as anywhere else in the south— endless expanses of rice fields divided by dikes and canals, each extending from horizon to horizon, as straight as arrows. As usual, our transportation to war was one of those old H-21 death traps.

The operation produced very little contact with the enemy, and in the early afternoon I called it a day and hitched a ride back to Saigon.

To explain what happened next, I need to mention a frailty to which all helicopters are prey. If a helicopter loses power and it is high enough, the pilot can put its nose down, pick up speed, and get the rotor (or rotors) spinning like a falling maple leaf. The lift this produces is enough that the pilot can glide to a safe landing.

But if something goes wrong below seven hundred feet, there isn't time or altitude to put the rotors into autorotation, as the maneuver is called, so the helicopter is apt to fall like a rock.

That afternoon we took off for the return trip to Saigon almost empty; besides the pilot, copilot and two enlisted crew members, I was the only passenger.

I can still hear the scream and vibration H-21 transmission shafts made on takeoff; even when it was working properly, the H-21 always sounded and felt like a banshee dying of palsy.

The moment we left the ground our pilot dropped the nose to gain speed for a rocketing ascent, hoping to get quickly away from anticipated Viet Cong groundfire, and to get above seven hundred feet. We left the operation far behind us, the crew chief was breaking open a package of C-ration cookies and the pilot had begun his steep climb when we were hit.

In Wagner's opera *Siegfried*, the hero forges a sword which he tests by chopping an anvil in two, and this moment is accompanied by an earsplitting orchestral crash. Whenever I hear that sound I think of the sound an enemy bullet made that day when it pierced the chopper's skin about one foot above my left shoulder. We lost power to the rotors almost instantly.

The H-21 lurched violently, slid to one side and began its roller-coaster descent as someone yelled, "We're going in! Hang on!" I glanced out a window, saw that we were headed almost straight down and then spent the worst twenty seconds or so I can remember.

Actually, I just quit thinking or feeling anything during the descent; only afterward did I remember the stark terror I must have been feeling at some lower level of consciousness. I lay on my back, braced myself between two aluminum girders and shut my eyes.

I don't remember the actual impact because it must have knocked me out. When I came to, the silence at first was overpowering, but by degrees I became aware of the pinging and ticking noises of cooling metal, and the soft moaning of one of the crewmen. The crew chief and I were bleeding from assorted cuts, but neither of us was badly hurt. The moaning man, an enlisted crew member, was not bleeding, but he fell back in pain each time he tried to rise, and it was obvious that his leg was broken.

The cockpit was a shambles, with blood spattered on the instrument panel and on the smashed windshield panels. But as the pilot recovered consciousness he seemed more stunned than injured. "The switches are off and we're not burning, but we gotta get out of here," he said. "Dave doesn't look too good."

The copilot, in fact, was unconscious. His cracked flight helmet lay behind his seat and blood was welling from a large head wound. The pilot fished a sterile pad out of an aid pack and applied it to the copilot's injured head, but at that moment there was a loud bang—the sound of another bullet hitting our aluminum skin. We were under fire.

"C'mon, buddy, we gotta keep 'em down," the crew chief yelled, handing me an M-2 carbine with several banana magazines. Then he dragged a machine gun from the wreck, hastily set it up and began firing long, unaimed bursts in the general direction of the Viet Cong fire. Hardly knowing what I was doing, I popped away with the little carbine, hoping without much confidence that the noise would scare off our persecutors.

After five minutes or so the Viet Cong left us alone, and the great sweep of rice fields fell silent except for the angry cawing of a distant crow. Our helicopter's radio had been smashed and there was no way to call for help, but the pilot was confident that a search-and-rescue operation would retrieve us soon.

He was right, but during the forty minutes it took for a pair of H-21s to find us, we felt lonely and naked in the middle of that rice field.

The copilot began to regain consciousness. While the pilot looked after him, the crew chief and I looked around and discovered that our bird had been brought down by just one rifle-caliber bullet—a lucky fluke that had cut an essential hydraulic line. A bullet that had cost a dime to manufacture wrecked a machine worth hundreds of thousands of dollars and had put at least one highly trained and valuable aviator *hors de combat.*

Cost-effective weaponry was a hallmark of the Viet Cong, and on another operation in the An Xuyen area I saw how the guerrillas made some of their munitions. The Saigon government unit I accompanied rooted out a Viet Cong weapons factory hidden in the jungle, where guerrillas were manufacturing primitive but useful mortars and infantry shotguns. They made the shotgun ammunition from short lengths of brass tubing, to which they soldered old French ten-centime coins, the kind with a hole in the middle. The workers crimped percussion caps into these holes and loaded the finished cases with powder and shot. The homemade weapons from which these rounds were fired were called "skyhorse guns," for some reason no one could ever explain to me.

Battered and shaken after the crash, I got back to Saigon's Tan Son Nhut airport early that afternoon, hitched a ride to the main gate and grabbed a blue-and-white Renault taxi into town. The driver barely glanced at me, despite the bloodstains and mud adorning my ripped shirt; a lot of fares picked up at Tan Son Nhut airport looked pretty messy in those days.

Back at my office on Rue Pasteur I stuck a carbon-paper manifold in our old Underwood and began typing out a story describing the operation I had just covered. But I hurt all over and nothing I wrote seemed to capture the flavor of the action. It's astonishing how often war correspondents face writer's block after witnessing dangerous battles, often falling back on stupid clichés just to finish some kind of dispatch.

Just as I finished counting the words in my rather pedestrian cable, my phone rang. The caller, a diplomat I assumed to be an intelligence spook, was inviting me to a black-tie cabaret show that very night, where the guest list included a couple of senior Vietnamese officers I'd been trying for weeks to interview. I naturally accepted.

I showered, bandaged up my lacerations and donned my new tuxedo, feeling rather foppish as I stepped into the street. But once inside the Caravelle cabaret I was among similarly attired men, including, I noticed, some American officers I had seen out in the mud during the day. There were beautiful women there, too, and the drinks were cold. I relaxed.

These many years later, I no longer remember what the Vietnamese generals told me that night, but I do remember that the chanteuse was Juliette Greco, straight from Paris and in top form. Her sultry songs were balm to her footsore listeners, and it crossed my mind, not for the first time, that Saigon was a city of astonishing contrasts.

As the seductive tunes washed over us I chanced to glance across the room through a window overlooking the Saigon River. Streams of red tracers were arching through the darkness beyond the river, and occasional yellow flashes marked the impacts of shells. *"Adieu, mon coeur,"* sang Greco.

I felt much restored as I walked back to my little apartment, past rows of sidewalk cots occupied by drowsing policemen and night watchmen.

But the evening's pleasant afterglow dissolved the instant I stepped into my room, where three blue-and-white envelopes stuck under my door awaited me. Rockets from New York! "Unipress has three choppers downed but your crash has only one stop if correct need matcher sapest foreign," one read. (Translation: "Regarding your crash story, UPI is reporting that three helicopters were shot down instead of just one. If you can confirm this, we need an equivalent story as soon as possible.

From the Foreign Desk.") I wearily picked up the phone and began trying to raise a U.S. military spokesman.

Saigon's cultural diversions in those days were welcome respites from the war. Many of the best-known Paris vedettes came to sing or perform in Saigon during the early 1960s, as did German chamber orchestras, the Martha Graham dance troupe, art shows and much more.

Diem and his powerful brother Nhu sometimes invited foreign artists and entertainers to command performances, for which the government rolled out the red carpet. Diem's entire cabinet and several thousand lesser officials were required to attend a political play called *The Year of the Tiger* produced by Moral Rearmament, an international politico-religious society that Diem admired. The play, which was about the riots and demonstrations that took place in Japan during the 1950s, was supposed to be an object lesson for Vietnamese officials in how to deal with rebellion, the fear of which was always in Diem's mind.

Another performance Diem's cabinet had to sit through was a special screening of *The Guns of Navarone*, a Gregory Peck war movie. The movie lesson the Ngos hoped to impress on their officials was that high morale and courage can triumph over any odds.

The State Department was eager to export American culture to Viet Nam, and paid plenty to do it. To ease the financial burden on Vietnamese who might wish to buy English-language reference books and literature, Washington subsidized the sale of such material in Saigon, where customers could buy it at ridiculously low prices. I paid only $35 for an *Encyclopaedia Britannica,* and I acquired a splendid library of other books. I don't think there were many Vietnamese customers for these bargains, but I, at least, was grateful to the American taxpayers who paid for them.

Each time a new American weapon system arrived in Viet Nam I tried to spend some time in the field watching it in action. Rarely did the performance of new gadgets live up to early expectations. I particularly remember the arrival of the first squadrons of M-113 armored troop carriers, which had been billed as the ultimate answer to rice-paddy warfare.

The M-113, which was something like a slab-sided tank, looked formidable, but its thin armor was made of aluminum instead of steel. This made the vehicle much lighter than a tank, so light and watertight that it could float and propel itself on water as well as on land. The Mekong Delta is a hybrid of land, water and mud, so the planners expected the M-113 to be able to chase enemy guerrillas across all types of terrain.

Early one morning I found myself clinging for dear life to the upper deck of an M-113 that was jolting at high speed over a dry paddy field in Long An Province. We were supposedly in hot pursuit of a Viet Cong battalion, and as we bumped along, our ragged line of M-113s presented a striking battle tableau as their little unit flags flapped from the tops of radio antennas. Cavalry charges were ridiculous anachronisms in Viet Nam, but they could still stir the soul.

By and by we came to a canal, just the kind of obstacle the M-113 was designed to overcome. Still advancing line-abreast, a dozen M-113s lumbered down the bank into the water, their tracks spraying sheets of mud and canal water over onlookers. But the crossing was a dismal failure. As the personnel carriers reached the opposite bank their drivers struggled like bears in a pit to climb out, but the harder the engines pushed, the deeper the tracks dug themselves into the slippery ooze. Five minutes after the charge had begun the day's operation was over, with our whole force of M-113s trapped like rubber ducks in a bathtub. I was unwilling to wait around for a tank retriever to pull them out, so I headed home.

The M-113 had other shortcomings that became more obvious as the war developed. One major weakness was the frailty of its aluminum armor, which could be pierced by 12.7-millimeter bullets and ripped apart by the Viet Cong's B-40 rocket grenades. Once set afire, an M-113 was soon enveloped in white flames that quickly consumed the vehicle and often killed its occupants.

Unsatisfactory though it was as a fighting vehicle, the M-113 proved to be ideal for a very special kind of mission: the overthrow of governments. M-113s figured prominently in all of South Viet Nam's coups, as they did in revolutions in Latin America, Africa and elsewhere in Asia. (After M-113 crews helped to overthrow them, President Diem and his brother Nhu were executed inside an M-113.) The M-113 became one of America's greatest contributions to political unrest, and this veteran king-killer is still soldiering on in many third-world countries.

The most useful thing I learned was that the war in Viet Nam had very little to do with weapons and everything to do with popular support. Some of my education came from intelligence spooks.

When I arrived in Viet Nam I was told that the CIA station chief, William Colby, was an amiable fellow who sometimes talked to reporters. This did not mean that he communicated anything of substance, however. My only contacts with Colby and his subordinates were casual and strictly social.

But the intelligence services of several other countries were more informative. I got to know a man called Peter, who was nominally an official of the British Information Service but was actually a seasoned MI5 operative. Peter never disclosed any secrets, but he introduced me to the writings of Vo Nguyen Giap, the victor over the French at Dien Bien Phu and Hanoi's chief strategist in the war against the United States. Reading

Giap, I began to understand Viet Cong tactics and strategy, and it was as if I had suddenly found the key to a perplexing puzzle.

Giap's best-known book, *People's War, People's Army*, was written in smugly turgid Marxist-Leninist style, and its broad message paralleled Mao Tse-tung's injunction to swim among the people as fish swim in the sea. But the book also contained so much practical good sense that it seemed to me a lot of American officials were missing an important part of their education by neglecting it. *People's War*, like T. E. Lawrence's *Seven Pillars of Wisdom*, is a classic textbook of politico-military warfare, a type of warfare Americans should have studied more closely in Viet Nam.

Giap's catechism to his troops included injunctions to pay for anything they confiscated from the people, to behave modestly, to help villagers out with farming and other rural chores and to concentrate their terrorist tactics against government officials the common people already disliked. Despite Giap's rules, the Viet Cong committed many atrocities and tactical blunders, but discipline in Hanoi's forces was generally tighter than that imposed on Saigon's troops.

Giap's combat strategy was simple: to move fast and keep the enemy off balance; to keep his guerrilla units dispersed and invisible until the very hour of battle; and to fight only when the local odds were overwhelmingly favorable.

After a successful skirmish or a large-scale ambush of a government convoy, the guerrillas were supposed to melt swiftly away and disperse, blending indistinguishably into communities of sympathetic farmers once again. Only when *de quoc my*— American imperialism—was worn out by years of piecemeal bloodletting would communist forces be expected to mass in large units for conventional warfare. By then, Giap promised his partisans, the "liberation army" would be buttressed by a popular uprising of the entire Vietnamese people.

Giap always considered the political war far more important than military action alone. The destruction of a guerrilla village by American napalm was a Viet Cong victory, he knew, if it turned Vietnamese against the Americans and their Saigon allies. Hanoi's leaders were also conscious of the importance of their image abroad, even in the United States. Giap counted heavily on the shift of American public opinion toward his side as the war wore on.

Giap's ideas were vindicated in 1975 when his tanks smashed into Saigon's presidential palace and put the American rear guard to flight. He had won, and his victory, he knew, had been achieved in hometown America as well as the rice fields of Viet Nam.

Thanks to Peter and other wise observers, I began to get a sense of "people's war" almost from the day I arrived in Saigon. My daily work, however, consisted mostly of trying to guess where news would break and being on the spot when it did. I sometimes guessed painfully wrong. One memorably bad guess took me to Ca Mau when I should have stayed in Saigon, and I suffered one of the worst beatings I've ever had at a competitor's hands.

February is South Viet Nam's hottest, driest month, and in February of 1962, the country was relaxing after the festive Tet New Year observances. I thought the holiday season would be a good time to spend away from Saigon, so I bought a ticket on an Air Viet Nam Cessna and flew to Ca Mau to see what was going on.

Ca Mau, the capital of An Xuyen Province, is close to the southern tip of the country, and much of the region is covered by swamps and bamboo jungle. A prevailing sea breeze moderates the oppressive temperature, but potable water is scarce, life is primitive, and the region will never attract many tourists.

The day I arrived, a Vietnamese marine unit was being readied for an emergency mission intended to find out why radio

communication with a nearby district capital named Dam Doi
had gone dead. All that was known in Ca Mau was that Dam
Doi's district chief, an army captain, had led a detachment of
troops into the jungle a few days earlier and had not been heard
from since.

That relief operation taught me the value of sturdy combat boots. At that point in the war I generally wore the sneaker-
like canvas shoes manufactured by Bata for the Vietnamese
army. They were light and they dried quickly after immersion in
water and mud. But Bata's combat shoes met their match in the
slime of An Xuyen's bayous, where they quickly filled with
detritus and leeches. Their soles were so slippery that I took
many falls while balancing across log "monkey bridges."

It was an arduous hike for an ill-coordinated civilian, and
because I was tired I became careless. On combat patrols in Viet
Cong territory, the rule was to watch one's step carefully for
booby traps, but as we neared Dam Doi I was stupidly staring
straight ahead when I stepped into a water-filled ditch. The Viet
Cong had planted a pattern of dagger-sharp bamboo stakes under
the water, and an excruciating pain informed me that one of
these devilish spikes had pierced the rubber sole of my shoe and
deeply penetrated my foot.

With visions of septicemia dancing in my head, I ground
up several of the halizone tablets I'd brought to sterilize drinking
water, and rubbed the resulting powder into my wound. It must
have worked, because I survived with two feet.

That night I slept on the tiled floor of the absent district
chief's office. Villagers told us that the district chief had ordered
a march into the jungle after one of his agents told him a Viet
Cong unit was camped nearby. If the local militia moved fast, the
captain was told, it could surprise and annihilate the enemy. The
district chief had taken this bait and marched away two days
earlier.

In the morning we started down the trail the district

chief's detachment had taken. Our marines cautiously assigned a point man to scout the route and guards to protect our column's flanks as we walked into the jungle; we were entering territory controlled by the Viet Cong's dreaded U Minh Battalion, and our marine commander was taking no chances.

My foot hurt like the devil, but we didn't have far to go. Barely five miles west of the hamlet we came to the ghastly end of our journey. There, in the center of a muddy clearing churned by the tracks of cattle, was a water hole, and arrayed around the water hole like spokes in a wheel were the bodies of the missing district chief and his men. The corpses were already bloated and stinking, enveloped by droning clouds of flies.

A bamboo pole had been erected next to the pool, and flying from it was a red-and-blue flag with a yellow star, the Viet Cong colors. A marine approached to yank the flag down, but was stopped in his tracks by the shouted order of a lieutenant. The officer had correctly guessed that the flagpole was booby-trapped.

A marine trained to detect mines cautiously inspected the pole and found a half-buried artillery shell the guerrillas had fused with a hand-grenade detonator and a trip wire.

Most of the dead government militiamen had been executed in cold blood. Their hands were bound behind them, and most had been shot through the head at point-blank range, so that gray powder smudges were left on their skin. Several had been beheaded. The Viet Cong had made its point: an enemy venturing into the U Minh Forest could expect no quarter.

Screams of grief met us as we trudged back to Dam Doi with our pathetic caravan of bodies. One woman threw herself into the mud, rhythmically banging her face against the ground and moaning. As village carpenters banged together a fresh batch of coffins, our officers decided to call off further operations for the time being, and we marched back to Ca Mau. Even the tough Vietnamese marines had had a bellyful of the U Minh Battalion.

An ugly surprise awaited me in Ca Mau. Radios were blaring the news that two Vietnamese Air Force fighter pilots had rebelled against the government, taken off and bombed the presidential palace in Saigon. It wasn't yet known what had happened to the Ngo family, but a state of siege had been declared.

Stunned and cursing my rotten luck, I asked Colonel Ut, the An Xuyen Province chief, if he had any idea what was going on. "It appears there has been a coup," he replied. What did he personally plan to do about it? He gave me a suspicious look and replied, "I'll have to see what develops."

But there was no question what I had to do: somehow, by hook or by crook, I must get back to Saigon and try to catch up with the competition. UPI, Reuters, Agence France Presse and everyone else had already beaten me, I knew, and my only hope was to make up for their long leads with some sharp reporting of my own.

I rented a car, but the driver refused to drive through territory controlled by the Viet Cong until I promised him three times his normal fare. Colonel Ut insisted on giving me an escort, two truckloads of troops, to accompany my car as far as the province border twenty miles northward. I didn't much care for an escort that would advertise me as a target, but I would have been rude to turn down the colonel's offer, so we set forth.

The troops crammed into the escort trucks sat with their backs facing outward, perfect targets for an ambush, and off we went, our ramshackle Buick sedan sandwiched between two trucks. We drove at breakneck speed to the province border, where the troop commander stopped, and like the White Knight taking his leave of Alice, he gave me a cheery wave.

Barely ten minutes later six men wearing green military jackets and farmers' black pants stepped into the road from a patch of banana palms and ordered my car to stop. One of them carried a Chinese AK-47 assault rifle. I held my breath.

The guerrillas inspected our car registration and questioned the driver for about five minutes. By turns, they stuck their heads through a window to look me over, and I felt the sweat starting from my brow. But after a while the tension seemed to break, and one of the guerrillas smiled at me, saying, "Peace, American. You go." "Peace," I replied, and off we went.

"VC think war is over because maybe Diem killed by bombs," my driver said. "You and me very lucky today, I think."

When I reached the AP office I ripped open the hateful blue-and-white envelopes that had accumulated in my absence. The first few were panicky pleas for stories. Later missives demanded to know why I had not filed. The last couple of cables plaintively wondered if I needed emergency assistance. I knew I was really in trouble.

SOME PRINCES
AMONG MEN

It wasn't long after arriving in Indochina that I began mingling with more of the mighty than I'd ever seen concentrated in one region, and at first it was an agreeable novelty. Besides the local big shots, there was an endless stream of envoys from the United States, some with names as prominent as Kennedy and Nixon. Visitors from many nations included chiefs of state, cabinet ministers, movie stars, evangelists, arms merchants and generals, all peddling politics or merchandise, all seeking publicity, and all eager to be photographed in dramatic settings with warlike backdrops. The "in" trip for conspicuous people in those days was to Viet Nam, in somewhat the same spirit as they might visit a Kenya game preserve or the South Pole today.

The flow of high-ranking officials visiting Indochina during the war years afforded newsmen some advantages they would not have enjoyed at home. A cabinet minister, senator or agency chief might be as aloof as a pharaoh in Washington, but in Viet Nam he was just another tourist who appreciated a few tips from the local newsmen. Exhausted by the snares of doing business with scheming Vietnamese leaders, the prominent visitor from Washington, London, Canberra or Tokyo was often happy to relax over an evening drink with a seasoned American correspondent and trade candid notes.

Informal contacts with newsmen helped the visitors by supplying them with a great deal of out-of-the-way information unavailable from official sources. Such meetings helped newsmen in two ways: we could sometimes pry loose a bit of news, and we gained standing with the lower-ranking officials with whom we had to deal every day. American diplomats in Saigon were apt to be more helpful than usual to a correspondent who was on friendly terms with some mover and shaker in Washington.

One of the main tasks of all reporters is to seek out newsmakers, and chiefs of state, like saints and serial killers, are newsmakers. Foreign correspondents see a lot of them.

Meeting a local potentate is usually quite easy. Resident representatives of the foreign press in most countries are automatically inscribed on diplomatic lists, and they receive a steady flow of gold-embossed invitations from presidential palaces. This may seem very grand, until one recalls that many third-world chiefs of state are simply former corporals or outright gangsters who led successful coups. The rat steering the average ship of state is likely to have seized power by shooting his predecessor, and he is no more a statesman than Nero was.

But while the national boss may lack moral fiber or diplomatic polish, he can rivet the attention of the foreign press with one redeeming quality: "color." He makes outrageous public statements, he flaunts his sexual prowess, he conducts impromptu public executions and he heaps egregious insults on any foreign dignitary who slights him.

It is often he, not the Nobel laureate or saintly statesman, who adorns the cover of *Time*, and splashy news coverage can attract foreign credit, favorable trade terms, weapons and bribes. The ambitious national leader therefore takes care to throw newsmen the color they demand, even if it is not sympathetically portrayed.

Symbiotic relationships between dictators and newsmen

are sometimes born that ill serve readers or viewers back home. Tacit bargains between the mighty and their pet scribes are sometimes struck, and it is not uncommon to find a reporter from one of the major world capitals enjoying special status in the palace of some dictator, king or party first secretary. If the leader happens to be a womanizer, his most-favored correspondent is likely to be female, pretty and an object of loathing by some (but rarely all) of her male colleagues. A male protégé of the big cheese usually buys his favored status by couching news dispatches about the leader in flattering terms.

Ready access to the leader's palace can yield spectacular news scoops, but for honest reporters the rewards are usually not worth the price. Once branded as a flack for some government, a newsman will never find work again with a respectable news organization, and will be all the more at the mercy of his or her ruler-patron. Of course, a male journalist may make enough money to retire, simply by serving as the ruler's chosen scribe. A female reporter who goes that route may win riches with a best-selling kiss-and-tell book, or perhaps with a brilliant marriage.

But the overwhelming majority of American foreign correspondents are immune to such lures.

One tends to remember a few corrupted correspondents, however, precisely because they are rare. There was an American magazine writer whose friendship with Kremlin leaders not only gave him a steady flow of exclusive stories but kept the KGB off his back, allowing him to prosper from an illegal-currency racket. This fellow (now dead) used American dollars to purchase cheap black-market rubles in Moscow, with which he would buy round-the-world tickets on the Soviet Aeroflot airline. He would then fly only as far as Western Europe, cash in the unused part of his ticket for hard currency at the legal rate, and increase his capital some tenfold.

If any honest correspondent had attempted such a scam,

he would have been summarily arrested, jailed, expelled or even shot. But this magazine writer was safe because he was in the Kremlin's pocket.

But even incorruptible journalists can sometimes find themselves squirming between the antithetical demands of hard-hitting journalism and the goodwill of some national leader.

During crises, hundreds of foreign newsmen swarm to even an obscure national capital, but during quiet periods, the local ruler must court a handful of resident foreign correspondents if he wants any attention. Consequently, the chief of state and his cabinet get to know all the local correspondents by name and by their vulnerabilities, idiosyncrasies and sympathies. If the president or generalissimo is seeking foreign capital, weapons or political backing, he will concentrate his charms and implicit threats on the local newsmen, whom he treats as surrogate diplomats from their respective countries.

Potentates are not always offended by ridicule; they sometimes accept disrespectful treatment from foreign correspondents in the same spirit that kings once encouraged jesters to gibe. My friend and former AP colleague Roy Essoyan was a tough critic of Soviet totalitarianism and expansionism, but Soviet communist leaders liked him, all the same. Roy is fluent in what he calls "gutter Russian." He delighted Nikita Khrushchev with his vulgar Russian wisecracks, and Roy once horrified a group of American officials and Soviet apparatchiks by pulling a baseball cap down over Khrushchev's ears. Khrushchev was delighted.

There wasn't much cause for laughter at the time. It was the era of the Cuban missile crisis and developments that brought the world close to the brink of nuclear holocaust. But Roy managed to make even the mighty laugh, and he rooted out many a story denied to sober-faced colleagues.

In the early 1960s, Indochina's princes exuded color.

In Laos, a country whose national emblem was a three-headed elephant, three princes ruled jointly: Boun Oum, the right-winger, Souphanouvong, the communist, and Souvanna Phouma, the neutralist. Laos was also the home of such colorful instigators as General Phoumi Nosavan, a right-wing maker of coups, and Colonel Kong Le, an eccentric paratrooper who also fomented coups.

In North Viet Nam, a commoner prince held sway: Ho Chi Minh. Ho's color stemmed partly from the mystery and intrigue that cloaked his past. He had lived in many countries, that much was certain. During his sojourn in France he helped to found the French Communist Party. But other periods in his life were hazier; did he, as some Hanoi historians asserted, earn his living as a dishwasher in New York City at one time?

South Viet Nam was ruled by Ngo Dinh Diem, who dressed in business suits and rarely smiled, and his color, for the most part, was gray. But making up for Diem's drab mien was his pepper-pot sister-in-law, Madame Ngo Dinh Nhu, a stubborn woman who at times fancied herself as a latter-day Joan of Arc. As beautiful and cold-blooded as Turandot, she was constantly in the news with her decree against public displays of affection, her tirades against the Americans and her ungovernable rages against foreign newsmen.

Madame Nhu was as brave and cantankerous as she was colorful, and whether they admired or hated her, foreign newsmen never ignored her. Her detractors took to calling her the "Dragon Lady"; because she seemed so much larger than life she became almost a cartoon character.

Madame Nhu told me once that she must have been favored by heaven because she had been spared so many times by events that could have proved fatal. During the early years of the Ngo reign, her fiery rhetoric had transformed hostile street mobs into supporters of the regime. In the 1962 bombing of the presidential palace by a mutinous Vietnamese fighter pilot, Madame Nhu fell two stories through a hole made by his bomb, but survived with a minor injury.

Madame Nhu had shared an attitude with most Vietnamese that many American officials failed to appreciate until it was too late: she despised being ordered around by anyone. "When I was a child," she told me, "if someone told me to stand up, I would sit down even if I wanted to stand up. I'm still like that. Can't you Americans understand that we don't like being told to do things?"

By late 1963 Madame Nhu and her husband, Ngo Dinh Nhu, were thoroughly distrusted and hated by official Washington, and Nhu, who served his president and brother as a political counselor, regarded the Americans as hostile colonialists. When relations between Washington and Saigon reached a crisis that summer, the Nhus made secret overtures to Ho Chi Minh in North Viet Nam, with the object of ending the war and throwing the Americans out.

Considering how few friends the United States won in Viet Nam, it still amazes me that we were able to hang on there as long as we did.

My journalism greatly annoyed the Nhus, but they never got around to expelling me, as they had several other reporters, including Francois Sully of *Newsweek*. Despite the fact that my name was on a palace list of supposed enemies, I even continued to meet the Nhus from time to time; Madame Nhu said that although I was a foe of Viet Nam I was fairer in my reporting than some of my colleagues. I wasn't flattered. A compliment from her of even the backhanded variety could tarnish a newsman's career.

In October 1963, when Madame Nhu went to the airport to leave for a conference in Europe, her husband came to see her off, and for the first time, I saw the two of them simply as a worried, affectionate married couple. He actually kissed her in public, violating her own ban. It was obvious that a crisis was coming and the Nhus were aware they might never meet again, so their airport parting seemed rather poignant.

A few weeks later Nhu was shot to death, and Madame Nhu never returned to Viet Nam.

Tragedy and foreign newsmen continued to dog Madame Nhu in exile. Her daughter Le Thuy was killed in a 1967 car accident in France. In 1986 Madame Nhu's brother, a lawyer named Tran Van Khiem, strangled both their mother and their father at the parents' Washington, D.C., home, afterward going to jail for the crime. Madame Nhu's estranged father, Tran Van Chuong, had been Vietnam's ambassador to the United States during Diem's rule, but resigned in 1963 to protest Diem's treatment of the Buddhists.

Another member of Vietnam's ruling house, Ngo Dinh Can, ruled central Viet Nam as a virtual viceroy of the region under his brother's presidency. A firing squad ended Can's life after the Ngo family was overthrown.

But another Ngo brother kept the family in the news long after his siblings' violent deaths. Archbishop Ngo Dinh Thuc made a career of stirring up trouble for the Catholic Church.

I crossed Archbishop Thuc's tracks in Spain in 1976, where I was covering the aftermath of Franco's death. The archbishop, it seemed, had visited a mysterious hilltop near Seville, witnessed miraculous apparitions in the sky and seen leaders of a local religious sect heal the sick through a laying-on of hands. Enormously impressed, the Vietnamese archbishop consecrated one of the faith healers as a bishop in the Roman Catholic Church, and ordained several other healers as priests.

The Vatican, infuriated by Archbishop Thuc's unauthorized ordinations, excommunicated him. The Pope later forgave him, but in 1983 Thuc reiterated his refusal to recognize John Paul II as Pope, and he defiantly consecrated three more renegade bishops. Mother Church threw him out once again.

Newsworthy though Vietnam's Ngos were in their heyday, the most colorful of Indochina's leaders, by far, was Cambodia's Prince Norodom Sihanouk. At this writing, he is still one of Cambodia's major political figures.

In the 1960s, when I first met him, Sihanouk was called "Samdech Sahachivin," or "Comrade Prince," a title that faithfully described his peculiar style of ruling, combining the rhetoric of Marxist revolution with the autocratic despotism of an absolute monarch. No one could really blend two such contradictions, but Sihanouk made the mixture seem plausible.

Sihanouk would hate the comparison, but I came to think of him as a modern version of Thailand's King Mongkut, the ruler who inspired Margaret Landon's novel *Anna and the King of Siam*. For years, the many-sided prince kept the international press and its readers gasping with surprise, delight and even admiration.

Like President Clinton, Sihanouk is a saxophone player, but he has many other talents. He composes serious music, he is a playwright, movie producer, director and actor, and while he ruled, he was the patron of the Cambodian Royal Ballet. He is also an essayist, a jurist and an astonishingly canny politician.

As absolute ruler of Cambodia in the sixties, Sihanouk delivered frequent radio addresses that delighted listeners by exposing scandals, including some in the royal family itself. One of the Comrade Prince's most memorable speeches warned the mothers of Cambodia against his son, Prince Yuvanath, who had acquired a national reputation for getting pretty young commoners in the family way. Sihanouk announced that he would take no further financial responsibility for his bastard grandchildren, and that parents should lock up their daughters when Yuvanath was in the neighborhood.

Some newsmen and diplomats, failing to understand why it was that Sihanouk commanded such loyalty in his own country, painted Sihanouk as a clown. This portrayal certainly influenced policymakers in Washington in their eventual decision to back a military coup that overthrew him. But what the Americans eventually got in place of Sihanouk and his successors was the Pol Pot regime, which slaughtered hundreds of thousands of Cambodians and thrust the country into a barbarism unequaled even in the country's bloody antiquity.

Sihanouk was the founder of modern Cambodia. In 1953, one year before Viet Nam fought France to its knees at Dien Bien Phu, Cambodia, under Sihanouk's stewardship, gained independence through negotiation. Sihanouk's de facto kingdom was more or less at peace and it prospered until North Viet Nam invaded it and the United States moved against the invaders.

Maintaining peace for Cambodia was not easy during a period when predators from all sides—North and South Viet Nam, Thailand, China and the United States—were nipping away at the national territory.

Soon after I arrived in Indochina Sihanouk granted me my first interview with him.

Flying from Saigon to Phnom Penh offered a stunning contrast. Saigon's streets were full of military traffic and exhaust fumes. Mambo music blasted from the Saigon bars, where bored Vietnamese hostesses drank fake whisky. By contrast, Phnom Penh, only a half hour away by air, was an enchanted tableau of old Asia, where temple bells paced a leisurely and graceful existence.

Even while high over the countryside in one of the propeller-driven DC-6s operated by Royal Air Cambodge, a traveler could spot the architectural demarcation between Viet Nam and Cambodia. The shacks and stucco-faced buildings of Viet Nam looked commonplace and drab, while the red-tiled roofs of Cambodia, with their turned-up corners and gilded woodwork, evoked an image of old Asia. Even simple Cambodian farmhouses, open-sided structures perched atop stilts, could charm a traveler's eye.

Phnom Penh's Pochentang Airport itself had regal touches, including a huge canvas-topped pavilion where "Monsigneur le Prince" received arriving potentates in a style to which very few were accustomed.

Some of the planes parked at the airport were interesting in themselves. There were the MiG-17 fighters of Sihanouk's air force and late-model French Alouette helicopters. But there were also antiques of great interest to aviation enthusiasts, including one of the last Boeing 307 Stratoliner transport planes in existence.

The Stratoliner was itself a bit of history. Aigle Azur, a French charter airline, flew several of the 1939-vintage Stratoliners for the International Control Commission, a military watchdog group made up of representatives from India, Poland and Canada. Members were supposed to monitor truce violations of the 1954 peace agreement that ended the first Indochina War, and to prevent a resurgence of fighting. As peacekeepers they failed miserably, but they kept flying the beautifully streamlined airliners all through the war between the capitals of the former French Indochina—Saigon, Phnom Penh, Vientiane and Hanoi.

I was a passenger on Aigle Azur's Stratoliners a few times, and they reminded me how much more comfortable airliners were in the thirties than they are today. Aigle Azur's Stratoliners were infested with roaches, their upholstery was faded and frayed and their cockpit windows bore green stains where pilots had spilled their crème de menthe in turbulent air. But a passenger could really wallow in those big, comfortable seats.

Phnom Penh was a city of broad boulevards, stately palaces and temples, a big, busy marketplace, and of course, the Phnom itself—a little hill surmounted by a white Buddhist stupa resembling an inverted wineglass. (Phnom Penh means "Mrs. Penh's Hill.") I liked it at first sight.

For my first visit in 1962 I stayed at an unpretentious little hotel called the Mondial, and it was there, while I was washing away the heat and grime of my trip under a primitive shower, that a uniformed footman arrived from the Royal Palace with a summons from the prince.

"Monseigneur" was out of town, I was told, but had sent a car to take me to Kep, a seaside town overlooking the Gulf of Siam, where he maintained a palace. The car was a Soviet Volga, my driver was in a hurry, and we rode like a pogo stick over the endless potholes. But between jounces I looked at the Cambodian landscape and was fascinated. Most of southern Cambodia is as flat as Vietnam's Mekong Delta, but it looks kinder and gentler, to borrow a phrase. For one thing, towering palm trees dot the Cambodian landscape, relieving the delta's monotonous vista of rice fields. For another, houses and farms in Cambodia are built with beauty in mind, not just utility.

The reception rooms of Sihanouk's Kep residence, resplendent in the trappings of a wealthy monarchy, had open sides so that occupants could enjoy passing ocean breezes. The prince, wearing *sampot* trousers and a silvery tunic, strolled in, greeted me in English, and flashed the traditional Buddhist salutation, pressing his palms together and slightly bowing.

We settled into comfortable chairs and the prince gestured toward a dark speck on the distant horizon of the gleaming Gulf of Siam. "Out there," he said, "you see an island the Vietnamese call Phu Quoc. It is a Cambodian island illegally seized from us, and it is one of the reasons we do not consider the Annamites good neighbors."

The interview had opened with a provocation. The word "Annamite," a hangover from French colonialism, is considered almost as objectionable to Vietnamese as the word "nigger" is to

American blacks. Prince Sihanouk wanted me to harbor no illusions about his feelings toward Viet Nam.

"The Annamites and the Siamese would eat us alive if they could get away with it," he added. Another provocation. Thais hate to be called Siamese.

Prince Sihanouk went on provocatively with a list of grievances against the United States, and as his temper warmed, he switched to the French language, in which he felt more comfortable for his diatribes. He branded Americans as cold-warriors ready to sacrifice his little country without hesitation just to win a round or two against the USSR and its satellites.

Deeply suspicious of both Washington and Moscow, Sihanouk was juggling his political ties and cultivating the friendship of China, India, Yugoslavia and France as buffers in his diplomatic rows. He could change diplomatic tack with lightning speed as political winds shifted.

When I took my leave of the Kep palace, Sihanouk was smiling angelically and handed me a little package of fruit, as if to tell me that his harangue had not been meant to target me personally. Sihanouk's unfailing charm has disarmed many an adversary and diplomat about to lose his temper.

Knowing that I was likely to report his outbursts in my news dispatches, Prince Sihanouk sometimes used me as a conduit for expressing his anger at Washington over one thing or another; he seemed to think complaints relayed through me would get more attention than diplomatic notes, and he may have been right.

One time a new American ambassador arrived in Phnom Penh to present his credentials, and the prince made sure I was present at the routine ceremony.

I arrived at the palace to find Sihanouk in the full fig of a Khmer king, with silver lamé *sampot*, gold-embroidered tunic and all the emblems of the royal house.

The new American ambassador arrived at the exact moment of the appointment, wearing the gray striped trousers, tails and top hat demanded by the occasion. He took about three minutes to convey greetings from the White House and to read a bland but friendly prepared statement, and then Sihanouk let fly. The prince, speaking in high-pitched English, unburdened himself of a half-hour tongue-lashing, in which he intimated that the United States was an imperialist foe intent on subjugating Cambodia. The ambassador was stunned and embarrassed. He glanced at me, looking acutely discomfited by the presence of an American newsman.

When Sihanouk perceived the effect he had made, he reassured the American that he harbored no personal malice, and hoped the American would take his remarks in a friendly spirit. He had made his point, and I would report it, he was confident.

On one of my frequent visits to Phnom Penh, the prince invited me to a reception for Liu Shao-chi, the president of China (subordinate, of course, to Chairman Mao), and General Chen Yi, one of the heroes of the Long March. Sihanouk hoped to impress on the world that Cambodia, while weak in itself, had a powerful Chinese protector against both Moscow and Washington.

Since I was Sihanouk's guest, Liu and Chen Yi apparently surmised that I was trusted by their host, and they spoke almost apologetically of the modest financial help China hoped to extend to Cambodia. Peking was always clever in avoiding self-aggrandizing rhetoric when it donated factories, roads, weapons or food to allies like Cambodia and Pakistan, and China's humility made a good impression on these countries. Third-world countries generally received vastly more aid from the United States than they ever did from China, but the paternalistic and boastful speeches of American donors sometimes converted friends into opponents.

A feature of many of Sihanouk's state receptions was a performance of the Cambodian Royal Ballet, in which one of his sons and his ballerina daughter, Princess Bopha Devi, were the lead dancers.

Bopha Devi, petite, beautiful and as graceful as only a Khmer or Thai classical dancer can be, stole the hearts of audiences as she danced the ancient *Ramayana* legend of the White Monkey. She was a star, and she played the part to perfection.

Not all visiting potentates succumbed to the charms of the Cambodian Royal Ballet, however. At one performance I attended the main guest was General Maxwell Taylor. Taylor had arrived as an emissary from President Kennedy to express (among other things) Washington's displeasure with Cambodia for letting Viet Cong guerrillas use its territory as a sanctuary.

I hadn't expected to do any socializing on that trip, and had not brought along a tuxedo. But my invitation to a command performance of the Royal Ballet in Taylor's honor called for *tenue de soirée,* so I had to get a tuxedo somewhere or risk being beaten on what looked like a good story by some better-attired journalist. The rainy season was at its wettest, but I made a dash for the St. Hubert restaurant to ask the French proprietor, a friend of mine, for the loan of a waiter's outfit.

I arrived at the Royal Theater in a leaking cyclo pedal taxi, wet as a sewer rat, and wearing a tuxedo so small and tight I had barely managed to pull it on. The Chinese ambassador, wearing a severe gray uniform, gave me a broad smile and winked as I slunk into my seat.

The ballet sparkled that night, but General Taylor, probably exhausted by constant travel and the tension of delicate negotiations, fell asleep. Seated next to the Cambodian ruler, whose own children were the stars, Taylor listed toward one side as a horrified corps of diplomats and courtiers watched, and he finally pitched over sideways, awakening with a violent start. I heard the Chinese ambassador chuckle.

Alas, the war dimmed even the glitter of Phnom Penh's princesses. The last time I saw Princess Bopha Devi, her father had fallen from power, and she was washing clothes as the hardworking mother of a large family. Her sister, Princess Bothum Bopha, had emigrated and was working as a checkout clerk at a supermarket in Australia.

Sihanouk sometimes acted on vindictive impulse. He once held a trial in a football stadium of an alleged traitor who had joined forces with Khmer Rouge guerrillas. After a furious speech, Sihanouk condemned the defendant to death, and had him summarily shot.

But the prince never let his deeply religious people forget that he was a nonviolent Buddhist at heart. When the World Court decided a festering border dispute with Thailand in Cambodia's favor, Sihanouk shaved his head in the manner of a Buddhist monk and led a religious pilgrimage to the site. Stopping to urinate along the way, he asked startled journalists if they wouldn't like to photograph the Chief of State irrigating the sacred soil.

Sihanouk was at his regal best while presiding over *audiences populaires*, impromptu judicial hearings he conducted in Cambodian villages as well as the capital, in which he adjudicated quarrels, punished villains and bestowed gifts on the poor and on families he judged to be victims of injustice. If a local official or even a member of his royal entourage was found at fault, the prince meted out reprimands or punishment on the spot.

Whether seated on his throne in Phnom Penh or alighting in rural hamlets from his Alouette helicopter, the prince dispensed Solomonic justice that was usually more beneficent than harsh. It's hard for an outsider to judge these things, but I had the feeling that his people really appreciated the attention, and even when his actions left them unsatisfied, most of his subjects gave him the benefit of the doubt.

I came to like and admire Sihanouk, for all his obvious faults. He seemed to me an effective ruler for a country where parliamentary democracy was as alien as military or communist dictatorships. Cambodia was a kingdom from earliest times, and it is still a kingdom in search of a king.

I had many reasons besides Sihanouk to cover Cambodia and I enjoyed every visit. In the heat of the day, the glare of Phnom Penh's streets was unbearable, but at sunset strollers and lovers took to the luscious green parks or lingered over ice cream and lemonade at sidewalk cafes. The gentle tolling of temple bells (and sometimes the gongs and xylophones of the Royal Ballet) blended in the late afternoon with the bells of bicycles and three-wheeled cyclo bicycle taxis. Dusk brought cooler air, and the city came to life.

The government's news agency issued its daily bulletin at sunset, and I used the pretext each evening to hire a cyclo for a leisurely ride to the office. Phnom Penh has greatly changed since then, but I'll always associate the city with the gentle tinkle of bells at dusk.

The people were incredibly graceful. Even the cops, who could act as brutally as thugs on occasion, directed throngs of cars and cyclos with the choreographed gestures of ballet dancers.

The great powers considered Cambodia a backwater in the greater drama of the Viet Nam War, but the French, ever appreciative of the good life, swarmed to their former colony as advisers, instructors, translators, artists and scholars. Some worked as antiquarians and art dealers, others as simple school-teachers fed up with the noise and bustle of metropolitan France. There were novelists, journalists, drifters and dope peddlers among them, all drawn to Phnom Penh to savor an easygoing existence where physical beauty, good food, intense sexuality and the odd whiff of opium cast a powerful spell.

One of my friends in Phnom Penh's large French community was Bernard Fall, a journalist and historian who was one of the most perceptive of all analysts of the French Indochina War. He had covered crucial phases of that war, and reported French military blunders in stark detail—blunders that some Americans believed were being repeated by the Pentagon.

In the early 1960s Fall chose Phnom Penh as a quiet and comfortable retreat in which to work on his books. If only he had remained there instead of returning to Viet Nam to cover the American phase of the war, he might have survived. But in Viet Nam, he stepped on a mine and died.

Cambodia's natural wealth included ruby and sapphire mines as well as rice fields that could produce three crops a year, if a farmer chose to work them that hard. For protein, Cambodians could rely on a bountiful harvest of fish from both the Gulf of Siam and the great Tonle Sap Lake. The lake swarms with fish, and when it abruptly empties out into the Mekong River at the end of the rainy season the fish are stranded and easy to gather up. By and large, Cambodian peasants as well as princes used to enjoy easy lives.

But with the arrival of American troops and advisers in 1970, Cambodia no longer bothered to produce bountiful rice harvests, and the country had to start importing rice. The economy fell apart and the good times ended.

Somehow, everything we touched in Indochina withered, and I still find it hard to understand how a people with intentions as ostensibly good as ours could have wrought so much ill. In Cambodia, after inadvertently wrecking the little country's fragile economic and political bases, we simply pulled out, leaving the people to the mercy of the Khmer Rouge, a gang of murderers Washington supported on the strength of their hostility toward Hanoi.

Small nations are wise to consider carefully before accepting American patronage.

There were some other Indochina princes I never cared

for. Three of them lived in Laos, jointly ruling as an improbable triumvirate. The worst of the three was Prince Souphanouvong, the titular head of the communist Pathet Lao, a guerrilla group whose brutality won an evil fame.

Souphanouvong's counterpoise in the triumvirate was Prince Boun Oum, a large and rather stupid aristocrat dependent for support on his military deputy, General Phoumi Nosavan, commander of the country's rightist army.

At the center of the trinity was the dour and wily neutralist, Prince Souvanna Phouma, who later became the sole ruler.

In 1962 the three Laotian princes, related by blood, were locked in combat. When Souphanouvong's guerrillas captured noncommunist Laotian troops or Americans, the captives could expect little mercy. One of the unlucky ones was Grant Wolfkill, an NBC cameraman, who was accompanying four other Americans on a clandestine military operation when they were taken prisoner by the Pathet Lao. One was killed outright and the others began a dreadful ordeal. When Wolfkill was finally released, he told of a yearlong nightmare in which he and the others had been tortured, starved and confined in bamboo cages. Shortly before the surviving prisoners were released they were turned over to Vietnamese guerrillas, the Viet Cong, for some fattening up, but the prisoners were still sick and exhausted men when they were released.

Wolfkill and his companions were still captives at the time I attended a garden party in Vientiane that the three princes threw for the diplomatic corps. All three princes, mortal enemies to each other, stood side by side as they greeted arriving guests. The princes even chatted with each other, in a surreal mockery of the horrors unfolding in the nearby jungle.

Laos was as improbable a country as the Looking Glass world ruled by the Red Queen, the White Queen and Alice. Its towns and trackless jungles swarmed with guerrillas, communist

agents, Special Forces troopers, armed tribesmen, opium grow-
ers, an international corps of mercenaries and sundry camp followers.

Vientiane was awash with the dollars pouring in with the
foreigners. The Chinese-owned gold shops along Samsentai
Street did a booming business in twenty-four-karat gold bracelets, each weighing five ounces or more. Customers included
pilots of the CIA's Air America, French military advisers, Belgian
mercenaries, spooks, assassins and journalists. Foreigners bought
gold bracelets on the theory that if they were shot down and
wounded, they could pay for help from tribesmen with gold, the
only currency universally respected in Laos.

My wife, Le Lieu, had given me a one-ounce packet of
sheet gold for the same reason. The gold fit conveniently into my
wallet, and it stayed with me until 1992, when a New York
robber relieved me of it. I regard New York's legion of hoods as
far more dangerous than Indochina's guerrillas, by the way.

Evelyn Waugh's novel *Scoop* was set in a mythical African
country modeled on Ethiopia, but could as well have described
the Laos of the 1960s. Laos, like Waugh's fictional "Ishmaelia,"
dominated front pages around the world for a time, without ever
having the slightest impact on real world events. The only Laotian feature that made some difference was a strip of jungle along
the Vietnamese border known as the Ho Chi Minh Trail, a
supply route through which North Viet Nam sent supplies and
troops into the western flank of South Viet Nam. No American
correspondents ever visited the Ho Chi Minh Trail or other
Laotian territory that mattered to the real war, so they covered
the shenanigans of the Laotian princes, politicians and generals.
By hawking inflated stories about endless Laotian crises, the
Western press created a Laos that never was. The newsmen had
fun, but it was not journalism's finest hour.

In the early years, most resident foreign correspondents

lived in the downtown Constellation Hotel, the bar of which, during the rainy season, filled with stray dogs and mud tracked in from the unpaved street. Cables to correspondents from their home offices were placed in the slots of a rack the French hotel owner hung up in the bar, and ever eager to steal a march on competitors, correspondents constantly opened and read each other's messages.

One newsman who had relatively few worries about competitors in the early sixties was a free-lancer named Peter Arnett. Arnett later won fame and fortune from Saigon to Baghdad, but in 1961 in Laos he was struggling to make ends meet. Arnett contrived to get simultaneous stringer assignments from three news services, including the AP. He sent each one a different version of every story he wrote.

The Constellation was often filled with visiting correspondents hot on the trail of the latest coup or military "victory," or simply writing up the inexhaustible supply of Laotian color. In their spare time, of which there was generally plenty, newsmen would buy gold trinkets, explore the markets for curios, or sometimes, I have been told, visit Lulu's whorehouse or one of the local opium dens.

I visited the most popular opium den once, and found it disappointing. I had envisioned a sinister establishment resembling the Limehouse dives of Victorian London, with tiers of wooden berths for the smokers and swarthy Malay attendants to stoke the glowing pipes. Instead, this den was a small wooden shack with a fluorescent light, a few pillows on the bare floor, a noisy Coke machine in a corner, and a bad-tempered old woman who collected a few *kips* (Laotian money) for each pipeload of opium.

The raw opium, black goo with the consistency of molasses, was served from a little squeeze bottle. The proprietress would smear the stuff on the rim of an opium pipe bowl, hold it over a spirit lamp, and let it boil and cook. After the opium reached the consistency of tar, she would stick a needle in it and gather some up on the point. She would then hold the needle over the flame, melt the dollop of cooked opium into a ball about the size of tapioca and insert it in the pipe's tiny brass bowl. Withdrawing the needle with a twist to leave a small hole in the opium, she would finally hold the pipe bowl upside down over her spirit lamp and pass the mouthpiece to the smoker. The customer was supposed to consume the entire vaporized opium ball in one breath. If he failed, the hole would choke up, annoying the server and forcing her to repeat the whole complicated ritual.

After about four pipes I felt very drunk and went home to throw up and sleep. For the following week, I could taste the sickly-sweet flavor of opium in everything I ate, and I resolved to forgo black gold.

But opium may, after all, offer some lessons even to nonusers. Eddie Tan, an Indonesian reporter who worked in Taiwan for a long time, told me how his native village in Indonesia dealt with the drug. Anyone younger than sixty who smoked the stuff was treated as a pariah, and there were very few people who violated this unwritten ban. But after the age of sixty, a person had presumably met his obligations to family and society, and was entitled to take up opium with the full approval of the community. The notion of reserving vice to the elderly has a certain appeal.

Civilization eventually arrived in Vientiane and the scruffy Laos of the 1960s faded away. In 1973 my wife, my dog and I were living in Vientiane's comfortable and respectable Lan Xang Hotel, which had a swimming pool and a restaurant-bar with good French cuisine and no mud on the floor, and a caged bear out back. Even the Pathet Lao had become respectable by then, holding daily tie-and-jacket peace parleys with the Vientiane government and conducting real press conferences. Kidnapping and murder were kept to a minimum.

But correspondents and diplomats never began taking the country so seriously as to quit playing practical jokes on visiting dignitaries. Many a high-ranking diplomat, statesman or editor was taken by his local subordinates to one of the restaurants specializing in delicious soups, unwarned that Cambodian and Laotian soups are often seasoned with a liberal pinch of marijuana. World-famous statesmen would walk into the night giggling softly to themselves, stoned to their socks and wondering why.

In the end, the communists of Indochina got rid of all the princes and papier-mâché politicians, and Laos changed in many ways. Even the owner of the Lan Xang Hotel finally ended up in a French jail for dope smuggling.

Viet Nam's equivalent of royalty, the Ngo family, were also driven from history.

As the tumultuous Vietnamese summer of 1963 boiled dry, martyrs were slain, rioting mobs took to Saigon's streets, prophecies of doom and rumors of miracles circulated and an aura of chaos prevailed as people waited for something momentous to happen. The Diem presidency barricaded itself inside Gia Long Palace, stubbornly waiting for its last stand.

Henry Cabot Lodge, the new American ambassador, came to Saigon that summer with a mandate from President Kennedy to straighten out the Diem regime or get rid of it, and Lodge went about the assignment with vigor. I liked him immediately. Unlike his predecessors and most of the other Americans guiding Viet Nam policy, Lodge spoke bluntly and honestly, and newsmen rarely if ever felt they were being misled by him.

He tightened the squeeze on the Diem government a little more each day, while encouraging a CIA overture toward certain Vietnamese generals. The idea was to get them thinking about the possibility of overthrowing Diem and replacing the regime with a government more acceptable to the South Vietnamese people, most of whom were Buddhists.

Details of Lodge's squeeze play were mostly secret, but he sometimes signaled his intentions in diplomatic ways. A week or so before the coup, for instance, he told me he had cut off Public Law 480 assistance to the regime as a means of starving it of funds to pay the armed forces, a good way to get them to revolt. (Under P.L. 480, the United States government donated surplus agricultural commodities like powdered milk to friendly governments like that of South Viet Nam, which could then sell them to their people and use the income to fight wars.)

Not realizing that Lodge had given me this information off the record, I filed a story reporting what he had done, and the news caused a considerable stir. Lodge was furious, accusing me of having put sensitive diplomatic strategy in jeopardy by publicly proclaiming its purpose. I was duly repentant, he quickly forgave my unintended breach, and he later wrote the preface of a book of mine about the Viet Nam conflict, *The New Face of War*.

Because of my acquaintance with Lodge I had some contact with his associates in the Republican Party. In April 1964, Richard Nixon, whose vice-presidential running mate Lodge had been in the 1960 election, came to Saigon for a visit. Ostensibly, he was there on behalf of his client, Pepsico, but his real purpose was to talk politics with Lodge; another election was coming up. Robert Kennedy stopped by that summer also. He made the rounds of diplomats, Saigon officials, generals and journalists as if he were making a campaign trip, shaking every hand in sight and flashing that boyish grin.

I spent an evening with some other people in Nixon's room at the Caravelle Hotel, and one of the things we talked about was public opinion. I asked the future president how he thought Americans were feeling about the war in Viet Nam, and he replied, "Well, I have faith in our people. They'll follow the flag."

I was appalled by his bland assumption that Americans would accept almost any war policy blindly, but at the same time I could see that he was probably right. Americans are enthusiastic about their wars, provided victory comes quickly. In Viet Nam, of course, it never came.

The standoff between the Ngo family and Washington grew more threatening by the day.

Our little AP office in Saigon was just around the corner from the Gia Long presidential palace, and in late 1963 our antennas were tuned to any change that could presage an upheaval. I could not openly inform my employer that a coup was imminent, because cable traffic and the few radiotelephone circuits available were strictly censored at that point. But there had been several false alarms before, and we had worked out a signal.

Le Lieu, my dear wife-to-be, had been in our office during one tense episode of street violence and had taken refuge in the office toilet. Ed White, the AP's splendid, imperturbable Tokyo news editor, had been in Saigon at the time, and from then on, he understood that in the event of an impending coup, I would message Tokyo that "Le Lieu's in the john."

In the last week of October I sent the coded message, and Ed White immediately flew down to Saigon with some other AP recruits to help out with the crisis.

I must mention here that Saigon was regularly visited by many nonresident American newsmen, some of whom had launched distinguished careers covering World War II and the Korean War. A substantial group of these veteran correspondents believed unshakably that Ngo Dinh Diem was doing a great job and that his critics were maliciously undermining him. They backed Diem's government not merely because of their conservative political views but because they saw Viet Nam as fundamentally similar to World War II and Korea. Viet Nam, for them, was another conventional conflict pitting the home team against the bad guys, and provided Americans would quit whining and buckle down, our side could win.

These men and women therefore regarded such of their younger colleagues as Dave Halberstam, Neil Sheehan and me as wrongheaded purveyors of political rumor and baseless forecasts. One of our detractors, Keyes Beech of the *Chicago Daily News,* frequently chided "young and inexperienced" reporters for suggesting that all was not well in Viet Nam, and on November 1, 1963, his paper published a piece by Keyes reporting that rumors of an impending coup were completely unfounded.

I kept a clipping of that story on the AP bulletin board for some years, as a cautionary reminder. The very coup Keyes had archly discounted began just as we Young Turks had expected, on November 1.

The first inkling came at about noon, when palace guards erected barricades blocking all streets around the palace, including Rue Pasteur, the street where I lived and where all the AP people worked. Shooting was soon reported around several military garrisons, and our staff took to our cars to scout.

The real action began that evening when rebel forces with tanks and artillery laid siege to the palace. We soon had to evacuate the AP office, which by then was in a cross-fire zone and beginning to take hits. Some of us moved to hotels, but most of us were up all night trying to cover the action and figure out ways to get news of the coup to the outer world.

All night long, downtown Saigon blazed with tracers and shells, many of which hit Gia Long Palace. From a block away we saw great slabs of masonry fall away from the handsome white building, and we guessed that everyone inside must have died. At one point a tank battle developed on Rue Pasteur, and an M-48 directly in front of our office was hit by a rocket and burst into flame. The crew tried to escape but was cut down by blistering machine-gun fire, and the fire ignited the tank's ammunition load with a horrifying explosion.

At about dawn the battle ended and we learned that Diem and his brother Ngo Dinh Nhu had fled to a church in Cholon, the Chinese half of the city. Later, the insurgent generals assembled newsmen in a government office building and told us that a junta headed by General Duong Van ("Big") Minh had seized power. The generals had nothing to say about the fate of the Ngos, but twenty minutes later some of us were told that both Diem and Nhu had been slain.

A Vietnamese captain came to my office that afternoon while we were cleaning out the battle debris, to try to sell me a photograph of Diem's body. I turned him down, partly because I could not be sure the photograph was real, but mostly because I was revolted by the prospect of rewarding anyone for hawking such carrion. The officer, I later learned, was none other than Captain Nhung, one of the two rebel soldiers who had shoved the Ngo brothers into an M-113 personnel carrier and then shot them, on orders from Big Minh.

The long succession of failed South Vietnamese governments that began that day in 1963 ended when North Viet Nam's tanks smashed into Saigon's Doc Lap Palace twelve years later. Indochina's princes had been swept away and America's costly adventure in the peninsula was forfeit.

MEMORIES OF HELL

MOST OF THE BATTLES I saw in Viet Nam over the years have blended in my memory into a collage of fear and horror dissociated from any particular times or places. Vignettes remain vivid, though.

I remember a time in the Plain of Reeds near the Cambodian border during an operation in which I was riding across a dry rice field on the deck of an M-113 personnel carrier. As we jounced along, two small figures emerged from a hut and dashed away from us toward a line of trees. With the reflexes and killer instincts of a cat, a Vietnamese soldier manning our vehicle's machine gun opened fire, and the two targets dropped almost immediately. We pulled up next to the bodies and a wave of rage washed over me as I looked at the mangled remains of two boys, both about ten years old, neither one armed.

Viet Nam was nearly never a war fought in traditional fashion with an easily identifiable, uniformed enemy and well-defined battle lines. Americans and their Vietnamese allies, hardened by having been shot at, ambushed and bombed by peaceful-looking peasants, yearned for a simplicity summed up in a saying: "Kill 'em all and let God sort 'em out."

For their part, apolitical Vietnamese farmers soon realized that they were just as likely to be targeted by American and Saigon forces as was the real Viet Cong. For many a peasant, joining forces with the Viet Cong was merely an act of self-protection.

I have an especially stark recollection of one of the fights the Viet Cong won. It happened along a stretch of Route 14 traversing uninhabited jungle north of Saigon in Darlac Province, where a large government convoy of troops, supplies and armored vehicles was ambushed. I reached the place by helicopter about thirty minutes after the brief battle to find every truck, jeep and armored car in the long procession burning, their smoldering tires pouring black smoke into the sky, and scorched ammunition popping like strings of firecrackers. The one hundred or so soldiers in the convoy had died to the last man, but they had gone down fighting: dead guerrillas lay all around the roadside ditches and in the nearby scrub jungle, along with bamboo canteens, shreds of black and green clothing, and great pools of blood left where men had fallen and been carried off by comrades.

To try to reconstruct what had happened I walked a short way from the road, where I found one of the electric exploders the Viet Cong had used to fire a battery of mines they had buried in the road. The exploder stood next to a bush, and in one of the branches was a human brain, popped from its cranium as neatly as a hard-boiled egg from its shell. The body was missing, apparently removed by surviving guerrillas.

The mines used by the Viet Cong in that ambush, a few of which had not been detonated, were made from American 105-millimeter howitzer shells captured by the guerrillas from South Vietnamese gun batteries. The guerrillas had simply replaced the shell nose fuses with electric blasting caps and strung wires to makeshift magnetos.

The Viet Cong were ingenious explosives manufacturers. They made their mines and bombs from captured American artillery shells when they could, but they also improvised. Early in the war they discovered that Unicel 100, a synthetic rubber-like polymer manufactured by the DuPont Company, is a potent explosive when detonated by a blasting cap.

South Viet Nam imported enough Unicel 100 to make soles for eight or nine million pairs of combat boots used by the South Vietnamese army, but in 1966, American investigators discovered that only a very small fraction of Unicel 100 had actually been used for boot soles. The rest had found its way into Viet Cong bomb factories. Secretary of State Dean Rusk promptly halted shipments of Unicel 100 to Viet Nam, but by then, the Viet Cong had acquired plenty of the stuff.

Some of the bloodiest fights occurred at outposts, fire bases and isolated forts besieged by North Vietnamese or Viet Cong guerrillas. When the attackers won, as they often did, everyone inside the fort was usually killed; when the guerrillas lost, they usually suffered a slaughter before retreating.

One time in 1972 I was visiting an American compound in the central Vietnamese highlands city of Kontum when guerrillas struck. The attack came at night, and began when a Viet Cong sapper started cutting his way through the several aprons of barbed wire surrounding the compound. Somehow he must have triggered an alarm, because American sentries on guard opened fire on the perimeter, spraying the general area where penetration had been detected. There followed a gigantic explosion that threw many of us to the ground and smashed every window in the vicinity. We heard some desultory fire and a few enemy bullets snapped by us, but the attack ended.

In the morning we found fragments of the unfortunate sapper all over the compound, his severed hand still gripping a strand of wire. The American experts said that one of the sentries' shots must have hit a blasting cap in the guerrilla's field pack and detonated his entire load of TNT.

Every now and then a handful of guerrillas would inflict

major military damage, and on February 7, 1965, a devastating raid by a ridiculously small group of Viet Cong provided the pretext Washington had needed to openly enter the war.

A dawn telephone tip from a military friend roused me from my Saigon bed that day, and within a half hour I was on a plane bound for Pleiku, the military nerve center of the Vietnamese highlands. We approached the big American-built air base cautiously to avoid ground fire, and as we circled we could see the wrecks of aircraft strewn around the apron, some still burning. Smoke was also rising from some barracks buildings used by American helicopter crews and advisers, and the entire base was a shambles.

By the time I arrived the Americans had taken stock of their losses: eight killed, 126 wounded, nine helicopters and a transport plane destroyed and another fifteen aircraft damaged. A celebrity, the great military cartoonist Bill Mauldin, had been visiting his pilot son at the base when the attack occurred, and had witnessed the debacle. He was appalled.

The senior American adviser at Pleiku was Lieutenant Colonel Ted Metaxis, a no-nonsense field officer who scorned deceptive language and public relations euphemisms. He furiously remarked, "It was just a handful of VC, maybe a dozen, who did all this. The bad guys were smart and gung ho, and our side was just asleep at the switch."

Defense of the Pleiku base perimeter had been primarily the responsibility of Vietnamese troops, who failed to detect the guerrilla penetration and were caught completely off guard. The Tet new year holiday was still being observed and everyone had relaxed, never expecting the Viet Cong to violate what many supposed would be an unofficial holiday cease-fire. (Three years later during the 1968 Tet holiday, American and South Vietnamese forces were again caught off guard when the Viet Cong overran five provinces, seized four cities and even briefly captured the American Embassy. The allies beat back the enemy and inflicted heavy Viet Cong losses, but the enemy's strength and daring had a powerful political impact on the United States as well as Viet Nam.)

The Viet Cong penetration squad at Pleiku had carried bundles of yellow TNT bars wrapped in palm leaves, tied with bamboo twine and fitted with blasting caps. After penetrating the air base they had dashed from aircraft to aircraft, placing their bombs at strategic points and lighting the fuses. Most of the charges went off, but a few were duds the Americans could examine later.

Some local villagers told the Americans how the raid was organized. Weeks earlier the guerrillas had smuggled mortars and ammunition disguised as logs into a hamlet near the air base, holding several farmers hostage while they stowed their equipment in a couple of huts, loosening the bamboo-and-palm-thatch roofs for easy removal.

No warning ever came from these farmers to the occupants of the air base, another of the endless lapses in allied intelligence that continued until the end of the war.

First, the Viet Cong sappers cut their way through the base's perimeter wire, rushing around with their explosive charges. As they finished, other guerrillas waiting in the hamlet simply pulled off the roofs of the huts and opened fire with their mortars on the airport barracks and supply buildings, with devastating effect. Metaxis said he believed that after they exhausted their ammunition, the Viet Cong quietly slipped away without suffering a single casualty.

That afternoon some high-ranking visitors flew up to Pleiku from Saigon in a specially equipped C-123 (the "White Whale") provided by Air Force General Curtis E. LeMay, the officer who proposed to "bomb 'em back to the stone age." Among the brass visiting Pleiku were the country's prime minister, General Nguyen Khanh (who had seized power in a coup), General William C. Westmoreland, Ambassador Maxwell Taylor and several White House officials, including McGeorge Bundy. Westmoreland fixed General Khanh with an icy stare and remarked, "This is bad. Very bad."

Metaxis briefed the celebrities, giving his opinion that the raid had been the work of a small but expert group of guerrillas, probably numbering no more than a dozen. This kind of candor was appreciated by newsmen on the scene, but certainly did Metaxis's career no good. A year or so later he retired from the army and became a professional arms merchant.

After Metaxis's briefing the American and South Vietnamese leaders retired to the privacy of the White Whale, which contained equipment allowing them to communicate directly with Washington. Barely an hour later, steam catapults on the Seventh Fleet's carriers were launching U.S. fighters and bombers for their first attacks on North Viet Nam, and the United States' entry into the war as a full-fledged combatant had become official. In the next few days, American combat troops, no longer labeled as advisers, began pouring into the country.

The White House said raids against North Viet Nam had been launched "in response to provocations ordered and directed by the Hanoi regime," notably an attack by a "regimental-strength main-force North Vietnamese unit" against the base at Pleiku.

The United States may or may not have been right to enter the war openly at that point. What news correspondents objected to was Washington's persistence in lying about enemy strength at Pleiku, when there was no longer any good reason to prevaricate. The motive may have been to quash the public image of a Viet Cong David besting an American Goliath, but even newsmen who applauded the subsequent American escalation felt Washington might have won more support with frankness.

A steady stream of American leaders visited Viet Nam at each critical point in the war, and their attitude toward the local correspondents was initially pretty arrogant. I particularly remember a large press conference in 1963 held at Saigon's Tan Son Nhut airport by Admiral Harry Felt, commander in chief of U.S. forces in the Pacific. I asked the admiral why it was that American military officials persisted in trying to hide the "gray war" from the American public, even though the war (and American casualties) were impossible to conceal. Felt testily replied, "Why can't you get on the team?" There was a roar of ironic laughter from the hundred or so newsmen present, and Felt lost a lot of media friends that day.

Later, visiting American senior officials, including Defense Secretary Robert S. McNamara, were friendlier. McNamara made a point of inviting a few of us to lunch whenever he visited Saigon, ostensibly to hear our observations and comments. On one occasion he asked a couple of us what effect we thought a major influx of American troops would have on the Vietnamese economy.

It was obvious, of course, that the effect on Vietnam's fragile economy would be staggering, and we said so. The U.S. forces and an army of civilian contractors were about to lure hundreds of thousands of Vietnamese to high-salaried (but obviously temporary) construction and clerical jobs, jobs that would take them away from planting rice, fishing and making an agrarian economy function. Mountains of American consumer goods were about to flood the country and its black markets, and enterprises ranging from fast-food stands to used-car lots were about to displace the traditional commerce that kept Viet Nam going in normal times.

And then there were all those other Vietnamese who joined the growing legions of dope peddlers, bar girls and racketeers catering to the lucrative GI service trade.

McNamara seemed attentive, but our remarks had not

the slightest effect on events, and the Vietnamese economy was wrecked.

A small but revealing effect of the American occupation was the destruction of Nha Trang's lobster fishery. Nha Trang, a beach resort on the South China Sea, had been a Mecca for international lobster lovers for a century or more. The fishermen of the area mostly trawled for ordinary fish in the open sea, but also set some lobster traps close to shore to supply Nha Trang restaurants catering to the local carriage trade, French planters and wealthy Vietnamese businessmen. The lobsters bred about as fast as they were eaten.

But when Nha Trang became an American base, all that changed. The Americans brought an insatiable taste for Nha Trang lobsters, and the price of a lobster meal rocketed. Soon, fishermen realized they could make a killing on the delicious crustaceans, and they gave up conventional fishing to concentrate on lobsters, which they harvested using grenades.

Explosions exterminate not only lobsters but their habitats as well, and in a short time, Nha Trang's fabled lobsters were no more. If they ever returned to Nha Trang, I have not heard, but before the Americans left, many a former Nha Trang fishing family had abandoned the sea to take up drug dealing, prostitution or theft. In the space of a decade, America overwhelmed the Vietnamese economy, which is still very far from recovery.

In my own coverage of the expanding war, I tried to vary the fare for readers by breaking away from the monotony of meaningless ground skirmishes. Several times I sat in the backseats of Vietnamese and American fighter-bombers to see what the war on high was like.

Sometimes my seat was in the back of an old, slow T-28, a plane used in the United States as a trainer, but operated by the Vietnamese throughout the war as a tactical fighter-bomber. The missions I accompanied usually lasted several hours, and since the T-28 had a big greenhouse cockpit enclosure but no air conditioner, flying around in the tropical sun was an exercise in sweat-drenched misery.

Most of the dive-bombing and strafing attacks were against reported enemy positions in densely forested areas like D Zone northeast of Saigon. On those runs, I could see the tracers or bombs boring through the green canopy below us, but neither the pilots nor I ever saw the results. The air war usually spared fliers the ugly sights of war, but it also kept them from knowing how effective (or ineffective) their attacks were. As a matter of fact, military statisticians calculated in the late 1960s that it was costing more than $100,000 to kill a single guerrilla using bombs.

To make up for the cost-ineffectiveness of bombs, we dropped lots and lots of them, and at one point, this led to a very embarrassing shortage. In the early 1960s Pentagon experts predicted that ordinary explosive bombs had no future in war, and the Defense Department decided to sell off a large part of its bomb stockpile. In 1964, 7,562 surplus 750-pound bombs were sold to a German chemical company, Kaus and Steinhausen Co., which planned to convert them into fertilizer. But two years later an acute shortage of 750-pound bombs developed in Viet Nam, and the air force was forced to buy back most of the bombs it had sold, bringing the German company a 1,000 percent profit on its investment. And people wonder why Viet Nam plunged America into a series of economic crises from which it has never recovered!

Flying with the U.S. Air Force meant riding jets, either the two-seat version of the F-100 Supersaber, or the backseat of an F-4 Phantom. Dreadful though the effects of these sorties may have been on people on the ground, the experience itself was thrilling.

Getting ready for a flight was quite a ritual. Passengers, like the pilots, had to wear G suits, which are singularly uncomfortable. Before a flight the passenger also had to be instructed and drilled in the operation of the ejection seat, an emergency device that blasts its occupant through the plastic canopy of a disabled plane and parachutes him to safety. But these things are propelled by cannon cartridges, and all airmen dreaded the prospect of having to "punch out." Many of the crewmen who had done so after being hit over North Viet Nam suffered spinal injuries from the shock of ejection, and some were killed. To pilots, that ejection trigger bar, with its black and yellow stripes, seemed about as benign as a boa constrictor.

In level flight, jet fighters were more comfortable than T-28s because they were air-conditioned, and I remember one flight in which the cooling was so efficient it actually snowed inside the cockpit. But cool or not, ground-attack missions were anything but comfortable, and they could be downright painful. I wore a G suit, of course, which softened the physical effects of pulling out of steep dives and kept me conscious even when the blood was trying to leave my brain and settle in my toes.

Sometime in 1965 I went along on an F-100 mission over the Mekong Delta that left me in pain for several days. I foolishly insisted on going even while recovering from a mild head cold, knowing that colds block the eustachian tubes and prevent the equalization of air pressure between the inner and outer ear. Even pressure changes during a commercial flight can hurt, and a dive in a jet fighter from twelve thousand feet almost to the deck feels like an icepick driven into the ear.

The F-100 was one of the most beautiful of fighters, and as we left Saigon airport the Supersabers in our group gleamed like a school of silver fish floating over the endless paddies. Flying at nearly the speed of sound, we needed only twenty minutes to reach our objective, which was a clearing in a banana grove with a dozen or so huts believed to harbor a Viet Cong battalion. We circled briefly while the flight commander checked his coordinates and instructions from the ground controller.

Pilots tried to avoid shooting up friendly villages, but they committed some notorious errors, such as a U.S. Air Force raid on a friendly village in Cambodia called Neak Luong, where 157 civilians and government soldiers were killed. (Airmen were extra careful when a newsman was aboard.)

As we circled, the turns grew tighter and our G suits squeezed our bellies like vises, making it difficult to talk. Centrifugal force crushed us into our seats, and I needed all my strength just to raise my hand from my lap. Through the electronic hiss of the earphones I heard the lead pilot announce: "I strafe." Down he went, and I could see a stream of smoke puffs trailing from his gun pod, but little else. The only sign of life on the ground was an animal I took to be a dog, running for its life. I found myself desperately hoping that the dog would survive.

Another pilot said: "I bomb," and in he went. Two splashes of gray smoke bloomed over the village. Then our turn came, my pilot said "I strafe," and our nose dropped almost straight down. As a lifelong fan of roller coasters I ordinarily like this kind of maneuver, but that day my ears were in anguish.

As the cluster of hamlets rose toward us at express-train speed, I could feel our guns firing, even though I couldn't hear them; when high-speed electric Gatlings let fly, they make the whole plane vibrate. Streams of our red tracers were meandering over the village, but I could scarcely think about them, I was in such acute pain.

After a few more passes the huts disappeared in flames and smoke, and someone said, "Looks okay from here. Let's head home, Charlie Brown." On the way back my pilot let me fly for a while (in my youth I had learned to fly light planes) and when I tried lighting the fighter's afterburner my back felt an exhilarating shove as we plunged through the sound barrier.

One of our companions had trouble getting his wheels down and our return to Saigon airport was quite dramatic, but we all landed safely and at the debriefing everyone agreed the mission had been a great success. Since I hadn't seen a thing but burning huts and a running dog, I could hardly disagree.

Sometimes in both Viet Nam and Cambodia I was almost on the receiving end of such raids, by both fighter-bombers and high-altitude B-52s, and being bombed was very frightening indeed; the concussion of a large bomb exploding a few hundred yards away is paralyzing.

But canny soldiers can survive even bombing.

One afternoon I was with a U.S. airborne unit somewhere near An Khe in central Viet Nam when it encountered withering fire from a large enemy unit dug into foxholes spread over a fairly open field. The commander of our outfit decided the enemy could best be neutralized by an "Arc Light," a B-52 mission usually flown from Guam by three bombers, each one carrying thirty 500-pound bombs. So he sent off the order and our group exchanged fire with the enemy for a half hour or so while we waited.

And then the bombers, already en route to Viet Nam when our request reached them, appeared in the sky. They were just specks in the blue but they left conspicuous white contrails, and the Viet Cong must have seen them well before they attacked.

All ninety bombs were aimed to fall within a rectangle only about one square kilometer in area, and the blasts truly saturated this target. The bombs hit within hundredths of a second of each other so that individual explosions were indistinguishable, and the effect on the senses really was like "rolling thunder," the code name assigned to the U.S. bombing campaign over North Viet Nam.

The blast waves from this hellish bombardment snapped my clothes against my skin and rocked me back in my seat as I watched a brown curtain of dust and debris rise above the field where the enemy was dug in. I couldn't help hoping that at least some of the poor bastards out there had managed to survive the rain of death.

As it soon developed, many enemy troops had not only survived but were firing accurately at us and inflicting casualties. We had hoped to advance rapidly after the raid, but instead we were pinned down as badly as we had been before the B-52s arrived. I would never have imagined that anyone could survive such devastating force, but the fact is, disciplined soldiers with a little luck, who dig shallow foxholes for themselves whenever they are halted out in the open, have a fair chance of living through even an Arc Light carpet bombing.

Viet Nam reiterated the lesson from other wars that air power is not all it's cracked up to be.

From the time of World War II, Americans have been brought up to believe that bombers can crack the toughest nut and bring any nation to its knees. Disney wartime cartoons portrayed air power as well-nigh invincible. But I don't believe airplanes have ever been quite the wonder weapons we are often told, and although laser guidance and other innovations have improved bombing accuracy, an army of guerrillas is hard to hurt. When bombs were dropped on targets as dispersed as those in Viet Nam, a prepared enemy could usually cope. I myself survived attacks by MiGs in Pakistan a couple of times by sheltering in shallow ditches, so it's not impossible.

One of the most impressive things I saw when I first visited Hanoi in 1973 (to witness the release of American prisoners of war) was the speed and apparent ease with which the North Vietnamese repaired bomb damage. The Long Bien Bridge between Hanoi and Gia Lam Airport had been bombed constantly during the war, usually suffering heavy damage and sometimes losing entire spans. Still, when I saw it up close while crossing the Red River in a bus, patchwork repairs of every section were evident, but the bridge as a whole seemed perfectly solid, despite all the bomb hits it had taken over the years.

Besides spending quite a lot of time with pilots at such air bases as Da Nang, Cam Ranh Bay and Bien Hoa, I visited the *Hancock*, a small carrier in the South China Sea from which Navy A-4, F-8 and Phantom pilots were flying around the clock.

Those navy pilots were brave men, not only because of the deadly SAM missiles, antiaircraft fire and MiGs, but because they knew Viet Nam only as a remote, unknown hell, and because unfamiliarity can make a place seem even more dangerous than it is.

The sensation of landing on a carrier and slamming to a stop on its arrester cables was a novel experience for me, and so was being shot from a steam catapult. The acceleration of the catapult is so terrific that after a plane has been hurled into the air its occupants feel as if they have come to a dead stop, even though they are flying at 150 knots or so.

Air operations were almost like vacations from ground operations, with no sight of blood or suffering anywhere. But journalists could never enjoy the detachment of air warfare for long because the real action was down in the mud, not up in the clouds.

I kept going back to the village of Dam Doi in the far south of Viet Nam, because things kept happening to it, and it seemed to me to be a kind of bellwether of the war. Dam Doi was the town whose district chief had been suckered into a Viet Cong trap, prompting the Marine operation I had accompanied in early 1962.

One of my visits came several years after Dam Doi had been overrun and burned by the Viet Cong. The enemy had been chased out after a long firefight before I arrived, but there was almost nothing left standing. The corrugated sheet iron that had roofed the town's buildings was scattered over the ground and the smell of burned flesh was mixed with the stench of rubber and wood smoke. The bodies of about one hundred residents were strewn all over, and one surviving woman, her hair mostly burned off, sat among the smoldering embers and pottery fragments of her home, rocking a dead child in her lap. She paid no attention to the troops picking their way through the rubble around her.

Saigon itself was sometimes a battlefield between guerrilla terrorists and the police. The fight for Saigon reached its peak during the Tet offensive of 1968, but even in periods of relative peace, terrorist bombs frequently exploded. The government banned the sale or possession of electric timing devices of the kind used in ovens and washing machines, since these were often use by the Viet Cong to make time bombs. But neither this nor any of the other laws designed to hamper the terrorists had the slightest effect.

At all hours of the night, the thunder of explosions would awaken us newsmen and send us scurrying forth to look at the latest tragedy. One of the worst bombings occurred in 1965 at the Brink Hotel, a billet for American military officers in downtown Saigon. Two Viet Cong agents dressed as ARVN soldiers drove a stolen jeep loaded with explosives into the Brink's courtyard, set a timer and walked away. The explosion, which heavily damaged the building, blew out the glass in an office where I was sitting four blocks away, and threw the American residents of the Brink into such panic they began shooting at each other.

In two other terrible explosions I remember, an American movie theater was destroyed and the My Canh floating restaurant on the Saigon River was demolished. The My Canh blast killed forty-three, including, as I mentioned in an earlier chapter, my Special Forces friend Al Combs and his pregnant Vietnamese common-law wife. The bombing was meticulously executed. The guerrillas first set off a small and relatively harmless bomb that sent terrified diners running down the gangplank to the dock where the restaurant was moored. Then the terrorists detonated two American Claymore mines aimed to send their blasts of shrapnel directly up the gangplank, sweeping through the fleeing diners. The carnage was as ghastly as any I ever saw.

Saigon's police chief and interior minister, Colonel Nguyen Ngoc Loan, was one of the first officials to turn up at the scene after I arrived, and his eyes glittered with hatred and revenge as he scanned the bodies. Three years later, during the Tet offensive, Loan gained worldwide notoriety for his street-corner execution of a captured Viet Cong guerrilla, an act memorialized by Eddie Adams's shocking photograph. Loan may have been thinking of the My Canh bombing and countless other acts of Viet Cong terrorism when he shot that prisoner.

In most of the terror bombings, particularly those of bars, many more Vietnamese than Americans were hurt or killed. One bombing stands out in my memory, that of a bar on the street leading to the airport, where an explosion left five American customers lightly wounded but killed seven Vietnamese bar girls. In a corner of the room was a dismembered foot and ankle still wearing a fancy high-heeled shoe.

I remember a particularly poignant tableau in Cambodia.

In September 1973, Le Lieu was with me there while I was covering the beginning of the final showdown. Khmer Rouge forces were attempting to strangle the capital by blocking all roads, including the arterial lifeline to the sea, Route 4. During an eighteen-day battle fought around a pagoda, Wat Kruos, government forces finally opened the road, but it was too late for the government garrison that had been holding the pagoda. Every soldier had been killed, and when Le Lieu and I arrived the relief force had just finished stacking up the bodies of more than fifty government troops for cremation.

After the pyre had burned out, I remember, one of the

widows retrieved scorched fragments of her husband's skull from the ashes. She took them to a little stream for the ceremony of washing them, and then she carefully wrapped them in a clean kerchief for a Buddhist burial. She didn't weep. She went about her gruesome task as matter-of-factly as if she were washing the family dishes. Her husband's death had not been the first tragedy for her family, I learned, and perhaps by then she was a little numbed by suffering.

As the Indochina conflict ripened, the fighting underwent a transition from guerrilla conflict to large-scale warfare, and by 1972 real battles had become common.

In that year I was based in Pakistan covering Central Asia for *The New York Times* when North Viet Nam launched its "Easter Offensive," an all-out drive by large units and columns of armor pushing southward. The *Times* ordered me back to Saigon.

For once, Hanoi's forces had blundered miserably. By sending a conventional invasion force across the 17th Parallel, North Viet Nam played disastrously into American hands and suffered almost unbelievable casualties. One of my first tasks was to go north to look at the communist debacle along Route 1 south of Quang Tri, where the enemy had been stopped.

The long stretch of road at that point runs near the coastal beaches, mostly over dunes where there is no cover anywhere. The North Vietnamese tanks and trucks had driven south as if on a country outing, bunched closely together in single file along the road. For the U.S. and South Vietnamese air forces, it had been a turkey shoot; every last communist vehicle had been blasted in its tracks, and only a handful of prisoners survived. As a former tank soldier in the U.S. Army, I was astonished to see how little attention the enemy commanders had paid to the classic rules of armored warfare, which dictate that tanks should never bunch together, never move in line (either line-abreast or in column), and never do anything without plenty of infantry support (and, preferably, with air cover and artillery support, as well). The scorched hulks of heavy tanks and amphibious PT-76 light tanks stretched as far as the eye could see, and it was difficult to avoid stepping on unexploded shells and grenades littering the smashed roadway.

General Giap's army was never much good at conventional warfare, but luckily for his side, he rarely tried to play that game, a game at which the Americans were experts.

Later that spring I visited an American fire base along Route 14, the main road between Pleiku and Kontum, just after it had fought off a very heavy North Vietnamese attack and killed so many enemy troops that their commanders certainly must have been given pause.

Using bangalore torpedoes, North Vietnamese sappers had cut their way through the multiple aprons of barbed wire surrounding the base, and had braved the canister-shot blasts of dozens of Claymore mines the Americans had positioned around the perimeter. The attackers died by the score, but they came on in wave after wave all night long, saturating the American gun emplacements with machine-gun and rifle fire. Some of their sappers penetrated deep into the camp, occupying several strong points and killing some of the defenders.

But with the coming of daylight and the arrival of the air force, the attackers realized the cause was hopeless and faded away into the hills, pursued by napalm bombs and howitzer shells. The fire base, when I reached it, was a wreck. Bare-chested Americans sweating under a hot sun were manning a bulldozer and shoving scores of enemy bodies into a mass grave.

The place reeked of death, and anyone who has seen war knows that this is no figurative expression. Men killed in combat very often defecate just before or after dying, and the smell of feces mixed with that of burned and decaying flesh is a universal hallmark of war. That smell is something people don't encounter watching war on television, but soldiers and newsmen know it well. It can certainly dampen a war-enthusiast's ardor for shot and shell.

THE INDOCHINA CORRESPONDENTS

ONE OF THE MAIN disadvantages of reporting for a living, especially reporting wars and foreign affairs, is that competence in this line of work declines with age. It's fashionable these days to suppose that old people are just as productive as young ones, and in many fields this is probably true. But for beauty queens, mathematicians, chess players, fighter pilots, quarterbacks and reporters, age is a pernicious enemy.

For reporters, the problem is not necessarily one of slowed reflexes, short breath and poor vision; as the oldest newsman covering the Gulf War in 1991 (I was sixty at the time), I was easily able to keep up with younger colleagues, and I had the benefit of a lot of experience gained in other wars that younger newsmen had to acquire as they went along. The real problem of aging is one's loss of humility and a corresponding gain in one's intolerance of arrant foolishness. These are not assets for any reporter, and they particularly ill-served some of the men and women who covered the Viet Nam War.

The kid weaned from the bottom, starting as a clerk or copyperson— or a hungry young free-lancer used to begging for piecework assignments—comes to an exalted job as a staff reporter with hat in hand. The new reporter is accustomed to

The author at eight, in a seaplane hangar near Babylon, Long Island, where he sometimes spent long afternoons watching the float-equipped Cubs landing and taking off.

The young Browne family at the stone house, a Dutch colonial building in New York's Ulster County, built about 1680. The author's grandmother bought the house in the 1920s for use as an art school, and Browne spent many formative years there. In this pose, Douglas and Dorothy Browne are shown with their first two children, Miriam, two, and the author, seven.

The Wilde-Browne family's stone house in 1954, with the author's first car, an old Renault. The wooden lean-to is modern, but the stone main building dates from 1680.

The author at his lab bench in 1953, while he was employed as a technician at Foster D. Snell, Inc., a consulting laboratory in New York City.

The author in 1957 as a soldier in Korea, standing before the quonset hut near North Korean lines where he began his career as a journalist.

Browne in a warlike pose in Korea, preparing to stand guard during an alert triggered by a feint by North Korean tanks just across the Demilitarized Zone.

Early days in Viet Nam. In 1962 a large government convoy was ambushed and destroyed by Viet Cong guerrillas near Dong Xoai. Browne arrived with a relief column to find the shambles shown here.

June 11, 1963 in downtown Saigon—the immolation of the Buddhist monk Thich Quang Duc. This was the sequence of photographs Browne made of the horrible suicide.

Thich Quang Duc in flames. These images played an important role in President Kennedy's decision to end support of President Ngo Dinh Diem's regime in South Viet Nam—an action that led to the coup in which Diem was overthrown and killed on November 1, 1963.

Madame Ngo Dinh Nhu, the power behind the throne in Saigon, 1963, smiled delightedly as she took a salute from girls in her Youth Corps. A few months later her family was ousted from power and she settled into exile in Italy.

The author on a 1963 mission in one of the new Huey helicopters. The helicopter is refueling at a pad in the Mekong River Delta.

The author entering American combat casualties on a makeshift tally sheet. This was the Associated Press office on Rue Pasteur, where Browne was bureau chief.

The author at a diplomatic reception in Saigon, with General Paul B. Harkins, commander of the U.S. Military Assistance Command Vietnam. Browne's war reporting had irritated General Harkins, and the smiles here were skin deep.

The cluttered AP bureau in Saigon during a 1963 crisis. Left to right are Horst Faas, the bureau's photo chief, Peter Arnett, Don Huth (chief of the AP's Southeast Asia bureau in Singapore), and the author. Faas, Arnett, and Browne were each to win Pulitzer prizes in the next few years.

The author with Attorney General Robert Kennedy during the latter's fact-finding trip to Viet Nam in 1963, shortly before his brother, President Kennedy, was assassinated.

Ambassador Henry Cabot Lodge with his former presidential running mate, Richard M. Nixon, who visited Saigon in 1964 to discuss political strategy with Lodge. Despite some differences in their views, Ambassador Lodge and the author became good friends during Lodge's tenure. It was following this meeting that Nixon assured the author that Americans would "follow the flag" in Viet Nam.

The three "young Turks" of the Saigon press corps in 1963—strong professional competitors, but all thorns in the side of the Saigon administration and its American supporters. Shown during a helicopter operation all three covered are David Halberstam, then of *The New York Times*, the author, then with the Associated Press and Neil Sheehan, then of United Press International. Sheehan holds a map of the day's operation. (*Photo by Horst Faas*)

One of many meetings the author had in 1964 and 1965 with Viet Nam's president, General Nguyen Khanh. After Khanh was deposed in 1965, he settled in France.

Le Lieu and the author on their wedding day in Saigon, July 18, 1966. The photograph was taken on the balcony of their one-room apartment on Rue Pasteur, upstairs from the AP office.

The New York Times office on Tu Do Street, Saigon, 1972, with *Times* staffers sent from various parts of the world to help out during a crisis. Affecting nonchalant poses, left to right, are Craig Whitney, the author, Sydney Schanberg, Fox Butterfield, Joseph Treaster, and Henry Kamm.

An artillery firebase on the road between Pleiku and Kontum, summer of 1972. Seconds after this photograph was made, the position was heavily hit by North Vietnamese mortar shells and several soldiers were wounded.

On the battle line south of Quang Tri in 1972, a U.S. Army captain chats with the author. This photograph was taken by Alex Shimkin of *Newsweek* a few days before he was killed near the same spot.

A lull in the Quang Tri fighting in 1972. With the author is an Italian newsman also covering the campaign.

With Kurt Waldheim, United Nations secretary general, on a plane lent by Imelda Marcos, wife of the Philippines' president, en route to Hanoi, Pyong Yang (North Korea), and Peking, 1979. Waldheim's object was to find some peaceful settlements in Asia, and the world was not yet aware of his past as an intelligence officer in the German army.

The author with Prince Norodom Sihanouk in New York, 1979. No longer ruler of Cambodia, Prince Sihanouk was lobbying for support at the United Nations.

The author during one of his trips to China's Great Wall.

The author with the offspring of his first and second marriages: son Timothy and daughter Wendy.

1983—The author at the South Pole during one of his four trips to Antarctica. To walk around the world, a visitor needs only to walk around the flag marking the South Pole. (*Photos by Michael Parfit*)

Three *New York Times* staffers during the 1991 war in the Persian Gulf, photographed in a Dhahran hotel room: the author, Walter Baranger and Philip Shenon.

A 1991 reunion of Viet Nam hands, during Columbia University's observance of the 75th anniversary of the Pulitzer prizes. David Halberstam, the author, and Neil Sheehan.

suppressing his or her own thoughts, and to beseeching others for theirs. Success in the job depends in large measure on being a good listener able to stimulate newsworthy responses from people without intruding one's own persona into the conversation. Above all else, this requires humility.

But reporters inevitably think about what they observe and hear, and this leads to the nucleation of opinions and an end to innocence. Unobtrusive opinions are fine, but when opinions harden and proliferate to the point of coloring almost all of a reporter's observations, humility weakens and dies. The ultimate result was perhaps approached by the great H. L. Mencken of the *Baltimore Sun,* who, toward the end of his career, had managed to efface any hint of humility from everything he wrote. Mencken had become a superb commentator but a lousy reporter, at least by today's standards.

Which brings me to the press corps in Indochina.

During the 1960s, press critics perceived the correspondents covering Indochina as polarized into two camps.

One camp, it was said, consisted of inexperienced, dovish amateurs trying to make names for themselves by bucking the fight against communist expansionism President Kennedy had enthusiastically taken over from his predecessors.

The other camp was perceived by its critics as consisting chiefly of headquarters-bound men and women who had covered World War II and Korea, and whose idea of war reporting consisted mainly of interviewing conservative diplomats and generals of their own generation.

Neither perception corresponded to reality, and opposing viewpoints were certainly shaped in part by the generation gap rather than real differences of principle.

Conservative criticism during the early years focused on David Halberstam, then with *The New York Times,* Neil Sheehan, then with UPI, and myself. Peter Arnett and Horst Faas, both members of my AP Saigon staff, also began taking hits from our critics almost from the time they arrived in Viet Nam, as did Morley Safer of CBS and several other television reporters.

We Young Turks had detractors in many walks of life. Some were fellow journalists, others were American and Vietnamese officials, but many more were ordinary citizens who wandered through Viet Nam for one reason or another. For instance, a steady stream of entertainers came to Indochina, and most of them seemed to be press-haters, eager for publicity but with little knowledge of the real war.

One evening in Saigon I got into a particularly nasty argument with Van Heflin after he had announced to a room full of people that journalists and traitors had a lot in common. Another row erupted at a Marine officers' club in Da Nang, where I was suckered into a noisy discussion with John Wayne, who was fulminating to a group of Marines against "the panty-waisted liberal sensationalists" of the American press.

In my view, Wayne and some like-minded actors bear part of the responsibility for deluding Americans about the facts of the Viet Nam War. By the time most people realized the war was something other than a Green Beret crusade for Mother, God and Apple Butter, it was far too late to change the course of history and avert the corrosive trauma from which the United States is still recovering.

Of course, there were show-business doves as well, but the problem with polarization into rival hawk and dove camps is that even people with good instincts tend to abandon critical detachment and take up the cudgels, at the expense of reasoned thought.

Joan Baez was an opponent of the war, but she avoided bitter invective, offered kindness to American troops and made few enemies in either camp.

I admired Jane Fonda for her courage in espousing a very

unpopular cause; my own mother had to endure many a verbal brickbat for sticking to her pacifist principles during World War II. But Miss Fonda, in my view, was just as unrealistic in her idealization of Hanoi's motives as John Wayne was in his idealized view of the Special Forces. Neither of these extreme views corresponded to the shades-of-gray distinctions we newsmen saw. There were no unalloyed good guys in Viet Nam. There were plenty of bad guys on all sides, and everyone sometimes stooped to savagery when it suited them.

One of the real heroes of the Viet Nam War was Wes Gallagher, who, as general manager of the Associated Press, had sent me to Saigon. In my view, Wes did more to keep a free and critical press alive during a key period than any of the other top news executives of the era.

Unlike many another news executive, Wes had paid his dues as a war correspondent. During Operation Torch, the American invasion of North Africa in 1942, Wes was severely wounded when the jeep he was driving overturned and caught fire. He was dragged from the jeep and saved by a young American officer, William C. Westmoreland, who was later to become the commanding general of U.S. forces in Viet Nam. Wes not only cut his teeth on World War II but had a special reason for listening to his friend and lifesaver, General Westmoreland.

For a while after I got to Viet Nam, Gallagher had trouble reconciling with his own experiences of warfare the reports I was sending back. In his war, massive amphibious landings, battles for ridgelines, bridges and towns, 1,000-bomber raids, and territory won or lost were the things that counted. The war I was reporting had almost nothing to do with any of those criteria; one side or the other could seize a town or strong point without making the slightest difference to the overall course of the war. There were no front lines.

What really mattered, most resident newsmen quickly

realized, was whether or not the population of a town, village or region was willing or unwilling to inform against the Viet Cong. Without intelligence provided by the ordinary people, efforts by Saigon and Washington to come to grips with the enemy were of no more avail than trying to sink a floating cork with a sledge-hammer.

Gallagher was under constant pressure from conservative publishers and editors. The AP, unlike all other American news organizations, is a nonprofit cooperative, of which all user publications and broadcasters are "members." The publishers and editors of AP member organizations exercise a powerful influence on AP policies. I remember a lunch at which I sat next to Gallagher and one of the most influential member executives of the time, William Knowland. Knowland, an archconservative, had been a powerful senator, dubbed by his foes as "the Senator from Formosa" because of his support for the Chiang Kai-shek regime in Taiwan. At the time I knew him, Knowland was the publisher of the *Oakland Tribune,* and I remember the dissatisfaction he expressed during that lunch with "overly liberal" reporting from Viet Nam.

But Gallagher's instinct was to trust his people in the field implicitly until and unless the trust was betrayed.

In 1963 Gallagher decided to pay me the first of a series of visits in Saigon. Naturally, I arranged for him to see his friend General Westmoreland, as well as the U.S. ambassador, and many other senior American and Vietnamese officials.

But I also invited him for a ride through the Mekong Delta in my four-wheel-drive Land Rover, which I had had painted red and prominently marked with the legend BAO-CHI— "press." Knowing Gallagher fairly well by then, I suspected that what he really wanted was a chance to get out and see for himself something of the war and its setting.

We didn't have to travel far to see how the Viet Cong had come to control a vast sweep of villages, villages that Washington and Saigon had declared to be securely in friendly hands. We talked to farmers, militiamen and minor officials, who told of how the Viet Cong ruled by night, and how informers against the guerrillas were brutally slain.

We heard of profiteering and extortion on the part of government troops. In Long An, we talked to Earl Young, a province representative of the U.S. Agency for International Development (USAID). Young, one of the few American civilian officials who lived in the field in those days (a "muddy boots" American, as they were called), had keen eyes and a taste for candor.

While rosy reports of pacification and enemy body counts were flowing through Saigon to Washington, Young was seeing (and reporting on) a countryside falling inexorably under the control of the Viet Cong—and this, barely twenty miles from Saigon. He told of ambushes, the bleeding dry of government convoys, the seeding of rural roads with nail boards to puncture the tires of government relief columns, and the nightly routine of carnage, in which the Viet Cong were steadily increasing their stocks of captured weapons. During our tour, Gallagher got a chance to see evidence of all this for himself.

Never a man to allow preconceived ideas to color direct observation, the gruff-voiced Gallagher changed his perspective. From then on he backed his AP Indochina correspondents more than ever, despite threats by the Pentagon, State Department, and President Johnson himself. When reporters were wrong, Gallagher himself rapped their knuckles. But when it came to protecting their freedom to do their jobs, Gallagher was a tower of strength. Would that all American news executives shared that quality.

Too many of the newspeople of Gallagher's generation failed to see the Viet Nam War through his perceptive, sharply focused eyes.

Among our occasional visitors was the columnist Joseph

Alsop, whose usual routine on arrival was to stop around at the news agency offices for briefings by people like me. He would then make the rounds of his high-level acquaintances, perhaps driving down to Ben Tre to visit his old friend Colonel Pham Ngoc Thao, the official I described in an earlier chapter who was revealed after the war to have been a high-ranking Hanoi agent.

Joe would then return to the United States and inform his readers that the resident correspondents in Saigon were maliciously misrepresenting the war, and that in reality, the Saigon-Washington alliance was winning.

The late Mr. Alsop, in common with Richard Nixon and Senators Knowland and Joseph McCarthy, believed that China had been lost to the communists in 1949 partly because of the alleged perfidy of pro-Mao American diplomats and news correspondents like Edgar Snow. Alsop believed that Viet Nam was facing danger from the same quarters. He was wrong both times.

Another of the most vocal disparagers of the Young Turks of the Saigon press corps was Marguerite Higgins. Maggie was a brave and indefatigable reporter, she had been a very beautiful woman, and she had a large and loyal readership. In 1951 she shared a Pulitzer Prize with Homer Bigart—her fellow reporter on the *New York Herald Tribune*—along with Keyes Beech and Fred Sparks, both of the *Chicago Daily News,* and Relman ("Pat") Morin and Don Whitehead, both of the AP. With that award, one of the great personal feuds of our profession came to public attention.

Homer and Maggie bitterly hated each other in Korea, where they were forced to cover the war as *Herald Tribune* colleagues, and later, in Viet Nam, where Homer worked for *The New York Times.* The Bigart-Higgins fight was something more than mere competition for stories, although Bigart said later that Higgins had nearly killed him by driving him to cover ever more dangerous actions in Korea.

In Indochina, younger newsmen came to see Higgins and Bigart as symbolizing a historic rift between two camps of journalists. On the one hand, Bigart seemed the very model of a hard-bitten, hard-driving reporter—infuriatingly dogged, abrasive, honest, brave, unmoved by political rhetoric and surprisingly learned. Most of his colleagues admired and liked him.

On the other hand, Higgins, the wife of an air force general, regarded the American press corps in Saigon as what she described to me as "arrogant upstarts" whose loyalty to their country was at best questionable.

In Viet Nam, Bigart was my friend and occasional collaborator, but I always hated feuds, particularly those between newspeople; the lives of reporters are tough enough without our rubbing salt into each other's wounds.

Sometime in late 1965 or early 1966, I happened to be working in Phnom Penh while Maggie was making her first visit there. With both of us away from Viet Nam and the lacerating quarrels Maggie was forever picking with some of her colleagues, I thought it might be nice if we could bury a hatchet or two, so I invited her for dinner at the Lotus d'Or, a floating dockside restaurant renowned for its delicious noodle soups.

My peacemaking initiative was a failure. I tried to steer the conversation away from the coverage of news and the Viet Nam War, but we kept coming back to what Maggie considered the lack of experience and patriotism in most of the Saigon press corps. Her attacks were mainly aimed against David Halberstam of *The New York Times,* who had left Viet Nam but remained, in Maggie's eyes, a reincarnation of her archnemesis, Homer Bigart.

What I remember most of that evening was the discovery that Maggie, despite her years of reporting from Asia, was still unable to handle chopsticks. Since the restaurant had no Western tableware, she resorted to picking up her noodles with her fingers, to the evident surprise and embarrassed snickering of the other diners.

Maggie returned to the United States and died a few months later of leishmaniasis, a parasitic disease spread by the bites of sand flies.

One of the main sources of strife between the so-called Young Turks in Viet Nam and our critics was the latter group's presumption that we harbored some political agenda, such as advocating American withdrawal.

I think it's true that eventually all of us came to believe America could not win what was essentially a civil war between Vietnamese. But in my case, that conviction came only after years of experience and reflection.

Like me, Neil Sheehan, my opposite number as the United Press International correspondent in the early 1960s, was a former soldier accustomed to military ways and to following orders. Neil and I had also been through the wringer of wire service indoctrination, which unequivocally suppresses the injection of personal opinion into news stories.

David Halberstam, who replaced Homer Bigart as *The New York Times* correspondent in Saigon, had worked on the Harvard Crimson and was grounded in the journalistic rules demanding fair play in news stories. As a newspaper writer, of course, he was given somewhat freer rein than was granted to wire service people in commenting on the news.

Sheehan, Halberstam and I, along with our colleagues from the TV networks and other news organizations were friends at heart, but we were also determined adversaries in a rough and tough competitive game.

The charge by some of our critics that we colluded to produce similar news reports was nonsense. We were friendly colleagues in the same spirit that a prosecutor and a defense lawyer may sit down after hours for a beer together. But competing news reporters can no more discuss news stories with each other than can the officers of opposing armies discuss strategy.

Neil gave me many a sleepless night with his UPI scoops that my AP employers expected me to match on short notice. I hope I may have turned the tables on Neil a few times.

Youth is the ally of good reporting. One reason is that young people are insecure and apt to be more polite and modest than older reporters. Modesty and diffidence are attractive qualities in beggars, including reporters who make their living by begging people for news, visas, assignments, airline seats and everything else.

Young reporters also have the stamina needed to fight through a pack of snarling colleagues, all out after the same story and all prepared to skewer each other for the sake of three seconds of TV tape or a paragraph of news copy.

Which brings me to a deplorable specialty of modern journalism, the news feeding frenzy.

Individually, most reporters are educated, knowledgeable folk, who are often grounded in music, humane letters, history and fine arts. Most reporters are good talkers and popular dinner guests. But when reporters are loosed in packs on some locus of concentrated news, an atavistic reversion occurs and they become cannibals.

Wars bring out the worst in us because they draw us like moths to a flame, congregating in great and grossly counterproductive numbers around "the news." During the peak of the Viet Nam War some seven hundred newspeople were accredited to the U.S. command in Saigon. More than double that number descended on Dhahran during the Persian Gulf fight of 1991, and we can expect future wars and catastrophes to be covered by thousands or tens of thousands of newsmen.

Newsmen as well as readers and viewers are disgusted by these feeding frenzies, but they're tough to avoid.

Savvy editors try not to force reporters to squander time and effort by joining media mobs, because experience has shown that the really good stories are usually turned up by loners. But unfortunately, too many assignment editors are compelled by pressures from their own superiors to become bandwagon followers rather than innovative journalists.

The reflexive reaction of many news directors or editors to a major news break is to send everyone available to envelop the story and to club it to death from all sides. My own guess is that readers are more interested in quality than volume or dazzling successions of quickie news flashes. Loners produce more interesting news than mobs because they are unobtrusive and inoffensive to the newsmakers they are covering. As a rule of thumb, the quality of coverage of a news event is inversely proportional to the number of reporters covering it.

Still, we reporters squander much of our lives on what we consider news junk. I remember one newsless press conference in the 1970s given by Marshal Tito, Yugoslavia's dictator, which I, as a member of the Belgrade press corps, was obliged to attend. On the bus to wherever it was we went I sat next to Dessa Trevisan, a longtime reporter of the Yugoslav scene for British periodicals, who was as bored and annoyed as everyone else on the trip. After staring glumly out at the flat Serbian countryside for a while, she sighed and remarked, "This is surely the most soul-destroying job in the world." I knew what she meant.

Foreign correspondence has another obvious shortcoming, especially where wars are involved: it can be dangerous. Journalism in general is becoming a riskier trade by the year. The International Federation of Journalists, which keeps track of these things, reported that in 1991 alone, eighty-three journalists were killed in twenty-three countries—twenty-one in Yugoslavia alone.

While the casualty rate for journalists in Indochina never

approached today's murderous toll, about fifty journalists were killed in the Indochina War, including quite a few men and women I knew as friends. At least one hundred were wounded, and some were permanently maimed or disabled. (I was nicked by flying metal a few times myself.)

I have no statistics to prove it, but I think two groups of war correspondents are especially at risk. One category consists of newcomers with little or no battle experience. The other consists of older hands, who lose their life-preserving terror of war. In combat, familiarity certainly can lead to fatal contempt.

One of the first in our AP family to die was Bernie Kohlenburg, a young free-lancer who arrived in Saigon in 1963 with press accreditation from the Albany (New York) *Times Union,* with very little money in his pocket, but with a burning desire to prove himself. He told me he wanted to "string" for the AP, which suited me fine; perpetually understaffed, we always welcomed news tips, photographs or stories from reliable free-lancers, although my budget for paying them in those days was pretty lean.

I explained to Bernie how to get a canteen and field gear from the Saigon market, I briefed him on the war and how we covered it, and I gave him a copy of a mimeographed booklet I had written as a confidential guide for AP Indochina correspon-dents. This little compendium contained names, phone numbers and my personal assessments of a lot of our military, political and diplomatic sources, and it described some of the social tactics I had found useful for prying facts out of these and other knowl-edgeable people. My guide to the Indochina War included sketches of most of the aircraft a newsman would be likely to encounter, as well as tips on everything from sterilizing water to avoiding booby traps. A lot of AP correspondents (and outsiders who managed to get bootleg copies) told me my guide had really helped them in getting started.

Bernie resolved to start his career covering the air war, and he persuaded the Vietnamese Air Force to take him along on a ground-attack mission. On the fatal day, Bernie climbed into the backseat of one of a pair of T-28s and took off. The two planes reached their objective, a suspected Viet Cong position on a forested hillside north of Saigon, and flew their first strafing run.

The rest is surmise. Evidence found by crash investigators suggested that the pilot of the lead plane was not satisfied with results. Since he was a young officer keen on impressing his superiors (and, possibly, the American newsman in the backseat), he swooped in for a second attack at treetop height—too low, as it turned out. Both T-28s slammed into the hill, the planes exploding in flames.

Another newcomer died in 1968 because of his unshakable belief in the fundamental goodness of human beings.

At the time, I was based in Buenos Aires covering South America for *The New York Times*. My wonderful secretary, Ana Ezcurra, had a journalist brother named Ignacio Ezcurra, one of the brightest young lights on *La Nación,* a leading Buenos Aires newspaper. Ignacio had reported brilliantly on the explosion of racial strife in the United States during the mid-1960s, and on the strength of his record as a reporter of dangerous mayhem, he had persuaded his newspaper to send him to Viet Nam.

A few days before leaving he dropped by my office for some pointers, in the course of which the young Argentine told me that one of his main goals was to reach the Viet Cong, in the hope of becoming one of the very few non-Vietnamese journalists covering the guerrilla side of the war.

I pleaded with him not to try. Making contact with Viet Cong representatives in Phnom Penh, Vientiane or Moscow was safe enough; I had talked to some of them myself. But to try to meet them in battle would be suicidal, I believed. In the eyes of a Viet Cong guerrilla, I told Ignacio, any "big nose" (a pejorative

Asian expression for an Occidental) must be an enemy American, and therefore a target.

With the fire of the good reporter in his belly, Ignacio set off on the long trip to Saigon, and the end of his life. Within a few days of his arrival, the great Tet offensive of 1968 began, and the Viet Cong quickly occupied much of the capital, including, briefly, the U.S. Embassy. At one point, while Ezcurra was with a group of American correspondents watching the fighting, he thought he saw the chance he was seeking, and he darted away from his American colleagues toward the Viet Cong positions.

How he died is not known. But one body among the hundreds killed in Saigon during the Tet calamity wore an Argentine belt and buckle that his sister Ana later identified as Ignacio's. He had been in Viet Nam less than two weeks.

The Tet offensive added luster to the name of an already lustrous American correspondent: Charlie Mohr of *The New York Times*. In the heat of one of the battles and under heavy fire, Charlie valiantly tried to carry a mortally wounded American serviceman to safety, an act for which he was awarded the Bronze Star. We already knew Charlie for another kind of courage. In 1963, when his employer, *Time,* was trying to pillory American correspondents in Saigon with a barrage of lies, Mohr resigned in protest, even though he needed the job to support his growing family. His courage was vindicated, however, and Charlie went on to a distinguished career with *The New York Times* until a heart attack killed him in 1989 on his sixtieth birthday.

Many brave journalists working as loners died in Indochina. Some were free-lance reporters lured by the big money some news organizations had begun to pay stringers. A young French teacher at a Luang Prabang secondary school in Laos was among the news recruits, and he set off to cover the Laotian jungle war. He simply disappeared. Only a year later did we learn that he had been captured by the Pathet Lao and forced to run through a sadistic gauntlet, where he was finally beaten to death.

Welles Hangen of NBC, my predecessor as press fellow of the Council on Foreign Relations, was captured, along with Sean Flynn (the son of actor Errol Flynn) and several other newsmen at a Khmer Rouge roadblock in Cambodia. The entire group was slaughtered.

Frequent fliers in Viet Nam faced poor odds if they kept flying long enough. Among the victims were two of my closest friends: François Sully of *Newsweek* and Jerry Rose, who had worked for *Time*, the *Saturday Evening Post* and other publications.

Sully was a suave ex-colonial with good contacts in the francophile Vietnamese aristocracy, and a good eye for news and pretty girls. He had a bumpy but successful journalistic career in Viet Nam. Sully's reporting for *Newsweek* of the political blunders of the Diem regime brought him a storm of outcries from conservatives in the United States, and he was eventually expelled from Viet Nam for allegedly slandering the Ngo regime. (The Foreign Correspondents Association of Viet Nam, of which I was president at the time, protested vigorously, but all we ever accomplished was to give Sully a nice send-off party at the airport.)

After the 1963 coup Sully was allowed back into Viet Nam, where he resumed a career of distinguished reporting, drawing once again on his excellent sources within the Vietnamese military hierarchy. In 1971, while he was lifting off with one of the Vietnamese generals he knew, Sully's helicopter was blown up and all aboard were killed.

Jerry Rose had been a teacher in Gloversville, New York, before deciding to see the world and take a teaching job in Viet Nam. Ever restless, Jerry found that by supplying *Time* magazine with a regular stream of news from Viet Nam he could earn a decent living as a news stringer, so he became a journalist.

As the war heated up, Jerry established a reputation as an

excellent writer as well as an energetic and effective reporter, and he was offered a job by the *Saturday Evening Post* as its Viet Nam correspondent. He wrote some memorable articles for that excellent publication, but after a few years Jerry decided to assume a more active role in alleviating the suffering we constantly witnessed. He joined the Vietnamese government as an adviser in programs to help war refugees and other Vietnamese who were pauperized by the fighting.

On the way back to Saigon from a refugee camp in the central highlands, the Air Viet Nam DC-3 in which Jerry was riding was shot down. As one of Jerry's oldest friends I was summoned by the U.S. graves registration team to identify the body and deal with it. Jerry's wife, Kay, a former secretary at the USIS mission in Saigon, was living in Hong Kong with their children at that point, and it was impossible for her to come to Saigon.

We talked on the phone about what should be done, and I had to tell Kay that the air force planned to charge a sum none of us could afford, just to rent us an aluminum casket and fly Jerry's remains to Travis Air Force Base in the States. In the event, we decided to cremate my friend and ship his ashes to Hong Kong by ordinary air freight. The Buddhist crematory presented me with a big blue-and-white urn with a Chinese motif, and my wife, Le Lieu, helped with the shipping preparations. It was a painful act for her. Long before my 1961 arrival in Viet Nam, she had been Jerry's girlfriend for a while.

Although I flew a lot in Viet Nam, my luck was phenomenal: I was shot down three times and walked away from each crash.

The first time was in the H-21 I described in a previous chapter.

The second time I was in an HH-43 Kaman Huskie, a powerful little chopper used mainly to haul up airmen downed in jungles. We had just taken off from a jungle airstrip where an American fire base was being overrun when our Huskie was hit. The pilot made a safe crash landing, and all of us sprinted away from the wreck to a taxiing C-123 transport, the last planeload of defenders to get out of the doomed base, as it turned out. The plane had already begun its takeoff roll when the last of us jumped up on its rear loading ramp, and as we rose from the ground we could see several guerrillas running along the airstrip, firing at us as they ran.

In my third crash, Viet Cong fire disabled the hydraulics of an army Caribou transport, and for some reason, the crew chief was unable to crank down the wheels manually. We made a bumpy but safe belly landing somewhere near Quang Ngai along the coast of the South China Sea.

Some of the best newsmen kept coming back even after being terribly wounded. Huynh Cong La, a brilliant Vietnamese cameraman on our AP staff, had an eye shot out in a delta operation. After recovering, La went right back to work, with as much zest and as little concern for his own safety as ever. He was killed in 1965, and we had another tragic funeral to attend.

Tim Page, a young British free-lancer stringing for *Time,* was aboard an American patrol boat in the South China Sea when an American fighter-bomber mistook it for a Viet Cong blockade runner. In the ensuing air attack Tim suffered horrendous injuries that included brain damage. A long time later, Tim sued *Time,* which, unlike the AP, was reluctant to compensate its stringer casualties. In 1982, when I myself was working for one of *Time*'s magazines (Discover), I received a memorandum from the corporate high command informing us that because of the Page lawsuit, *Time* would no longer pay medical compensation to wounded stringers.

And then there were two old war dogs I've missed over the years. One was Dickie Chapelle, a kind of female Ernie Pyle who marched with the U.S. Marines in every conflict from World War II to Viet Nam, where she was killed by a mine.

I have a feeling that by 1965 Dickie had begun to think her life was charmed, however dangerous war might be. Cowards like me never forget that while walking through hostile territory or minefields, the safest course is to step exactly where the soldier ahead of you placed his own feet; if he doesn't blow up, you won't either.

Incidentally, the same cowardly strategy once saved my life while I was walking across polar ice in Antarctica, where crevasses concealed by snow bridges pose the same kind of danger as a mines on a battlefield. (We safely pulled the scientist in whose steps I was following out of that crevasse, so I didn't need to feel guilty.)

Whether or not Dickie momentarily forgot the step-following rule I have no idea, but in 1965, while covering an operation by her beloved Marines in central Viet Nam, she stepped on a mine, and a lot of us mourned her. (Dickie's stormy life was recapitulated in fascinating detail in a recent book: *Fire in the Wind, the Life of Dickie Chappelle*, by Roberta Ostroff.)

Another friend of mine who fell victim was Bernard Fall, the French journalist-historian whose accent and views seemed more American than French. Bernard was an unusual mixture of academic scholar and hell-for-leather war correspondent, and I remember him as much for the meticulously organized library of 5-by-7 filing cards he kept in his Phnom Penh office as for his brilliant battlefield coverage of the French Indochina War in 1953 and 1954.

Despite his fascination with war, Fall was a gentle soul emboldened by a keen sense of mission: at all costs, he hoped to convince American strategists of the need to learn from the French Indochina experience. Although I disagreed with some of his conclusions, no one has written more convincingly than he of the tactics of ambush and rapid dispersal developed by General Giap and the other enemy commanders.

It was near the "Street Without Joy," the bloody stretch of Route 1 that Fall had vividly described in his book of the same name, that he himself was killed by a mine in 1967.

There was also a fair number of suicides among newspeople who covered Indochina, and it's conceivable that the trauma of war had something to do with their tragic deaths. Dave Hudson, the American intelligence operative who also worked as a journalist, was one of the first to die at his own hand. An Italian cameraman who covered the Easter Offensive in 1972 hanged himself soon after returning to Rome. Jim Markham, a *New York Times* correspondent who had covered both the Lebanese and Vietnamese wars, ended his life without explanation in his Paris apartment some years later.

One of the saddest suicides was that of Sarah Webb Barrell, an American girl who drifted with the news and finally hit a reef. She had been a dancer at one time, but by the time she journeyed to Indochina in the 1970s she had become a free-lance writer and photographer.

Sarah, whose bronzed body often adorned the swimming pool at the Hotel Royale in Phnom Penh, frequently attached herself to some male colleague, endlessly seeking a protective wing and a lasting personal relationship. She was brave in combat and she cheerfully endured chronic toilet-paper shortages, suffocating heat, scorpion bites and all the other discomforts of wartime Cambodia.

The last time I saw Sarah was on April 29, 1975, in Saigon, the eve of the communist entry into the city. We journalists were covering a gloomy ceremony at which a new interim president of South Viet Nam was sworn in to make peace with Hanoi's conquering Hanoi army. A violent thunderstorm broke out and Sarah leaned against me, shuddering.

Four years later Sarah was covering the war in Southern Rhodesia (now called Zimbabwe), and had become attached to one of the mercenary officers serving in Ian Smith's government forces. In June 1979, her friend was killed in a skirmish with the rebel army that soon afterward came to power. Sarah's sad little life had run its course, and she shot herself.

There were a few murders, too. A very pretty and plucky American reporter named Claudia Ross who worked for the English-language *Bangkok Post* spent a lot of time covering battles in Cambodia in 1973. At home in Thailand, she covered the brewing student insurrection that eventually brought down Bangkok's military government, and another of her stories exposed the growing influence of some rather sinister religious sects.

In 1974 Claudia was found dead in her Bangkok apartment, stabbed many times in a pattern of wounds that suggested a ritual of some kind. The case was never solved.

In the slaying of two other correspondents I knew, South Vietnamese officials were at least partly responsible.

During the final phase of the war, anti-American and anti-Western feeling was running so high in South Viet Nam's armed forces that Western newsmen were treated as enemies.

In March 1975, less than two months before the communist triumph, Paul Leandri, a thirty-seven-year-old correspondent for Agence France Presse (the French news agency), filed a story from the provincial capital Ban Me Thuot, saying that mountain tribesmen of the region had defected from Saigon's forces to join a communist assault on the city.

The story was true, but Nguyen Van Thieu's government was sick of foreign messengers of ill tidings, and Leandri was summoned to the Saigon office of the immigration police for a grilling. During the long interrogation he was allowed to speak to a French consular official, first by telephone, and then face to face in a police courtyard. Leandri said the police were trying to learn the names of his Vietnamese sources, while the police said Leandri was acting belligerent and refusing to discuss his article.

The impasse went on for some time, but finally the exasperated French newsman simply walked out of the building. He refused to stop when police ordered him to return, whereupon a policeman fired one bullet through the back of Leandri's head, killing him instantly. His pregnant wife went into shock.

Many Saigon policemen were among the refugees airlifted to safety in the United States at the end of the war, and some of them continued their murderous ways in this country, participating in gang warfare and assassination plots against fellow Vietnamese refugees they regarded as enemies.

In 1972 Alex Shimkin of *Newsweek* was killed, and since he and I shared a car and a lot of adventures covering the brutal campaign south of Quang Tri that spring, I have strong feelings about his death. One is a suspicion that the South Vietnamese army was indirectly responsible.

In the first week of April 1972, the North Vietnamese Easter Offensive rolled southward across the 17th Parallel, spearheaded by T-54 tanks and several mobile infantry divisions. I was living in Rawalpindi at the time, but *The Times* asked me to grab a flight to Saigon and pitch in with coverage.

On May 1 the city of Quang Tri, the northernmost town of major importance in South Viet Nam, fell to the enemy, and South Viet Nam's 3rd Army Division collapsed in a rout. At the same time, major communist offensives in the central Vietnamese highlands threatened to cut the country in two, and heavy fighting between very large opposing units continued all that summer. The battle for Quang Tri continued until South Vietnamese forces recaptured the shattered city on September 15, and I spent much of that bloody summer in the thick of the action just south of the town.

A lot of us newsmen were living in the ramshackle shell of a former hotel in Hue, which we used as a base for covering the battles to the north. Life in Hue was a real comedown for me. In the old days when I covered riots or coups in Hue I generally lodged aboard one of the cool, comfortable sampans that plied the Perfume River, on which a comfortable pallet and good food—not to mention a respite from the civil war battles raging ashore—afforded many a good night's sleep. But in 1972 the sampans were gone and Hue was a sorely stricken city.

Cars in 1972 were always in great demand and very scarce, so Alex and I agreed to share expenses on one and work together for a while.

Driving to war is always tricky; if you go too far you may find yourself trapped in cross fire, and if you don't go far enough, you may miss everything of importance. One day in late July or early August, Alex and I drove up Route 1 to within about five miles of Quang Tri, where the crash and roar of artillery and air strikes told us we were getting too close. We spotted a clearing in some trees to the left of the road where a Vietnamese Army battery of 105-millimeter howitzers was in action, and we stopped to ask for information.

The battery commander, a first lieutenant, gave us a sour look and demanded to see our identification papers and credentials. I asked how things were going. "We win whenever you Americans stay out of our way," he replied. It was apparent that we could expect little help from the man, so we asked how to reach an advance airborne unit we knew to be accompanied by a couple of American military advisers.

"Straight up Route 1 about one mile," the lieutenant said. "Don't leave the road. You'll find the CP [command post] right by the side of the road."

I put the creaky old Citroën in gear and we crept up the road, but we hadn't gone more than a couple of hundred yards before I smelled a rat. The road was straight as an arrow without any sign of life all along it, and the thunder of the howitzers had abruptly stopped. I pulled the car over to the side and Alex and I got out to reconnoiter on foot.

Keeping to the trees on the left side of the road, we cautiously moved forward until something told us we were in trouble. About fifty yards ahead we detected shadowy figures crouching behind bushes on both sides of the road, and they were wearing green-and-black combat clothing—Viet Cong.

We couldn't tell whether they had seen us, but we hastily ducked into the woods on our left and found a trail headed westward away from the road. It wasn't thirty seconds before a concentrated bombardment began falling on and around the road—105-millimeter shells from our surly acquaintances down the road, along with earsplitting 155-millimeter shells fired from positions farther to the rear. Just then, the popping of small arms a short distance up the road ahead of us showed that Viet Cong gunners had spotted us. Alex and I found a ditch and jumped in, faces to the ground and hands over our ears.

The cannonade subsided after a while and the acrid smoke of shell bursts began to disperse. Alex and I took our first breaths and moved on, with a disquieting feeling that our own side had tried to kill us. If we had followed the directions given us by that Vietnamese artillery lieutenant, we would have walked right into the Viet Cong gun position the lieutenant must have known was there. This officer also knew he was directing us straight into a target box that was about to be saturated by artillery shells.

Following a compass heading, Alex and I crept through the forest until we came to a small clearing that seemed to have been overlooked by both sides. Large-caliber artillery shells still rumbled over our heads with a noise like the passing of freight trains, but the crump of their impacts seemed quite distant. The clearing seemed peaceful, so we sat down to rest and eat a couple of sandwiches. As I recall, our water canteens were supplemented that day by a couple of cans of mediocre French Bordeaux, which you could buy in the Saigon street market.

Alex was a tall, rangy kid with thick glasses, a ready wit and a wonderfully sardonic sense of humor. He was good company.

Eventually, we reached the advance CP we were looking for, where we found a couple of American officers fuming over the haphazard artillery support their Vietnamese unit was getting. "Everyone's groping around like blindmen up here, and we can't tell who the hell is where," one said.

The following week I was elsewhere, covering a military crisis in the plateau region between Pleiku and Kontum. It was then that Alex went out for another look at the Quang Tri battle line, at just about the same place where he and I had had a close scrape the last time. Alex apparently blundered into a patch of forest the North Vietnamese had just occupied, and some nearby government troops heard him yelling in Vietnamese, "Don't shoot! I'm a newsman!"

Alex's body was never recovered after he joined the ranks of the missing in action. No one will ever know whether South Vietnamese malice played a part in his fate, but I wouldn't be surprised to learn that it did.

It must be noted that despite problems American journalists often had with Vietnamese officials, many of us owed our lives to ordinary Vietnamese people who reached out to help at times of danger.

I remember an episode in 1965 when politically inspired mobs, some led by the Viet Cong, were rampaging through Saigon and beating up or killing people whose looks they didn't like. One night, John Wheeler of our AP bureau and I were covering these riots when a gang of young men armed with knives and pulling a cartload of bricks for use as missiles spotted us.

John and I ran as fast as we could through a maze of streets and alleyways, but our pursuers were gradually gaining on us. Almost exhausted, we rounded a corner and found ourselves trapped in a *cul de sac,* but at that instant an old man opened the door of his house, grabbed us by the sleeves and pulled us to safety. The puzzled mob leaders swept past without seeing us.

I'm not sure about South Vietnamese officials, but I don't believe United States officials ever connived at the deaths of American correspondents in Indochina. Still, some of Washington's diplomats certainly made life miserable for us in other ways.

I have particularly disagreeable memories of the U.S. mission in Cambodia at one time. In 1973 American bombers were regularly pasting Cambodia's jungles, partly to interdict the Viet Cong supply line into Viet Nam, but also to knock out Khmer Rouge units threatening to overwhelm the government forces commanded by Cambodia's president, General Lon Nol.

Correspondents knew that U.S. Air Force bombers were carrying out these raids, despite continued denials by both Washington and Phnom Penh. But one day Sylvana Foa, UPI's Cambodia correspondent, stumbled on proof. While listening to a shortwave broadcast on her Zenith radio she absentmindedly tuned to the VHF channel used in the United States for weather service broadcasts, and to her surprise, she overheard a conversation between B-52 pilots in the air and their controllers on the ground. The pilots were getting instructions that guided them to specific coordinates for bombing well inside Cambodia. The conversation was "in the clear," and could be heard and understood by any English-speaking listener with a radio equipped to receive VHF weather forecasts. Many Cambodians owned such radios, and enemy intelligence operatives almost certainly were listening.

Sylvana reported her discovery in a UPI dispatch that was published throughout the world and caused considerable embarrassment to U.S. and Cambodian authorities, who, as usual, hoped to conceal America's combat involvement. The breach of military security was not a legitimate issue, since it was the air force itself that had broadcast its game plan as openly as a Saturday football game. But on instructions from the U.S. Embassy, the Cambodian government charged Sylvana with violating military security and expelled her for her scoop.

On another occasion in 1973, the U.S. Embassy in Phnom Penh struck at my wife and myself in what appeared to be a grudge reprisal for what it regarded as my negative reporting. The incident began with a trip Le Lieu and I made to Hanoi.

The two of us (along with our dog, the highly portable Japanese spaniel Nif-Naf) were commuting between hotel rooms we maintained in both Phnom Penh and Vientiane at the time, and in the spring of 1973 we were offered a chance to fly to North Viet Nam to witness the release of the last group of American POWs held by Hanoi.

Air Force C-144 transport planes carried out the actual prisoner evacuation from Hanoi, but about thirty correspondents, including Walter Cronkite and representatives of all the major news organizations, were flown to Hanoi from Vientiane aboard a chartered Royal Air Laos airliner. Le Lieu (accredited as a *New York Times* photographer) went along.

It was a fascinating day. Some of the released prisoners hobbled on crutches, and all the men were stony-faced and grim. The general mien of the prisoners bespoke a terrible ordeal. Several journalists shouted greetings at them and a few smiled timidly, but the prisoners obviously wanted to avoid annoying their captors until they were really out of Viet Nam.

Simply being in the enemy's capital and politely shaking hands with smiling officials wearing green pith helmets was the strangest experience of all.

Le Lieu was the first Vietnamese American to visit North Viet Nam since the beginning of the war, and she instantly attracted the attention of officials and soldiers, all eager to talk to her. Although all were North Vietnamese by nationality, many were ethnic southerners separated from their homeland since the country was divided in 1954, and Le Lieu was deluged with questions about friends and family members in the Mekong Delta province where she was born, about what life was like, about long-lost homes.

Many of the comments made to Le Lieu were indiscreet, but no one seemed to worry about being overheard by political commissars. A lieutenant in North Viet Nam's regular army told my wife that he guessed all of South Viet Nam must be beautiful, and that he himself had been much impressed by the architecture of Hue when his side had occupied the city in 1972. The remark was a shocker. As far as I know, it was the first open admission by a North Vietnamese official that regular Hanoi forces, not just the Viet Cong, had invaded the south.

We strolled through the walled prison camp known as the Hanoi Hilton, where some of the American POWs were standing at attention in their purple-and-pink-striped prison garb. We were not allowed to speak to our long-suffering compatriots.

Later, the visiting correspondents got to tour the city. Having read accounts by earlier visitors of massive destruction in Hanoi, we were mildly surprised to find the beautiful capital virtually intact, except for an entire block that had been flattened when a B-52 with its bombs still aboard was shot down over the city center.

Hanoi's main lake with its picturesque island pagoda

looked charming, and young people packed the lakeside restaurants, laughing and chatting as they consumed their savory *pho* soup and barbecued shrimp. Some of them greeted us in Russian.

When the time came to leave we joined the convoy of buses taking the POWs to the airport, and bumped across the bomb-blasted bridge over the Red River. After seeing off the last of the C-144s, our press party was given time to shop at the airport souvenir store, which sold vile Hanoi beer and gimcracks that included aluminum combs and brooches made from the metal skin of downed American bombers.

There was an unpleasant aftermath for Le Lieu and me. We noticed on leaving North Viet Nam that Hanoi officials had stamped all the American correspondents' passports, and this posed a problem: the United States Immigration and Naturalization Service had decreed that no American could travel to North Viet Nam without special State Department dispensation. Since all of us had had less than eight hours' warning before making the trip from Vientiane, none of the correspondents had been able to obtain the required State Department clearance.

For all of us except Le Lieu, the only naturalized American among us, the State Department simply ignored the infraction. But several weeks later, Le Lieu visited the U.S. consulate in Phnom Penh to ask for a second passport, explaining that she could not enter South Viet Nam with a passport containing a North Vietnamese visa stamp. (Duplicate passports were routinely issued to Americans with similar travel problems—travel between Israel and some of the Arab states, for example.)

Instead of assisting her, the consulate, under instructions from the Embassy, seized Le Lieu's passport and issued a temporary document permitting her only to travel back to the United States. *The New York Times* raised hell with the Immigration and Naturalization Service and Le Lieu was immediately issued a new passport, but our adversaries at the U.S. embassies in Indochina rarely lost subsequent chances to play similarly spiteful tricks on us.

In the summer of 1972 I was constantly traveling between widely separated theaters of fighting but spending a lot of time at Pleiku. Pleiku was the fulcrum of resistance against the North Vietnamese High Plateau offensive, in a region of barren prairies and hills that somewhat resemble parts of Montana.

The allied viceroy of the High Plateau was an old acquaintance of the press, John Paul Vann, who in 1963 had been a maverick U.S. Army adviser to Viet Nam, and whose advice and observations often clashed with U.S. military policies. His unorthodox views eventually forced Vann out of the army, but by 1972 he was back in Viet Nam as a civilian, this time acting as both *de facto* military commander and *de facto* ruler of the High Plateau.

Early in the war, Vann had recognized that it takes more than cumbersome, slow-moving battalions to fight guerrillas, and that without good intelligence and quick reactions, forces opposing the Viet Cong would always be hamstrung. In some ways, Vann's approach to warfare was more that of a savvy field sergeant than of a general, and even at the end of his life, he lived with the troops, trying to stiffen backs and strengthen the resolve of South Vietnamese infantrymen facing North Vietnamese tanks.

Some Saigon newsmen in 1963 regarded Vann as a mentor; his "grunt's-eye" view of the war seemed more realistic than anything Secretary McNamara and his generals had dreamed up. Two correspondents in particular, David Halberstam of *The New York Times* and Neil Sheehan of UPI, regarded Vann as one of their most truthful and valuable sources, perhaps even as a kind of mentor. Only later when Neil began work on a book about Vann's life and career did he see Vann's dark and sometimes duplicitous side. Sheehan's book, *A Bright Shining Lie,* portrayed

Vann as a metaphor for the American experience in Viet Nam—a courageous idealist who believed he was doing good but who could nevertheless betray those closest to him, finally abandoning even his own ideals.

I remember Vann as a cocky little squirt, partial to the kind of matching ties and shirts sold at PX stores to NCOs preparing for a raucous night in civvies on the town. A man of very limited education, Vann parlayed the popularity he had earned in official and journalistic circles by maneuvering into a position of almost absolute authority in the central highlands of Viet Nam. Commanding B-52 strikes as easily as he did the affections of pretty Saigon girls, he thoroughly enjoyed the job.

But in the summer of 1972 Viet Nam was falling apart, and Vann simply had more to do than he could handle. Never adept at grooming subordinates to assume real authority, he frittered away nights on routine paperwork, phone calls to Saigon (some to his girlfriend) and nightly press conferences for the gang of newsmen and groupies who had assembled in Pleiku. By day, his eyes were red with fatigue. Running on coffee and nerves, Vann would board his LOACH helicopter and skip like a grasshopper from one crisis to another, redirecting ground troops, calling for air strikes and giving pep talks to exhausted and frightened Vietnamese troops.

On June 7 I had some business to attend to in Saigon, so I left Vann, urging him to get some rest. Two days later we heard that Vann's LOACH had flown too close to a hill overlooking the road from Pleiku to Kontum, and that he had been shot down and killed. For those who had come to think of Vann as a symbol of America in Viet Nam, his death seemed something of an omen.

But there are times when war is quite liberating for a correspondent. When death or capture seems inevitable, and there is nowhere to go but the shade of a tree or an abandoned building, and no chance of writing or transmitting news, and the heat and exhaustion have sapped the last ounce of initiative, one simply sits down and stares into space, no longer giving a damn about anything. I assumed that zombielike posture a couple of times during the summer of 1972, just waiting for something to happen. It always did.

War may deaden feelings but it can also stimulate the procreative urge, and young men and women correspondents thrown together in battle are much more likely to seek comfort from each other's bodies than they would be as coworkers in an office somewhere. The sex lives of correspondents underwent a change in Viet Nam, I think, because many more women covered Viet Nam than had covered previous wars. In former times, the predominantly male press corps relied for female companionship mostly on the local flesh markets, but in Indochina the pairing was more often between colleagues. The advent of the Pill in the early 1960s largely eliminated the risk of pregnancy, and this too certainly helped to fan the flames.

The physical setting of war can be an aphrodisiac, especially at night. Sitting in the poolside garden of the Hotel Royale in Phnom Penh, newspeople could look northward at the graceful red streams of tracer bullets floating through the night sky, and watch the faint flashes of distant shells and bombs. The light show lent animation to the gentle light of a tropical moon.

Very few of the wartime romances that bloomed between Indochina correspondents lasted for long; most ended when one partner or the other was reassigned. But many a correspondent will remember to the end of his or her days the fleeting beauty of an attachment formed while watching that dismal theater of death.

TRICKS OF THE TRADE

DURING THE TIME I spent in Indochina, something a little less than a decade, I worked for news agencies, a couple of radio networks, a television network, several large-circulation magazines and a couple of newspapers. While this track record may not attest to personal stability or corporate loyalty, I can at least claim a working acquaintance with "the media," that dreadful Latin plural our detractors use when they really mean "scum."

Because the various tentacles of our profession are supposed to constitute one of the main props of representative democracy, I thought I'd explain some of the differences in the ways we gather news and lead our lives.

First, it needs to be said that since the latter half of the nineteenth century, the backbone of the news industry in the United States has been the wire services (or, as these organizations prefer to be called, the "news agencies"). Nearly anyone who publishes or broadcasts news gets a major share of the raw material from the agencies, without which we would have to do without the broad spectrum of news we're accustomed to getting in our magazines, newspapers and broadcasting systems.

Respectable newspapers generally credit the news agencies that supply grist for their mills, and some publications (but not *The New York Times*) even accord wire-service reporters occasional bylines.

The flow of news goes two ways, incidentally. The AP supplies news to all its members, and in return, the agency is entitled to pick up, rewrite and distribute news from its members. Everyone gets due credit, of course.

The relations between the wire agencies and television broadcasters are somewhat different. The TV networks, fulsome in their never-ending self-congratulation, unearth very little news for themselves. Instead, they choreograph, dramatize and pictorialize the news fed to them by primary suppliers, notably the wire services.

Compared with the wire services, television networks have small news-gathering staffs, because their function is not so much to gather the news as to package it. The big TV news money goes for production, satellite communications, anchor salaries, transportation and hotel costs for the supporting crews and much more. When a network establishes a war-coverage bureau in, say, Dhahran, the staff includes producers, secretaries, clerks, gofers, cameramen, soundmen, engineers, communications experts, repairmen, makeup artists and God knows what else. The TV correspondents themselves sometimes feel lost in the crowd.

By contrast, the wires get by on a shoestring. Roger Tatarian, who headed United Press International during the twilight of its glory days, used to say that UPI was a "lean and hungry" agency. That description applied in some measure to all news agencies.

Those of us who could speak articulately were also asked to go on lecture tours, ostensibly to entertain and inform member publishers and broadcasters, but actually to sell our agencies' services to new subscribers and keep old subscribers loyal.

Despite the burdens of wire service reporting, there never was a shortage of young men and women willing to work themselves to death for a pittance, just for the chance to break into foreign correspondence.

Of course, some of the more enterprising agency men and women ended up rich. There was a UP correspondent I knew who had covered World War II, went to Japan to cover the occupation, married a Japanese girl and settled down. Gifted with real economic prescience, his wife persuaded him to let her invest $5,000 to buy a piece of property in downtown Tokyo. (*Gaijin*, foreigners, were not allowed to own Japanese property in their own names.) Fifteen years later the value of Tokyo property reached astronomical heights, and my newsman acquaintance later retired as a very wealthy man.

Many newsmen have started out as stringers. American stringers in my day formed little expatriate communities, much as American novelists and painters did in the Paris of the 1920s. As we shared adventures and hardships, some succeeded and others fell to alcohol or depression or suicide; love sometimes bloomed, and tragedy sometimes struck. Our lives were probably not much different from those of our Left Bank cultural ancestors, except that we produced precious few real artists or writers. I've often wondered why.

The transition from stringing to a salaried job is an important benchmark. When I became an Associated Press staffer I could count on regular pay and health insurance, and overnight, I became a respectable cog in the machine of mainstream journalism. My salary in Baltimore, where I was hired, seemed more than adequate, and my pay in Saigon seemed princely. Because I lived outside the United States my taxes were reduced to practically nothing, my rent was about $50 a month, my food and my maid's salary were cheap, and I began saving money. I also spent more than I should have on the kinds of gadgets correspondents bought whenever they stopped in Hong Kong to shop in the glittering duty-free stores.

Occasional shopping sprees probably compensated for

the anxiety of the job, which saddled correspondents with a permanent sense of guilt. No matter how timely and important any given dispatch might be, its author was conditioned by long training to assume that his work should have been quicker and better. Wire service people used to say there was a deadline every minute, and it was literally true.

For a wire service reporter, communications have always been the first priority, even ahead of digging up news. Every now and then, agency men and women become too engrossed in the stories they cover, forgetting that the important thing is always to get the news out. Their editors quickly bring them around, however. The first AP war correspondent to die in battle, Mark Kellogg, fell with Custer at the Little Bighorn, a sacrifice that was wasted, AP editors pointed out, because the poor fellow had failed to file his story before being scalped.

I never actually used carrier pigeons, but I was helped many times by human pigeons, particularly in Indochina. But it is not always possible to find a pigeon, especially if a nation's airports are closed down by a coup or some other military upheaval.

During the 1971 war between India and Pakistan, Pakistan imposed a total communications blackout on foreign newsmen in the country, forcing us to resort to expensive and time-consuming alternatives.

Most newsmen in Pakistan at the time made Rawalpindi their base of operations because of its proximity to battles along the Punjab front. Rawalpindi was also handy as the only major town from which one could expect to get news out in fairly timely fashion.

With a long day's drive, one could reach Kabul, Afghanistan, from Rawalpindi, traversing the Northwest Frontier Province and passing the city of Peshawar, the Khyber Pass and Jalalabad along the way. Provided a correspondent reached the

Kabul telegraph office before closing time, he could file his story and keep his employers happy. Copy moved slowly and it cost nearly a dollar a word, but at least the Afghan authorities did not censor news from Pakistan. One of the nice things about a twenty-four-hour respite in Afghanistan, which was much more relaxed than Pakistan in its practice of Islam, was that one could enjoy wine with dinner and bacon with the breakfast eggs.

But nothing is ever simple in such situations. It was easy enough to leave Pakistan and enter Afghanistan, because the two nations had agreed to waive the usual visa requirements for American refugees fleeing the war in Pakistan. (The main risk was in remembering to change from the left side of the road in Pakistan to the right side in Afghanistan.) The trouble came traveling back to Pakistan at the border, where newsmen lacking Afghan exit visas or Pakistani entry visas were always held up. On one occasion Afghan border guards at Torkham, the international crossing point in the Khyber Pass, hauled me from my car and administered a painful beating before deciding to let me pass.

In Viet Nam during the political upheavals of 1963, newsmen had to use all sorts of tricks to get their news out. When the Diem government raided the pagoda headquarters of dissident Buddhist monks and jailed their leaders that summer, the authorities closed down communications in hopes of blocking the news completely. For more than twenty-four hours I was stymied, and my chief competitor, UPI's Neil Sheehan, wiped me out. He had cleverly arranged with the captain of a ship tied up at the Saigon quay to use the ship's single-sideband radio to get at least a few nuggets of news to the outer world. As far as I know, Neil was the only correspondent in Viet Nam to report that memorable story as it broke.

But on another occasion, I got the better of competitors with a different technique. One day in 1963 I learned that Vu Van Mau, South Viet Nam's foreign minister, had resigned his post to protest the Saigon government's actions against the Buddhists, and had shaved his head in the fashion of the dissident monks. This was the first sign that the government itself was falling apart, and was clearly a major story.

The censors prohibited the transmission of all news stories from Viet Nam at that point, but the authorities permitted limited transmission of radiophotos from the government radio station, provided the pictures were approved by a censor on duty at the station. It occurred to me that I might use a picture to get out my story.

The radiophoto transmitters used in those days had revolving drums to which black-and-white photographs were attached. As the drum rotated, a light beam in the instrument scanned the photograph, and the reflected beam hit a photocell, which translated the variations in light intensity into electrical impulses that could be broadcast. Sending a single picture to our Paris office took about ten minutes.

I went to the radio center that day with a photograph I knew would pass censorship, a picture of the U.S. ambassador talking to some official. But I also brought along a piece of paper with an adhesive backing, and on this paper I wrote out a brief story reporting Mau's resignation and its political significance. After I'd placed the photograph in the machine and started the drum rotating, the censor turned away to chat with the operator, and at that moment I stuck my slip of paper on the revolving picture. Standing with my back to the radiophoto machine, I managed to block the censor's view until the transmission was complete, at which point I removed the paper and slipped it into my pocket.

But my scheme backfired. The following morning, the *New York Herald Tribune* published my story on its front page, just as I had sent it, as a handwritten scrawl on a slip of paper partly covering a photograph of the American ambassador. It didn't take long for Saigon authorities to find out what I had done, and the censors were harder to trick from then on.

Many censors lack the imagination and education to carry out their tasks effectively, but some I have known were real masters of their abominable trade. I encountered one of them in Rio de Janeiro.

I covered a military coup in Brazil in 1969, at a time when the foreign press was also reporting on government-sanctioned death squads roaming the streets. A wave of political arrests and "disappearances" had also broken out, and the new Brazilian regime was getting some pretty bad press.

The generals quickly moved to halt such reporting, and the authorities actually stationed a censor in our *New York Times* office in Rio. This army major had been educated in an American university and had specialized in American literature, so his grasp of semantic nuances was impeccable. If he struck out a phrase or paragraph in my story, he would always insist that I close up the excision without any visible seams. At first I tried leaving his cuts untouched, knowing that editors in New York would realize something had been removed, but the censor would say, "Now, Mr. Browne, let's have no childish tricks. You know that the syntax here will have your editors smelling a rat. Fix the prose, or I won't let you file any of it."

An entirely different set of problems confronted me when I switched to television. From my very first contact with the medium I knew that I had a lot of learning to do.

In 1965, a year after I got a Pulitzer for work in Viet Nam, I spent some time for the AP giving little talks around the United States at universities and meetings of publishers and broadcasters. One of the talks I delivered was at a lunch in New York hosted by Wes Gallagher, the AP's general manager, and the guests included a bevy of luminaries from ABC. One of them was Jesse Zousmer, vice president of the network's news division, whose distinguished career in journalism and television had included producing Edward R. Murrow's TV series for CBS.

A digression: several weeks later I went to London to speak at an international meeting of news organizations, and one night I spent some pleasant hours at Clarence House, where Princess Margaret was giving a reception. As a small boy I had seen pictures of the princess at her father's coronation in 1936, and I had contracted an ardent crush on her. Actually meeting the princess in 1965 was therefore a great occasion for me. She was shorter than I had imagined, but possessed a trim body and a face as pretty as her picture. She was married, alas, so I had to settle for touching her hand.

I got back to my hotel room to discover that Zousmer had been trying to reach me from New York with a job offer.

I didn't accept immediately, but went back to Viet Nam to think things over. I had grown up without television, and even as an adult in the 1950s and 1960s I had never owned a TV set. The snippets of shows I had seen in bars and hotel lobbies left me with the feeling that television was a toy; it might divert children, but it could hardly provide sustenance to an adult of average intelligence.

At the same time, I discovered that even in the 1960s an awful lot of Americans were already glued to their light boxes, photosynthesizing their views and biases from the TV images that passed for news.

Then as now, a television reporter who failed to find an expert to analyze the day's crisis in time for the seven o'clock news would often turn to some print newsman who could vamp intelligently and serve as a talking head. By the mid-1960s I'd often been interviewed myself, and whenever I appeared on the tube I received lots of letters from viewers—far more letters than I ever got from readers responding to my own AP stories. This surprised me, because my published or broadcast AP news stories were read or viewed by countless millions of readers every day.

So I began to consider television from a new perspective. As a news medium it offered pretty slim pickings, but it did command a vast audience ready to grab any crumb slipping down its rabbit-ear antennas.

In the end, I signed ABC's contract and resigned from the AP. Gallagher, my AP boss, defender and friend, grumbled an avuncular grumble and said, "If you had to ditch your AP family for television, you might at least have gone to NBC." I've had a good life and a reasonably productive career since leaving the AP, but I've always missed the AP family.

My first trip for ABC was to Mexico City, where the network was holding its annual meeting of stockholders, executives, affiliate radio and television stations, groupies and whatnot. Part of the annual ritual that year was devoted to "launching" Adam West as the star of the new "Batman" series, and in a much more modest way, I, too, was launched, as the new kid on the Indochina beat.

One of the most revealing chats I had was during a taxi ride with Elmer Lower, the president of ABC's news division. Elmer told me that the networks had a kind of gentlemen's agreement to broadcast their prime-time news shows simultaneously, and never to run a movie when competitors were broadcasting news. Otherwise, he said, the movie would steal the ratings.

But it wasn't until I got back to Viet Nam that I realized fully how much a part of the entertainment industry television news really was. Lou Cioffi, an old Asia correspondent for CBS and later for ABC, took me in hand to explain the right ways to apply pancake makeup and hair spray, which type of safari jacket to order and how it should fit and how to seek out pictorially appealing news stories. I learned from Lou that each half-minute "stand-upper" (the correspondent's on-camera spiel) filmed at a battle (or wherever) must first be typed out and then memorized, rehearsed and performed—perhaps four or five times. Only when the cameraman, soundman, producer and correspondent agreed that a take was satisfactory could the team move on to other things, such as finding a ride out of the jungle after the last chopper has left.

I learned that the real heroes of the TV news industry are the cameramen, who must carry killing loads under appalling conditions, and must produce exciting "actualities" even at the risk of their own lives. In the 1960s, the main instrument for doing this was the cumbersome 16-millimeter Auricon sound camera, a French product. This beast produced the very best quality sound-striped film, but it was extremely heavy. Since the Auricon needed electricity to run, the cameraman had to wear a belt fitted with lead-acid batteries, not unlike the lead belts worn by divers to neutralize their buoyancy.

On field trips the cameraman would usually bring along a second and somewhat smaller camera (an Arriflex), which required no external connections and was useful for "cut-away" shots, such as a close-up of a shattered doll in the debris of a shell-blasted house, or an "establisher"—a shot of a pagoda to tell the viewer he's looking at Asia.

But when the "natural" sounds of machine-gun fire or a correspondent's "voice-over" commentary were required, only the Auricon would do. A network of electric umbilical cords connected the Auricon to the soundman and his recording controls, and to a microphone clutched in the hand of the correspondent. Joined together as a cursed trinity, a television crew would leap together from an alighting helicopter and run in cadence through the ground fire like three monkeys holding each other's tails. Ron Headford, the Australian cameraman who generally worked with me, had the physique of a bull and the endurance of an Olympic marathoner.

Shipping film was always a crucial part of the job. Cutthroat competition has always dominated the TV industry, and the race between three networks covering the same story has often depended on which one could get its film to the States first. These days procedures are easier, because portable or semiportable satellite stations can operate practically anywhere a network wants to set them up. During the 1990–91 Gulf War, for instance, all three American networks and some other television organizations took over the athletic field and gardens behind the Dhahran International Hotel, and correspondents did their stand-uppers and interviews live, right in U.S. prime time. Peter Arnett in Baghdad could talk to American audiences even as American cruise missiles were screeching over his head.

But when I was in television, we had to ship undeveloped film by commercial air freight, or by chartered airplane. If only one charter plane was available and all three networks wanted it, success sometimes hinged on treachery, bribery or some other low trick, and anger sometimes accelerated to blows. Occasionally the networks would agree to share transportation, but only if there was no alternative.

From Viet Nam the film went to Tokyo, where a customs expediter would pick it up, take it to a laboratory for processing, and thence to a satellite transmission station. One's lead over a competitor could usually be measured in seconds or minutes, and the shipping of film from some battlefield was always a nerve-racking procedure.

Soon after my sojourn with ABC the networks began buying minicam video cameras, which were comparatively light and very forgiving of operator errors. Best of all, they used simple magnetic tape that could be viewed on the spot, rather than the fussy, vulnerable photographic film of the Auricon era.

I never got to benefit from the minicam revolution, so I missed many a ride to and from stories. It's a lot harder to hitch a ride in a river assault boat or helicopter if there are three of you linked together by wires and cumbersome equipment than if you are on your own.

Still, our ABC team did see a lot of action in Viet Nam, and a few of our stories were moderately interesting. The trouble for me was that I never felt my remarks were anything more than an accompaniment to the pictures, and that when the image and the spoken word clashed, the pictures always won.

I remember trying to do a moderately complicated story on the impact America was having on the Vietnamese economy, and at one point in my narrative, my voice-over was delivered as an accompaniment to pictures of a battery of howitzers blazing away. I'm certain that fascinated viewers paid not the slightest heed to what I was saying, so intent must they have been on watching the flash and smoke of the guns.

An irksome constraint was that the story line generally had to accommodate itself to the pictures. Really good footage required little more than talking captions from the correspondent presenting the spiel; if the pictures fitted what he wanted to say, fine; otherwise, it was up to the correspondent to fit his remarks to the pictures.

Old TV Asia hands of the 1960s, people like Jim Robinson of NBC and Pete Kalischer of CBS, knew how to live with the dilemmas and frustrations of TV reporting, and often managed to get something informative across, despite the limitations of the medium. But I never felt that I was doing much more than performing as a circus barker. I also had a gnawing feeling that although pictures do not lie, and although my commentary was always as honest as I knew how to make it, there was always something wrong. Even my most cleverly written monologues never told more than half the story, and despite their factual accuracy, they didn't convey the sense and feel of reality; at root, they always smelled of greasepaint.

Another problem for me was the producer ABC put in charge of our Saigon office. Unlike the great Zousmer, who even as a senior executive always remained a news-savvy journalist sensitive to the needs and instincts of reporters, the producer ABC sent to Saigon was mainly interested in his hobby, which was making forged credentials of various kinds for himself and the staff, all neatly laminated in plastic. If this man had stuck to the mechanics of air-freighting film shipments to Tokyo, paying the office bills and smoothing communications between New York and Saigon, all would have been well. But when he began to imagine that he knew something about Indochina, he became dangerous.

Disagreements between him and me, polite and collegial at first, degenerated into more serious quarrels that eventually led to my departure from the network. Two things brought matters to a head.

I learned one day that an American unit was going to try out new tactics called "Eagle Flights," rapid hit-and-run, helicopter-borne assaults by small, specially trained units. It sounded as though the U.S. command had finally realized that quick reaction rather than overwhelming numerical force was the key to success in Viet Nam, and I badly wanted to see whether the idea would work. The trouble was that the operation I wanted to cover conflicted with another event that ABC considered more worthy of coverage, the selection by a panel of experts of a young lady to be designated Miss Saigon 1966.

On the same day, I received a notice from New York that an expense claim I had filed had been disallowed, because I had asked for $25 to replace a pair of boots destroyed by barbed wire in an operation I had covered for the network. When I complained, our Saigon producer purred that there was no problem, that I should merely charge the $25 to "entertainment," or any of the other categories customarily used for padding. I was furious. Having been brought up to abstain from cheating, I could never reconcile myself to the slick accounting practices that have become all too common in the news industry.

At any rate, the issues raised by Miss Saigon 1966 and my ruined boots brought me to such a boil that I quit.

A great sense of peace came over me as I looked to the future. I've never regretted forgoing what might have been a TV career, except for an incidental consequence of my decision—the deaths of Jesse and Ruth Zousmer.

After I sent off my resignation cable, the two of them flew out from New York, partly to try to persuade me to change my mind. After he arrived in Saigon, Jesse and I had friendly talks over some lunches and dinners, but I finally convinced him that I had deeper reasons for quitting than a mere temper tantrum. Before he left, I agreed to do a couple of TV documentaries, as well as some work for the ABC radio network—a weekly series of nine-minute broadcasts on whatever topics I chose.

From Saigon Jesse flew up to Hong Kong, where his wife had been waiting, and they then departed for Tokyo, but their plane crashed at the foot of Mount Fuji, killing all 130 passengers. The Zousmers were wonderful, intelligent people, and I wondered whether they might have lived if I hadn't resigned from ABC.

It was rather a bad time for me on several counts. Three months earlier my mother had died in New York, and I had not been there to say goodbye. None of our family had believed that her symptoms—shortness of breath, anorexia and agoraphobia—amounted to much more than neurotic hypochondria. We hadn't realized that she was dying of emphysema, and on my last visit home, I thought her tears were just the normal sadness we felt at each parting. But she had known that she was dying and that she would not see me again.

My mother was only fifty-seven and deserved better of her short and mostly unhappy life.

For the documentaries I did for ABC the network assigned another producer, a seasoned professional and a very amiable man. The first show I did reported on the many-tentacled influences that Peking was bringing to bear throughout Asia. It was a fascinating assignment that brought me in contact with former war-criminal industrialists in Japan, the secret police in Taiwan, the vast camps housing floods of refugees from China and the cultures of a half dozen interesting countries.

My series of broadcasts for ABC radio struck some sparks and controversy. Instead of taping the usual military reportage, I tried to address war issues I considered more substantive. In one broadcast I contrasted United States propaganda with that of the Viet Cong, showing how a brutal enemy was outmaneuvering our side by convincing many Vietnamese that it was really motivated by the purest benevolence.

The suggestion that our leaders were botching the Viet Nam War was not popular among conservatives at home, particularly in southern states with large military installations. Several affiliate radio stations in the American South angrily refused to carry my broadcasts from Saigon.

Meanwhile, I had embarked on a new line of work, magazine writing.

I had been free-lancing occasional magazine pieces from Viet Nam for years before my work was noticed by the editors of *True,* the best (and last) of a venerable line of magazines for men. My new affiliation began during one of my home leaves at New York's Algonquin Hotel, the erstwhile haunt of such literati as Dorothy Parker and the *New Yorker* pantheon. My hosts were editors Howard Cohn and Charlie Barnard, and we hit it off immediately.

The fiction and articles in *True* could be about anything and did not necessarily epitomize hairy-chested machismo, but they had to be accurate, exciting, smoothly written and not about gardening, cooking, marriage, romantic scandal or other "feminine" subjects.

True's editors especially liked a piece I did on a U.S. Marine school for snipers in Viet Nam, whose students got to practice on human targets. They were less enthusiastic about a piece on the Viet Cong's women fighters, including the murderous Kim Loan, one of the most ruthless and effective politico-military tacticians on the communist side. Kim was a woman playing a man's role, and that put her outside *True*'s normal sphere. But the piece got published, and I found after a while that my articles in *True* were being read by women as well as men, especially the wives and daughters of American servicemen missing in action.

One of my pieces summarized all that was known up to that point of the fate and condition of American prisoners of war held in North Viet Nam's camps. After its publication I was flooded with letters from families of missing Americans, asking for any other scraps of news or information I might have. I answered the best I could, trying to include anything I knew that might be comforting. It was not until 1973 that I actually went to the Hanoi Hilton and saw for myself the wretched conditions under which Americans had been held.

A lot of Americans are still missing at this writing, and their wives and families are still tortured by hope, nearly two decades after the end of the war. I feel deep sympathy for them and can think of no way to assuage their suffering, even though I'm personally convinced that no American prisoners remained in Viet Nam unwillingly after the war.

After magazines, a step many journalists take is the writing of books, and I tried my hand at that, too. I've come to the conclusion (probably too late in life) that the best journalism often masquerades as fiction or prose—the kind written by Graham Greene, for instance, or George Orwell. Orwell's *Homage to Catalonia* remains a model of war reporting despite its intensely partisan viewpoint.

Of course, that sort of thing takes talent, which news writing, mercifully, does not.

HOME

In 1966 I got word in Viet Nam that I had been picked by the Council on Foreign Relations as its press fellow for one year, a really cushy berth that gave me a good salary, a commodious office in its Sixty-eighth Street headquarters, and a blank check to enroll in any university courses I chose. (I picked a tutor in Mandarin and some courses at Columbia on Arabic and African politics.)

Le Lieu packed up our belongings and shipped our dog Nif-Naf by what must have been a terrifying flight to my father's apartment in New York. We ourselves took a couple of months coming back, shaking off the dust of war on the Greek island of Ios and then visiting the Athens Acropolis, the Villa d'Este fountains of Rome and the shops and concert halls of Berlin. At last, we sailed to New York aboard the *Queen Elizabeth,* on one of that great ship's last voyages before it was retired as a floating school in Hong Kong and finally destroyed by fire.

My main obligation in New York was to attend weekly black-tie dinners at the Council on Foreign Relations for celebrity guests, often banana republic dictators, African potentates and others the State Department considered worth courting. As we dined, smoked our cigars and listened to dictators' explanations of why they were entitled to buckets of American aid, the speakers' personal bodyguards sometimes took station at the windows of our oak-paneled dining room, scanning the street below for assassins.

When the Robert Redford movie *Three Days of the Condor* came out, it seemed to me that the Council's genteel New York brownstone could easily have been the model for the inconspicuous CIA town house in which the movie's action begins. In fact, quite a few members and fellows of the Council had at one time or another served in senior jobs with the CIA. During my fellowship year I got to know Allen Dulles himself, retired but still conspicuous as one of the founders (and by far the most famous director) of the Central Intelligence Agency.

I remember Dulles as a down-to-earth, folksy sort of fellow, whose real enthusiasm was always for operations rather than "estimates"; he was not at all the Ivy League brand of spook epitomized by George Bush. Dulles was direct, blunt and sometimes startling. Once, I asked him what he would most like to see the CIA accomplish, and this was his reply, more or less verbatim:

"What we need is a deal with Peking, whereby the Chinese send us fifty spies. We would take them to Langley, give them intensive training in American history, politics, sociology, military structure, the English language, intelligence tradecraft, the works. Then we'd give them three-year visas and turn them loose."

"What would that accomplish?" I asked.

"No government really trusts anyone but its own spies," he said. "By giving China the best spies money could buy and giving them the freedom to look at America in its entirety, Peking would begin learning the realities of this country. From there, the Chinese could formulate realistic diplomatic and military policies, which for us would be easier to cope with than the nonsense we now confront."

It was a very biblical idea: "Ye shall know the truth, and

the truth shall make you free," and all that. It's a pity that things don't work out so nicely in real life.

That was a very strange year for me. Besides trying hard to be a proper college student once again, I found that my having just returned to America after a long stint in Viet Nam put me in demand as a speaker. In my innocence, I imagined that talks I delivered would be mere reports, not political statements. But I soon learned that the audiences I addressed at Cornell, Michigan State University and many other colleges and public forums were really interested in attending brawls rather than lectures. I usually found myself with several other speakers on a platform where I was expected to counterbalance hawks like Arthur Sylvester, the Pentagon's spokesman under both Kennedy and Johnson, and Brigadier General S. L. A. Marshall, a military analyst and author of many books on World War II and Korea.

As I have mentioned earlier, the polarized views implicit in the words "hawk" and "dove" always seemed to me completely at odds with the reality of Viet Nam, a war in which there were no good guys and very few good causes. My real beef with all camps in America's debate over Viet Nam was that too few people were willing to tell the whole truth, and too many let their prejudices color their conclusions. I wanted no part of a row that shed mostly heat and very little light.

My former AP boss and mentor, Wes Gallagher, had often counseled me to "never get into a pissing match with a skunk," and working newsmen generally tried to abide by that rule. But again and again I found myself behind a lectern facing the icy stare of Herman Kahn or one of the other Viet Nam crusaders, hearing myself and my colleagues described as "young and inexperienced," "taken in by the Viet Cong," "selling our great fighting men short," "undermining our loyal allies in Asia" and generally comporting ourselves like traitors.

In battle after battle, so the line went, the South Vietnamese and American forces had emerged as winners, with hamlets pacified, mountains of weapons seized, prison camps filled with the enemy. We were winning the war, as well as the hearts and minds of the people. That was the line.

But Americans with muddy boots, CIA people and U.S. military analysts as well as correspondents, knew better. We had watched the insidious progress the Viet Cong was making where it really counted, in mobilizing a nation's underclass for pro-tracted resistance against its rulers. MACV's claims of body counts (or heads collected in pickup vans, or ears hung to dry on clotheslines), or of territory recaptured and pacified, or of supply lines permanently interdicted—it all looked impressive, as por-trayed by the after-action reports sent to Washington. But real or imaginary, these victories hardly mattered in the context of growing Viet Cong control of the nation. In my talks and work-shops, I suggested that the statistics from Viet Nam were not telling the underlying story.

Because of my comments the antiwar activists decided I was their ally, and the Pentagon wrote me off as an adversary. And when Sylvester or Marshall or one of the others launched into a speech impugning my honesty, morality, intelligence, patriotism and vision, my Irish blood sometimes prompted me to respond with equal heat. If I was to be thought young and inexperienced (I was thirty-five at the time), so be it; the other side of that coin was that my detractors were World War II retreads, with no more idea how the Viet Nam "people's war" was fought than so many Colonel Blimps. Our dialogues often went like this:

"You're the kind that would have let Hitler run right over this country, Browne."

"I would at least have tried to turn his tactics against him. For your part, you've never even visited these villages you claim are pacified. You just believe what the local Vietnamese officials tell you."

"I learned about war at the Army War College, and I

fought in the hedgerows of Normandy and the hills around the Chorwon Reservoir in Korea. Are you telling me that someone as wet behind the ears as you is a competent judge of strategy?"

"I wore an army uniform in Korea myself, but in Viet Nam I had to unlearn a lot of the things I thought I knew before I saw how Hanoi's partisans wage war."

"The Viet Cong aren't ten feet tall. Are you saying that a nation with the technological and military might of the United States could be bested by an ill-trained peasant militia?"

"Yes, unless the United States is prepared to occupy and administer Viet Nam permanently. We can win any number of battles and pulverize the enemy's cities and towns, but we'll still lose, the moment we start pulling out."

"Well, Browne, loyal Americans have little use for your kind."

There was a lot of ill will in these exchanges, and I don't recall any of my more vehement opponents offering their hands (or accepting mine) after public debates. But time and again I was struck by the sober intelligence of audiences all over America—public affairs clubs, university gatherings, veterans groups and so forth—who really seemed to be concerned with issues rather than invective. Many people came to those debates to watch fireworks, of course, but most of all, their questions told me that they were thinking for themselves.

During my lecture and debating tours of the 1960s, I was constantly reminded how reasonable and decent Americans are, by and large, and how wise our founding fathers were in leaving the big decisions to the American people.

Occasionally I was invited to share platforms with friends rather than opponents. I remember trading impressions of the war with Martin Luther King, Jr., and hearing his views on the disproportionate numbers of black soldiers in Viet Nam. California's Governor Pat Brown was at that workshop, as were George McGovern, actor Robert Vaughn and Senator Ernest Gruening of Alaska, one of the real political heroes of the Viet Nam era. For once, I could shake hands amicably with everyone at the speakers' table.

Gruening was rarely if ever fooled by the Emperor's New Clothes, including the "Gulf of Tonkin Incident" of August 1964. After the U.S. Navy concocted a story about North Vietnamese torpedo boats attacking American warships in the Gulf of Tonkin, members of the United States Senate and House of Representatives trooped like sheep to the administration's call, and almost unanimously voted for the Gulf of Tonkin Resolution. That resolution gave the president a blank check to make war, thereby vitiating a constitutional tradition that the Senate must advise and consent in the making of war.

Only two hard-nosed senators refused to join the parade of sheep, Wayne Morse of Oregon and Ernest Gruening of Alaska. A few years later, a thoroughly contrite national legislature was forced to admit it had been hoodwinked, and in 1970 Congress repealed the Gulf of Tonkin Resolution. All the senators except for Gruening and Morse, in my view, should have been made to spend a year in Viet Nam as an act of atonement and self-education.

I admired Gruening and another great senator and statesman of the era, Mike Mansfield. A former Montana copper miner, Asia scholar and college professor, Mansfield was majority leader of the Senate at the time I knew him, and one of the few steadfast friends the press had in government. His reasoned and humane voice in the Senate and his later work as ambassador to Japan were important factors in keeping the United States from being mired even deeper than it was in various policy follies and an Asian quagmire.

In those days it was tough to avoid wearing a label of some kind, but some of us tried, and people like Mansfield made it easier.

SOME NAZIS AND
THEIR FRIENDS

LE LIEU AND I, clutching our Saigon-born Japanese spaniel Nif-Naf, arrived in Buenos Aires the week after New Year's Day, 1968. The temperature in New York when we left had been three degrees below zero, but ten hours later the thermometer at Ezeiza Airport stood at 90 degrees. After claiming our luggage we moved to the customs inspection platform where Nif-Naf, having restrained himself in the flight bag in which we always carried him, copiously relieved himself.

Meeting us was a *despachante,* a red-tape cutter, who had become as indispensable to *The New York Times* Buenos Aires bureau as he was to many another foreign business in Buenos Aires. This amiable fellow, Yetman by name, was to become my mentor in a skill essential to survival in the Third World—knowing whom to bribe, how much and when.

Since Le Lieu and I were moving our belongings more or less permanently to Argentina, customs arrangements had to be worked out then and there, tired though we were by the long flight. Yetman was magnificent. He, two or three Argentine officials and the Browne family trooped into a customs warehouse where we could talk in private, the customs men handed us gourds charged with steaming, sweetened yerba maté (a strong herbal tea), and we got down to discussions. In less than a half hour of congenial negotiations, we settled on a satisfactory bribe—a surprisingly small one, considering how much stuff we were bringing in.

Only later did we fully realize how much trouble had been saved by that short conference. About a year afterward a new American wire service correspondent arrived in Buenos Aires, and this man was determined to shun corruption of any kind. But he paid the inevitable price such virtue exacts. After six months of delays and red tape, my colleague was informed that his entire consignment of furniture and belongings had accidentally fallen into the River Plate and had sunk irretrievably to the bottom.

Sometimes during my stay in South America bribery was supplanted by smuggling.

While traveling through the hinterlands of Bolivia one time, my wife and I met a vacationing American FBI agent, with whom we shared some adventures. I mentioned to him at one point that Argentine restrictions on imports were sometimes a bit onerous, and that I particularly missed Campbell's canned soups. I had long forgotten our conversation when about six months later the Danish captain of a tramp steamer that put into Buenos Aires phoned me, requesting that I pick up a consignment from the docked ship for which "special" arrangements had been made. The mysterious consignment turned out to be three cases of contraband Campbell's soup my FBI friend had arranged to smuggle to me, and the Danish skipper explained how to bypass the wharfside customs shed. The pepper-pot soup tasted particularly wonderful.

As the new *Times* correspondent I was welcomed to Argentina with some slightly embarrassing fanfare. The weekly scandal-and-photos magazine *Gente* interviewed me, the Círculo Italiano (headquarters of the city's press club) issued me a membership card and the *ministro de gobierno*, Guillermo Borda, invited me to dinner.

The minister of government in a Latin American country is the chief of police, top spy, immigration chief and lord high executioner, something like a KGB boss under the old Soviet system. Naturally, I expected a grilling at Borda's home, especially since my wife had not been invited—a clear signal that the meeting was not to be entirely social.

But as it turned out, Mr. Borda himself did most of the talking, and his remarks went something like this:

"Argentina is the most advanced, educated and progressive nation in Latin America, for a simple reason: racial purity. In most South American countries there is a great deal of Indian blood. Brazil is populated largely by blacks. But we Argentines are white Europeans. That will help you to understand our country in the Latin American context."

The minister certainly knew that I represented a newspaper that viewed racism as abhorrent, and that I myself had a non-European wife. His remarks were deliberately provocative, intended to see how I would react.

Momentarily stunned, I assumed as frigid a demeanor as I could manage without being abusive. The reader should bear in mind that I had just arrived at a new post, and that my employer had invested a considerable amount of money in preparing me for the assignment. One learns to tread carefully in dictatorships, saving one's heavy artillery for occasions so important as to warrant the risk of expulsion or some other serious consequence. But I didn't forget Borda and the other racist ministers in a succession of quasi-fascist governments.

One of the things foreign journalists do well to avoid in places like Argentina and Uruguay is dueling, unless, of course, a reporter happens to be skilled with a sword or pistol. I discovered early that political squabbles, even some involving journalists, often end in nonfatal duels. During my tenure in South America, dueling was not only countenanced (especially when military officers were insulted), but was strictly regulated and refereed by experts at the jockey and military clubs of Buenos Aires and Montevideo.

It was about the time I got to South America that a celebrated duel brought unexpected glory to the name of journalism. In 1968, Yoliván Alberto Biglieri, owner of the periodical *Autonomía,* called Vice Admiral Benigno Varela, former commander of the Argentine Navy, a traitor. In the United States, a military officer would probably bring a libel suit under such circumstances, but in Argentina the traditional and expected response is the challenge to a duel.

When Varela sent his second around to the journalist, the Buenos Aires press corps was delighted but apprehensive for our colleague, who was fat, middle-aged and apparently outmatched by his lean, active opponent.

It must be explained that modern South American duels are fought with one of three stipulated weapons. The first and most popular is the dueling pistol, which is so wildly inaccurate it rarely even nicks anyone. The second is the épée, somewhat more dangerous than the pistol and therefore more honorable. The third is the saber, which can really cut and maim, and is therefore the most honorable (but least popular) weapon.

Our journalist colleague, to everyone's surprise, picked sabers. What few people knew at the time was that he had been a university fencing champion, and that he regularly worked out, using double-weight practice sabers, which had endowed his wrists and forearms with tremendous strength and suppleness.

When Biglieri met Varela in a secret place (secret, that is, from all but about thirty newspaper photographers), the journalist took less than two minutes to slice the admiral's ear and cut two slashes across his chest. The vanquished duelist stated in late editions of the city's newspapers that if only his opponent were as good a journalist as he was a swordsman, he would be a great man.

Dueling is one of many customs that make South America seem to an outsider as rather antiquated, much closer in tradition to Queen Isabella's Spain than to a modern country governed under the "Firmament of Law." Many South Americans live in the past and deeply resent change, and woe betide the journalist who fails to study and respect Latin American traditions.

Tradition includes even music, and the breaker of musical tradition faces retribution. One of the musical names that carry special weight in Argentina is that of Carlos Gardel, the celebrated Uruguayan tango singer and movie star, who was killed in a plane crash in 1935. Although he is long gone, his music is still heard everywhere in Argentina and Uruguay. Gardel is tradition.

But Gardel and the traditional tango faced a challenge. When the brilliant Argentine cabaret musician Astor Piazzola returned to his native land in the 1960s after many years in the United States, he brought with him a new kind of music, "modern tango." A few young Argentines were enchanted by it, but a lot of other Argentines so resented modern tango that Piazzola was flooded with death threats, which in Argentina must be taken very seriously. Callers told Piazzola that he had destroyed a tradition—and never mind that the tango was created in Buenos Aires' old brothels. By 1992, when Piazzola died, his music had finally become accepted in Argentina, but only long after Europeans and Americans had come to love it.

A more sinister nostalgia in the "Southern Cone" of South America was for Nazism, fascism and the right-wing populism of the 1930s, when the region (or at least its wealthy landowners) was far more prosperous than it is today. In the 1970s, three decades after the end of World War II, souvenir shops in Montevideo still sold picture postcards of the Nazi battleship *Graf Spee,* the sinking of which in 1939 was a high point of World War II for South America. As it turned out, the *Graf Spee* also figured in one of my own news projects.

There had been rumors and reports ever since the close of World War II that Nazi war criminals were living in South America, especially in Argentina, but I never realized until I arrived there how pervasive the Nazi ideology was, or how ubiquitous were the shadowy Germans clustered in scores of communities like Olivos, a suburb of Buenos Aires. Most of the Germans, of course, were perfectly respectable, politically innocuous Argentine citizens. But some were real war criminals.

The best-known Nazi in Argentina was Adolf Eichmann, head of SS extermination operations, who was found and spirited out of the country in 1960 by agents of Israel's Mossad. Eichmann was tried and hanged in Jerusalem two years later, but lots of other Nazis remained safely tucked away in South America.

One was Walter Rauff, a gentleman *estanciero* living in southern Chile, who in 1940 had been issued an SS patent for a device he invented that ducted engine exhaust into the back of a prison van, so that Jewish prisoners could be delivered directly to cemeteries. South American journalists occasionally visited Rauff in his pleasant Chilean sanctuary, and I remember one article that quoted him as saying (in English), "I'm working like a nigger."

Shocking though Latin America's tolerance of war criminals seemed to Americans, I had an acquaintance in the Mossad who told me that Israel cared little about the Nazi small fry. The Israelis merely wanted to nail one or two of the worst criminals as symbols of the Holocaust, he said. High on the list was Josef Mengele, the medical officer at Auschwitz concentration camp, whose abominable experiments on the inmates were among the most infamous of Nazi atrocities. It seemed to me that the Mossad's hunt for Mengele had the makings of an interesting news story.

But a journalist trying to investigate Nazi-hunting activities found himself obstructed at almost every turn. The German community itself was highly protective of its members and maintained the lowest possible profile. The Nazis also had a fair amount of official help; the Buenos Aires government of General Juan Carlos Ongania, for instance, was a right-wing military establishment that intensely disliked foreign probing, including any involving the local Nazis.

In Paraguay, General Alfredo Stroessner, the grandson of German immigrants, ruled as an absolute dictator, ruthlessly crushing anything that looked to him like a threat, and he never counted Simon Wiesenthal or any other Nazi-hunter as his friend.

To visitors, Stroessner seemed as jolly as a Bavarian innkeeper, until one listened to his outrageous perspectives on government. When I interviewed him on the eve of one of his totally rigged elections, he told me without embarrassment what the exact outcome of the election would be, predicting right to a percentage point his Colorado Party's victory margin. (He was right on the nose, of course.) Despite the blatant disregard of democratic norms he evinced in an interview Stroessner granted David Belnap of the *Los Angeles Times* and me, he seemed more naively brutal than cunningly evil. Of course, that didn't help his victims.

I knew some former students who regarded Stroessner as a sadistic war criminal. They explained why the walls of Asunción, unlike those of other Latin American capitals, were absolutely free of graffiti. "When anti-Stroessner slogans were painted on walls," one told me, "Stroessner's police would go into neighborhoods where dissident students lived and round a bunch of us up. They would take us to the walls and beat us, forcing us to scrape off the paint with our fingernails."

The governments of Brazil, Argentina, Paraguay and Bolivia generally left the vast Chaco wilderness alone, and plantations the size of European countries flourished in the region, sometimes providing sanctuary to German war criminals. I visited one plantation in the Paraguayan jungle that could be reached only by a long river voyage or by light airplane, there being no roads to the place. The plantation, which harvested the bark of giant quebracho trees for tannin, had its own internal railroad extending 100 miles or so to the Bolivian frontier, all within the company's private property.

After we landed at the plantation airstrip, my chartered plane was surrounded by very hostile armed guards who took me to their headquarters building for questioning. The authorities there examined my press credentials and asked suspiciously why I was so interested in quebracho agriculture, but in the end, they invited me to lunch.

The lunch was one of those leisurely *al fresco* South American banquets with lots of steak, Paraguayan cornbread, palm hearts and wine, and the diners were quite a select group, including the regional province chief, the police chief, the local army commander, a dozen plantation executives, and about twenty foreign engineers and advisers. As we chatted, I noticed that the foreigners spoke heavily accented Spanish, so I tried asking one of them a question in German. He happily replied, and soon several others joined the conversation.

But one of the engineers, seemingly a man in authority, abruptly brought the chatter to a halt, ordering quiet while he asked me why I was speaking German and what I was really doing at the plantation. My answer failed to satisfy him, and he barked a few words that brought all the Germans to their feet. As the leader marched them away from the table, he shot back at me, *"Verdammter jüdischer Spion!"* (Damned Jewish spy!).

In the 1960s and 1970s right-wing terrorists seemed to be everywhere. At Recife, Brazil, a gang of storm troopers caused an uproar by murdering a local priest they regarded as a leftist. The courageous Archbishop of Recife, Dom Helder Câmara, reacted by stepping up his denunciations of "gorillas"—military dictators who tolerate and encourage such excesses. But the assassinations and disappearances continued.

In Buenos Aires, a large Jewish community lived in terror. Merchants were murdered in their homes, businesses were burned down, and even an Israeli trade fair was put to the torch. Journalists themselves, particularly those who regularly reported state-sanctioned terror, were sometimes targets. Buenos Aires terrorists, probably the neo-Nazi Tacuaras, bracketed my AP colleague Lou Uchitelle (who now works for *The New York Times*) and myself with a single bomb. *The New York Times* office in the Edificio la Nación on Corrientes Street was one floor below that of the Associated Press, and the terrorists hit both of us with a bomb placed on the landing midway between our offices. It blew out glass doors but didn't hurt anyone.

Regrettably, some of my problems came from the Jewish community itself. Whenever one of my *Times* articles reported some new anti-Semitic outrage, many Jewish community leaders would react with angry letters and telephone calls to my editors in New York, charging that by calling attention to anti-Semitic violence in Argentina I was likely to provoke terrorist reprisals against Buenos Aires Jews. I never thought silence would help, myself. Only by labeling terrorism for what it is can one begin combating it.

South American Nazis were motivated by somewhat different cultural and economic backgrounds than were most of their German role models. Unlike German Nazism, which was rooted in an alienated middle class, South American Nazism bloomed amid the oligarchy, the wealthy and powerful old families that trace their ancestries to mother Spain. Curiously, it is the well-educated children of these select families who turn as often to left-wing, Cuban-style revolution as they do to Nazism.

A bit of history that I found instructive highlights this anomaly.

In Santiago next to La Moneda, Chile's presidential palace, stands a tall building that to this day is adorned with a monument to Nazism. Today the building houses the Justice Ministry, but in 1938, when it was the Ministry of Social Welfare, the building was the scene of a bloody drama that left wounds felt even now.

Inspired by Hitler's demand for a New Order, a gang of mostly rich young men had formed a Chilean Nazi Party, and had persuaded several army leaders to join them in a putsch against the elected government of President Jorge Alessandri. Veterans of the 1938 episode have told me that communications between the rebel army units and the Nazis were the responsibility of an American Nazi sympathizer who headed the local Ford motor car concession.

On the morning of the putsch, the Nazis took to the streets, shot a protesting cop and headed for the presidential palace, but for some reason, perhaps poor communications or a change of heart, the army failed to move. The *carabineros* (national police) regrouped, counterattacked, and herded more than thirty of the storm troopers, most of them college students, into the Social Welfare Building.

After some hours, the *carabineros* sent word to President Alessandri that the police needed guidance as to what to do about the young Nazis, and the ambiguous reply is supposed to have been something like "Get rid of them." The *carabineros* stormed in and slaughtered the whole group, many with blows of fire axes.

Chile's upper class was horrified by the massacre, in which some of the most socially prominent youths in the country had been slain. After the funeral ceremonies a large plaque cast in bronze was mounted on the corner of the Social Welfare Building, bearing the names of all the dead and commemorating the supposed dying words of one of the Nazis: "Don't worry, comrades, our blood will save the nation." The plaque is still there.

Infuriated by the actions of the *carabineros,* the Chilean public blamed the conservative President Alessandri and, in the kind of ironic twist that often shapes Latin American politics, elected a left-wing president.

The 1938 Santiago massacre seems trivial today, in comparison with the slaughter of leftist students by General Augusto Pinochet's dictatorship during the 1970s. Both Chile and Argentina have become textbook laboratories for forensic anthropologists whose specialty is digging up mass graves. These brave scientists, often threatened with death while they work, are looking for clues not only to the identities and manner of death of the victims, but to the identities of the state-sanctioned murderers responsible. Sadly, forensic anthropology is one of the few sciences that seem to be flourishing these days, as pogroms proliferate like cancer in many corners of the world.

At any rate, I thought I should do some investigative reporting of both the aging German Nazis and their younger Latin American admirers, who were exerting some strong political influences on the events of the day. Both Nazi groups regarded the veterans of the *Graf Spee* battleship as heroes, so I decided to start with them.

Florida Street is the main shopping and tourist street in Buenos Aires, and in the summer months of December and January the street is packed with strollers window-shopping the boutiques, antique shops, handicraft emporia, gaucho dagger-and-pistol stores and so forth. Recorded tango music issues from many of the shops, and the air fills with the savory fragrance of *asado* grills as street workmen prepare heavy meat lunches over glowing charcoal.

One of the restaurants in the neighborhood, the ABC, was run mostly by German immigrants, and I began my search there. No, a waiter told me, the staff at the ABC were mostly veterans of the Waffen SS; the *Graf Spee* sailors could be found at another popular restaurant. I inquired there, and after a few days gained an invitation to interview Friedrich Wilhelm Rasenack, a retired commander in the German Navy and the highest-ranking survivor of the *Graf Spee*.

To persuade Rasenack to meet me I used a ploy I have often found helpful: I asked for information needed to pursue my hobby. I have several hobbies, but the one I invoked in this case was model building. I used to build models of historic warplanes and naval ships, and when I needed information about color schemes and camouflage, I would often go directly to the people who had flown the planes or manned the ships. For Rasenack's benefit, I bought a plastic model kit of the *Graf Spee*, and went to him ostensibly to get information about the ship's markings.

He lived in Olivos, an hour's trip from downtown Buenos Aires, and he worked for the Orbis Mertig Company, a German-Argentine manufacturer of gas heaters. The company had helped to evacuate the *Graf Spee*'s crew from Montevideo, and was later active in assisting Nazi refugees escape from Europe to Argentina.

Commander Rasenack himself had had an adventurous life. Serving as chief gunnery officer aboard the *Graf Spee*, he had been aboard the "pocket battleship" during its fateful 1939 encounter with three British cruisers in the South Atlantic off the Argentine coast.

The mighty German ship mauled its attackers almost to destruction, but was damaged enough in the fight that her skipper, Captain Hans Langsdorff, decided to put into Montevideo, the capital of neutral (but unfriendly) Uruguay, for repairs. That began a diplomatic battle between the British and German embassies, the British at first demanding that the Uruguayans expel the *Graf Spee,* the Germans insisting that the ship be permitted to remain in dock long enough to make repairs. Then the tables were turned, with the British asking for a delay in the Uruguayan sailing permit to allow the Royal Navy time to muster more warships just beyond Uruguay's three-mile limit.

In the end, Captain Langsdorff decided that he was impossibly outmatched, so he set sail, with tens of thousands of spectators and newscasters watching from the windows and roofs of the Salvo Palace Hotel and other downtown buildings. The *Graf Spee* slowly moved a few hundred yards offshore and then blew up, erupting in flame and sinking to its deck in shallow water. Rather than risk the lives of his men in battle with a waiting British flotilla, Langsdorff had scuttled his ship in such a way that it could never be used against Germany.

A tugboat provided by businesses working for the German legation in Buenos Aires was waiting, and it rescued the entire *Graf Spee* crew, taking the men to neutral (but friendly) Argentina.

The pro-Nazi Buenos Aires newspapers pilloried Langsdorff as a coward, and after he had smarted for a few days under their barbs (and from some more sinister remarks from Hitler), the German captain shot himself, instantly regaining stature among Argentines as a brave commander. Langsdorff was buried in Buenos Aires' German cemetery under a handsome swastika-emblazoned tombstone (although he had not been a member of the Nazi Party), and his grave became a shrine for Argentina's Nazis. During my tenure in South America, Tacuara toughs wearing swastika armbands were still parading to Langsdorff's grave every year on the anniversary of his death.

Rasenack was interned in Argentina, but internship meant living pleasantly on farms, with no restrictions against traveling around the country. Eventually, the local Bund organization smuggled Rasenack across the Andes into Chile, where German agents gave him a Bulgarian passport, money and papers identifying him as a wine merchant. From Chile he traveled to Panama, where he discovered that the FBI, agents of neutral America, were helping the British government hunt down German escapees from Argentine internment camps.

Rasenack needed a pass and transportation to get to the Pacific end of the Panama Canal, where a ship was scheduled to leave for Yokohama, so with his usual gall, he went to the FBI for help. The Feds, he told me, obligingly escorted him (in his guise of Bulgarian wine merchant) to the ship.

In Japan Rasenack acquired a camera and took a ferry to Vladivostok, where he boarded the Trans-Siberian Railroad to Europe. Passing through European Russia (still an ally of the Germans at that time) and through Soviet-occupied Poland, he photographed every military installation and tank depot he passed, photographs that served the Nazis well in their subsequent invasion of the USSR.

Secretly hailed by the navy and the Abwehr intelligence organization as a hero, Rasenack seemed destined for a successful career, but bad luck dogged him. As a senior officer of the heavy cruiser *Tirpitz*, Rasenack was on the ship at Tromsö, Denmark, when British bombers attacked and destroyed it. He spent the rest of the war on the staff of Admiral Karl Dönitz (who succeeded Hitler after the latter's suicide), and then he emigrated to Argentina, along with about half of the *Graf Spee*'s original 1,100-man crew.

Through Rasenack I eventually established contact with other German émigrés, and at one point in my research, I believe I was only about one week behind Mengele himself. But Mengele moved fast and often, and I had a lot of stories to cover besides Nazis—coups, guerrilla campaigns, earthquakes and all the other things that keep correspondents hopping. Much of my work at the time centered on anti-American riots, as well as the nationalization of American businesses like the sugar plantations and oil-field concessions in Peru. Americans were kidnapped or murdered, too; but even today, very few Americans realize the depth of anti-American enmity that festers south of the Rio Grande.

My Nazi hunting came to nothing, but in 1979, long after I had left the region, some bones were dug up in Brazil that were subsequently identified as those of Mengele. The crafty old Nazi had avoided his pursuers throughout his life, and had finally succumbed to a drowning accident. Although some doubts were voiced that the bones were really those of the "Angel of Death," the forensic evidence was overwhelming and I, at least, was convinced.

The ghost of Nazism in Europe, which many believed had been laid forever, has reappeared. Moreover, it has reached out from Germany into Eastern Europe and even the former Soviet Union. I'm afraid that echoes of the "Horst Wessel Song" also linger in Latin America.

SOUTH AMERICA

WHETHER OF THE FAR right or the far left, Latin American guerrillas have always been a source of news. Today the most famous of them may be the terrorists of Peru's "Shining Path," but guerrilla groups in South America are all much the same in their methods and ideology of violence. Few, however, have had the glamour of the Bolivian group headed by the Argentine doctor and revolutionary Ernesto "Che" Guevara. ("Che," an Argentine slang word meaning something like "Mack" or "Hey, you," is used by many Latin Americans as a somewhat pejorative colloquialism meaning "an Argentine.")

In a way, Guevara was the reason I went to Latin America. *The New York Times* hired me during the year Guevara's Bolivian adventure was in full swing, and when my editors sent me to South America, it was largely because they thought I knew something about guerrilla warfare. Mind you, guerrillas in South America were never anything like those of Indochina; the latter were pros, whereas Latin American guerrillas are mostly romantic, intellectual, brutal, inefficient amateurs who almost invariably fail. (The Cubans were exceptions, of course, bringing to power the longest-lived communist presidency in the world.)

I'd met "El Che" a few times in Havana when he was

Castro's minister of finance, and he had seemed to me less pretentious and given to posturing than the other Cuban leaders. I could understand why this modest but highly educated, dedicated revolutionary had proved so attractive a leader to earnest young revolutionaries in several countries. Certainly, the Guevara legend glowed brightly for a long time after his death, inspiring the Montonero guerrillas in Argentina, the Miristas in Chile, the Tupamaros in Uruguay, the followers of the martyred Colombian guerrilla-priest Camilo Torres, and many more; walls throughout Latin America were plastered with posters displaying Che's beret-capped face.

In October 1967, Bolivian troops under the command of President René Barrientos Ortuño (with a lot of help from the CIA) cornered Che and his closest lieutenants near Santa Cruz in southeast Bolivia, and executed most of them on the spot. Che's hands were cut off and brought out of the jungle for fingerprinting and identification, and those hands were later to figure in my own adventures.

Guevara's guerrilla archivist, the French leftist Régis Debray, had been captured shortly before Guevara himself was killed, and Debray was imprisoned at a military jail in the jungle town of Camiri, initially under sentence of death. The son of an aristocratic French family, Debray enjoyed an enormous international reputation at the time as one of the world's leading revolutionary intellectuals, and his primer, *Revolution in the Revolution*, was as much in vogue in the Left Bank cafés of Paris as it was in the student hangouts of La Paz, Santiago and Buenos Aires. I applied to the Bolivian military authorities for a permit to interview Debray, and after a long delay, it was granted.

Camiri is a scruffy little village which in 1968 was studded with army checkpoints, barricades and other evidence that the government still took the guerrillas seriously, despite the recent death of their leader. When my wife and I arrived at the prison barracks, we were subjected to a two-hour grilling by a very hostile major, which included many irksome questions about our religion (we have none), political sympathies and so forth. At last, warned to speak only Spanish and not French, we were allowed into Debray's cell, which contained a desk, a shelf with some books and other amenities. Despite the fact that Debray expected to have to face a firing squad, his wealthy family had been permitted to provide him with a few luxuries.

The young prisoner was just as hostile as his jailers toward me. He spent most of my limited time berating *The New York Times* as the cat's-paw of the CIA, and he repeatedly demanded assurances that I was not using a hidden microphone to trap him in some way; he clearly believed that I was in league with his captors. I knew, of course, that he had reason to be suspicious of everyone. His guards had done all they could to trick him into various confessions and to demoralize him. Early in his captivity, Debray had been awakened in the middle of the night to look at the bloody corpse of his friend Tania, a young woman who had been one of Guevara's lieutenants until she was captured.

Debray had little to say about the nuts and bolts of guerrilla warfare, but plenty to say about the supposed evils of U.S. imperialism. I remember nothing original in his cant, and I came away with the impression that Debray really knew very little about the practical aspects of guerrilla warfare.

I went to Camiri expecting to see a fiery latter-day Trotsky, or at least a French version of John Reed. But instead I found a whining, quixotic youth who seemed more likely to be remembered (if at all) as a misguided martyr than as a revolutionary hero.

Debray was eventually released and expelled from Bolivia. But as time went on, I began to see the entire Castroite revolutionary movement in Latin America (which at one time sent shivers up the spines of State Department officials) as little more than a projection of Régis Debray himself, a blend of half-baked political ideas, romantic military posturing and an impetus toward martyrdom rather than success.

To me, the guerrilla partisans of violent revolution in Latin America seemed to picture themselves mainly as the subjects of song, story and legend. In this, they differed fundamentally from the Viet Cong, whose object was to win.

CIA operations in Latin America during the 1960s and 1970s were amazingly widespread and audacious, subverting governments and political movements in most countries in the region. Americans occasionally paid a heavy price. In Montevideo an acquaintance of mine, Dan Mitrione, was kidnapped by the Tupamaros, ultra-leftist guerrillas who had acquired a reputation as Robin Hoods because of their frequent bank robberies and occasional gifts to impoverished Uruguayans. Mitrione, chief of the public safety division of the US AID mission in Montevideo, was a genial retired cop who went to Uruguay as an adviser to the Uruguayan police in their struggle against the guerrillas.

After seizing Mitrione the Tupamaros demanded broadcast time on national radio and various other concessions as conditions for his release, but the hard-line president, Jorge Pacheco Areco, refused. As we journalists waited and Mitrione's family prayed, few of us believed the guerrillas would carry out their threat, but when the deadline passed the Tupamaros shot Mitrione and left his body in an abandoned car. That kind of thing appalls most Uruguayans, and the Tupamaros, with that slaying, lost most of their popular support.

In Bolivia, CIA operations were publicized dramatically by a stocky little double agent named Antonio Arguedas Mendietta, President Barrientos's minister of government and top cop. Arguedas's name made headlines in July 1968, when he left Bolivia, announcing that he had been working for the CIA for years, and that he intended to return to the true cause, revolutionary Castroite communism. Already, he said, he had thwarted the La Paz government and the CIA by smuggling a copy of Che Guevara's battle diary to Cuba, which had published its interesting contents. Arguedas then disappeared.

Arguedas was making waves that had considerable impact in the United States as well as Latin America. In the United States the Viet Nam debate was in full cry, and many Americans were ready to believe the worst of Washington's clandestine operations in other parts of the world. Arguedas was saying that the CIA had, in effect, taken over the Bolivian government and was trying to export an American counterrevolution throughout Latin America.

The Times asked me to try to find Arguedas and get some account of who he really was and what he was up to. After some digging, I learned that he had gone to ground somewhere in Lima.

In the Peruvian capital, Arguedas always seemed a couple of steps ahead of me as he moved daily from one hotel or rooming house to another, but I finally found him in an apartment owned by one of his intelligence colleagues. When he threw open the door, he looked at me with a resigned expression and asked (in Spanish), "Well, you found me. Do you plan to kill me?"

It took me a while, but I persuaded him that I was merely a journalist interested in his story, and he finally recounted his odyssey. How much of it was true I have no idea, but at least some of the details matched Arguedas's public record.

Early in his life, he said, he had become a communist sympathizer and had remained close to the party until the early 1960s, when he joined the Bolivian Air Force. It was there that he met Barrientos, who gave him a high post in government after Barrientos seized power in his 1964 coup. But the following year, Arguedas said, he was approached by CIA officials, who told him they knew he was a communist agent, and that unless he resigned his post as minister of government, all United States aid to Bolivia would be cut off.

He did resign, but later was told by the CIA that he could be reinstated and would be granted other emoluments if he would cooperate with the agency. Arguedas said he agreed to this condition. After that, he said, he was subjected to a series of interrogations in CIA safe houses in Peru, England and the United States, and having passed these tests, he was patted on the head by his CIA spy masters, who gave him money and some expensive gifts. He then returned to La Paz, where he was reinstated as minister of government, but was actually working as an agent of the CIA. That, at least, was his story.

Arguedas had been involved in the jungle operations against Che Guevara's guerrillas and had witnessed Che's capture, execution and mutilation. Arguedas was so disgusted by the treatment meted out to Che, he contended, that he decided to switch sides again and abandon his ties to Barrientos and the CIA.

At that point the CIA evidently suspected that Arguedas was about to rejoin his former communist allies, and so decided to remove Arguedas from Bolivia. The month before I tracked him down in Lima, Arguedas told me, the CIA had sent him an urgent message saying that for his own safety he must leave Bolivia, because a crisis had arisen. Arguedas, no stranger to intrigue, was ready to believe he was in trouble, and he jumped into a jeep and drove to the Chilean border.

But once inside Chile, he discovered that the CIA had tricked him into playing the part of a defector, which, he said, he was not. Believing that CIA men would use his alleged defection as a pretext to hunt him down and kill him, Arguedas next fled to Peru and went to ground.

By the time I found him, he told me, he was sick of running.

"I'll tell you what," he said. "I've decided to go back to La Paz tomorrow to tell my story to the world. Since you are probably a CIA agent yourself, I'm going to take you along, and if they kill me, they'll have to kill you too."

He was as good as his word. At the Lima airport some of Arguedas's friends (whoever they may have been) surrounded me and made sure that I remained at his side as we waited for our Braniff flight.

As we waited in the terminal we noticed a man on the balcony just above us with a parcel in his hand and his eyes fixed on Arguedas. At the moment he saw we had spotted him he tossed the package at us and yelled, "Here's a bomb, Arguedas, see how you like it!"

We scurried for cover. The Peruvian police evacuated the terminal building, arrested the supposed terrorist and checked his package, which proved to contain only a roasted chicken. Three hours late, we finally boarded our 707, in which the flight crew had reserved a large, empty section for just Arguedas and me. Arguedas took a window seat and insisted on my sitting right next to him. "You can take the bullet first, if it comes from the aisle," he said with a grin.

During the flight, Arguedas recited the names of all his alleged CIA controllers, with dates and places he had met them and other details of his history as a double agent. He also told me, "I've sent Che's diary to Cuba. And you know what else? I have Che's hands with me, preserved in salt!"

Arguedas's stories may have been mostly cock and bull, or they may have been intended as malicious provocations. Like so many of the other screwball shenanigans that passed for intelligence operations in Latin America in the 1960s and 1970s, Arguedas and his outrageous stories often seemed more like parodies than serious business.

At the same time, some of his confessions certainly rang

true. In 1970, after Arguedas fled from Bolivia a second time and reached sanctuary in Cuba, Castro gave a speech in which he mentioned the gruesome trophy of Che Guevara's severed hands. "Compañero Arguedas has brought us two treasures," Castro told a Havana crowd. "He has brought us Che's diary and Che's own hands. Should we build a mausoleum for the hands?" The crowd roared "*Sí!*"

Bolivia's troubles never end. Today the chief source of violence in that country is the struggle between impoverished Aymara coca farmers and the U.S. Drug Enforcement Agency; America's junkie population on the one hand and the anti-sin zealots who keep passing unenforceable drug laws on the other ensure that the Indians of the Altiplano remain pinned in the cross fire.

Despite all, though, Bolivia is a beautiful and fascinating never-never land, and La Paz was my favorite of all Latin American capitals during the time I was based in the region.

Lima, the city where I found Arguedas, also has some beauty points, particularly when the wind is not blowing from the direction of the fish-meal factories of Callao. It has wide, tree-lined boulevards, a beautiful colonial-era palace and a handsome cathedral (San Francisco) with catacombs where human bones are arranged in ornate arabesques and designs. A couple of decades ago Lima was also popular with the international cloak-and-dagger set, one of whose activists promised to kill me.

It happened in 1970, a year in which I spent a lot of time covering the presidential election campaign in Chile, which Washington feared would bring to power the first freely elected communist government in the world.

The candidates were Radomiro Tomic, the centrist Christian Democrat; Jorge Alessandri, the right-winger; and Salvador Allende Gossens, who represented the Castroite Chilean Socialist Party, plus a coalition of Moscow-line communists and some minor left-wing parties.

American officials were scared to death because there was every indication that Allende had enough popular support to carry the day and take over one of the most advanced nations in Latin America. Chile has some of the largest copper deposits in the world, but more important, the election of Allende would deliver a staggering blow to American efforts to stem what was perceived as the red tide in Latin America.

So the CIA went to work. It was only a decade later that the incredible extent of America's meddling in Chile was revealed by Congressional hearings, journalistic investigations and during the trials of some of the perpetrators.

Clandestine American operations in Chile were not new. In 1964 the Johnson administration had poured more than $20 million into the election of Washington's man, Eduardo Frei Montalva. It was natural that in 1970, the State Department and CIA should go all out to get Frei's Christian Democrat successor, Radomiro Tomic, elected.

With money and many other resources it brought to bear, Washington subverted several Catholic clergymen, journalists, American corporations, and scores of Chilean politicians, many of whom acted as conduits for CIA influence.

In the end, Washington failed to get Tomic elected, but America's spooks did manage to lay the groundwork for a military putsch that raised the curtain on the bloodiest epoch in Chile's history. Forensic experts are still finding and identifying the corpses of General Augusto Pinochet's holocaust, an atrocity for which Presidents Kennedy, Johnson and Nixon bear some indirect responsibility, in my opinion.

I didn't know all this in 1970, but I did get a nasty taste of things to come.

Three American former journalists were players in the CIA's campaign to defeat Allende at the polls and, subsequently, to destroy his elected government. I have always felt sorry that they allowed themselves to be suckered into such a game; besides the damage they did, they paid a terrible price themselves. All three were decent men.

One was Edward Malcolm Korry, a former UPI newsman who became U.S. ambassador to Chile during a crucial period of that country's history.

Another was Hal Hendrix, whose 1962 reports to *The Miami News* on the arrival of Soviet missiles in Cuba won him the 1963 Pulitzer Prize for International Reporting. Soon after his award, Hendrix went to work for the International Telephone & Telegraph Company (ITT) as its public relations chief, an unusual job for a man whose vocal cords were so impaired that he always had to speak in a whisper. Hendrix, a popular member of the Buenos Aires press corps, enlisted another veteran Latin America hand, Bob Berellez of the Associated Press, as an ITT recruit.

The Senate Select Committee on Intelligence and other organizations later proved that ITT had acted as an arm of the CIA in Chile, funneling vast funds into the coffers of cooperative politicians like Frei, while doing everything possible to undermine the Christian Democrats' leftist opponents. Hendrix and Berellez were up to their ears in this skulduggery. In 1973, former CIA Director Richard Helms and Hendrix were both convicted of perjury for concealing the roles they had played in trying to keep Allende out of power, while similar charges against Bob Berellez were dropped on grounds that prosecution would have damaged national security interests.

Korry, intensely critical of practically everything I reported from Chile, was no friend to me, but he always seemed forthright and honest. Hendrix and Berellez had been my colleagues and friends, and I could not understand how men molded by the strict rules of responsible journalism could have gone so far astray.

In the course of the campaign I got to know all of Chile's

leading politicians, who were as colorful, cantankerous, interesting and ultimately tragic a bunch as any I've ever encountered.

There was President Frei himself, a friendly man who rarely traveled with bodyguards—one whom a journalist could approach and chat with in the Santiago restaurants he frequented.

There was Gabriel Valdez, Frei's bullying deputy and foreign minister, who eventually threw me out of Chile. And there was Radomiro Tomic, the presidential candidate and Frei's former ambassador to Washington, who used to write letters to the editor of *The New York Times* denouncing me and all my works. I tried to avoid clashes and ill will in dealing with the Christian Democrats, but somehow we never became friendly. One reason may have been my reports of the rapid strides the Marxists were making in an increasingly impoverished country where the unemployment rate rose to about 20 percent in 1970. I also sometimes mentioned the help and support the Christian Democrat Party was getting from Washington, the kind of public association Latin American politicians shun at all costs.

Another group was the conservative and wealthy National Party, headed by its presidential candidate, Jorge Alessandri. The Nacionales, most of them old men, hung out at the Club de la Unión, an imposing downtown building adorned with marble nymphs, pastoral murals and a half acre of overstuffed chairs enveloped in cigar smoke. The Partido Nacional often invited me to the Unión to lunch on conger eels and sea urchins, but I accepted only once. The members wanted me to know they would fight against creeping socialism and all assaults on traditional values.

Then there were the Marxists, most of whom were much more interesting than their opponents. Allende, a medical doctor with the gift of gab, wore black horn-rim glasses and a leather biker's jacket while preaching the gospel of violent revolution.

But he was an intelligent, kindly man who listened to Mozart at home and practiced Freemasonry. I rather liked him, and he apparently thought well enough of me to invite me back to Chile right after he was elected president, voiding the ban the Christian Democrats had issued against me.

One of Allende's top lieutenants was Augusto Olivares, a former communist who had been expelled from the party and had joined the Castroite socialists. Olivares edited the weekly *Punto Final,* which, despite its blatant Marxist bias, often broke important political stories no other Chilean publication uncovered or dared to touch. On its masthead were such famous names as Jean-Paul Sartre and Stokely Carmichael.

I sometimes dined with Olivares and his cronies at a Chinese restaurant called Danubio Azul (Blue Danube) to keep abreast of things, and those dinners always sparkled with good conversation. Olivares himself never seemed consistent in his views of the world; for one thing, he constantly denounced United States imperialism, yet he also openly admired much that was American. When the University of Chile needed a Spanish-language commentator for its live broadcast of the *Apollo 11* moon landing, Olivares was picked for the job, and his informative broadcasts glowed with praise for America's space technology.

Both Allende and Olivares were killed, supposedly at their own hands, during Pinochet's 1973 coup. I was covering the war in Cambodia at the time, and when I heard of their deaths I felt a pang of real regret.

In that stormy summer of 1970 the Chilean Communist Party was also struggling for power, under the dour and fleshless leadership of Volodia Teitelboim. The communists wanted no part of violent revolution, regarding Castroite Cuba and the Chilean Socialist Party as troublemakers likely to damage the cause of Marxism-Leninism more than help it. But to stand any chance of participating in a leftist coalition government, the communists knew they had to go along with Allende, and they reluctantly did so.

If the communists in general were colorless, their greatest publicist, Pablo Neruda, was anything but. Neruda, who was awarded the Nobel Prize for Literature in 1971, was one of the greatest modern poets in the Spanish language, and one of the most insistently sensuous writers I ever read. All his poetic reflections and political ideas seemed to be ordered around his ravenous senses, which he fed with every kind of experience he could imagine.

Neruda was also a pillar of the Red Decade, the 1930s, which he never outgrew. As Chile's consul general in Madrid during the Spanish Civil War he immediately sided with the Loyalists against the fascist Falangistas (in defiance of orders from Santiago's foreign ministry), and when Spain fell to Franco in 1939, Neruda personally arranged the evacuation of hundreds of leftist refugees to Chile. The Spanish refugees formed a club under Neruda's protection, the Club of the Spanish Republic, and in 1970 aging veterans of the 1937–39 Civil War were still dining there, playing dominoes and swapping war stories, to which I sometimes listened. The club and its members are all gone now, of course.

Despite his powerful intellect, Neruda never lost his rather childish infatuation with Marxism-Leninism, although his unorthodox interpretations of communist ideology often embarrassed the party.

I visited Neruda's Isla Negra home one time, in the company of Georgie Anne Geyer of the (now defunct) *Chicago Daily News*. Miss Geyer, by the way, is one of the most sensitive and intelligent American writers who have covered Latin America.

Neruda's sprawling estate included a lawn on which he exhibited a large steam locomotive, one of his many eccentric toys. The interior of his house unsettlingly suggested the cubist surrealism of a Picasso sculpture; the high ceiling of his living room arched upward like the vaulting of a cathedral, but many of its angles were askew and dizzyingly asymmetrical. A huge picture window looked out over a rocky cliff, against which mountainous waves of the Pacific Ocean beat, spraying the window from time to time. Mounted on walls and plinths all over the house were dozens of painted wood figureheads from sailing ships that had been wrecked along the Isla Negra coast over the centuries, and Neruda relished the blend of sexuality and death he sensed in these wooden female icons.

Neruda loved all women, but at the time I knew him, he was confining his attentions to his strikingly beautiful young wife.

He loved esoteric forms of beauty, including some that other people considered ugly. Besides women, Neruda accumulated immense collections of paintings, antique furniture, rare books, butterflies and the kinds of implements sold by ship chandlers. I once offered to build him a model airplane, a good replica of one of the German Heinkel 111 bombers that destroyed the undefended Spanish city of Guernica in 1937, horrifying the world and inspiring Picasso's evocative painting. Neruda, a great friend of Picasso's, was delighted; a model Nazi bomber was just the sort of incongruity he liked to collect, combining beauty with evil.

I never got to give him the model, because I was expelled just before the 1970 election, and Neruda died in 1973, a few days after his friend, Salvador Allende, died in Pinochet's coup.

Neruda is remembered by many in Chile as a latter-day saint, not because of his flawed political ideas (which were expressed in some rather fatuous poems attacking institutions like the United Fruit Company) but because of the passionate warmth of his speeches, love poems and humanitarian deeds. He lent the communists a luster they could never have achieved without him.

My work as a reporter resulted in many an odd experience. I visited Santiago's public jail several times, where Carlos Altamirano was serving time. Altamirano, a Chilean senator, had been sent to prison by a court-martial after allegedly slandering an army general.

To me, Altamirano's incarceration gave the lie to one of the State Department's favorite predictions: that democratic Chile and Uruguay would never succumb to the kind of military rule that curbed free speech in most other Latin American nations. Foggy Bottom was wrong on both counts.

With the approach of the national election in Chile, I became aware that while I was watching the politicians, various shadowy characters were watching me. I would get peculiar phone calls in the middle of the night from people insisting on knowing my political views on Chile. (I had none, except the hope that democracy would prevail.)

One evening Hy Maidenberg, a *New York Times* financial writer, and I were having dinner at the wonderful old (now defunct) Crillon Hotel when a well-dressed, educated Chilean asked to join us. In polite and courtly Spanish, he questioned me for a half hour on Chilean politics, remarking that there were people in Chile who suspected I was a spy. At the end of our conversation he professed himself satisfied with my answers and said that I wasn't at all the kind of person he had expected to encounter.

Three days later I read that he had died of a heart attack, and I wondered whether the poor gentleman's heart might have been stopped by a bullet.

On another occasion, a very pretty Chilean journalist with ties to the Christian Democrat Party invited me to join her in a Sunday swim at the Prince of Wales country club, where she was a member. As we stretched out on the grass, she first chatted about politically neutral things, some of them sexually suggestive, but she gradually steered the conversation to the election campaign. I realized that she, like the man who had joined me at the restaurant, had been assigned to find out what she could about me.

American newsmen in Latin America and much of the rest of the world never seem able to convince people that they are simply journalists, not spies or provocateurs. Of course, spies and journalists are both in the business of collecting information, but while the spy conceals his harvest, the journalist publishes his.

Shortly before the Chilean election I had to go home to Buenos Aires for a few days to take care of a developing Argentine story. Then, on the eve of the Chilean election, my wife and I boarded a flight to Santiago, where we intended to remain through the voting and its aftermath.

But arriving at Pudahuel Airport we were in for a shock; grim-faced *carabineros* led us off none too gently to a detention cell, where, after a few hours, we were informed that I had been banned from Chile by order of Gabriel Valdez, the foreign minister, and would be put aboard the first plane out, whatever its destination might be. (Le Lieu asked whether she, too, had been banned. "Of course," the official snarled.)

The first flight turned out to be headed for Lima, which lay four jet hours to the north and was completely out of our way. But off we went, escorted to our seats on the plane by two Chilean cops. The sympathetic flight crew plied us with drinks and eager questions throughout the flight.

In Lima I decided on impulse to check into the pleasant old Hotel Bolívar rather than the more modern Crillon, and Le Lieu and I had barely opened our suitcase when the phone rang. "We're watching you, Browne, and if you don't watch your step, we're going to kill you," the voice said. Death threats are fairly common for journalists, but what I didn't like was the realization that someone was dogging my steps pretty closely, even outside Chile.

The threatening caller might have been from any one of a number of organizations, but I couldn't help suspecting the fine Italian hand of the CIA, which sometimes surprised me with the reach of its arms. About six years after I was expelled from Chile I was covering Czechoslovakia, where, in due course, I met the political counselor at the U.S. Embassy. He told me he had known of me not only from my newspaper reporting but from the transcript of a conversation he had read. The conversation had taken place during a party in my home in Buenos Aires, at which the Czech ambassador had been one of my guests. The CIA spy at my party, whoever he may have been, had filed a long memorandum of the conversations he overheard, not only mine, but of the Czech ambassador representing Alexander Dubcek, the president who tried vainly in 1968 to pull his country out of the Soviet orbit.

I left South America soon after the Chilean election because a war was brewing in Pakistan and I was needed there. In some ways I was fed up with the vicious chicanery of Latin American politics by the time I left, but I guess South America wouldn't be quite the same without intrigue, romance and a hint of murder in the air.

And there was much, much more for me than strife and tragedy. I carried away delicious memories: the *Carnaval* devil dancers of Oruro; the mystic Inca ruins at Machu Picchu; the menacing black headwaters of the Amazon in Peru; a submarine expedition in search of Inca treasure in the depths of Lake Titicaca; a school for thieves and cutthroats at Buenaventura, Colombia; the glowering *moais* of Easter Island where "short ears" and "long ears" mingle with foreign spies; and Patagonia,

Tierra del Fuego and the Galápagos Islands of Darwin, where feathers and fur still make scientists ponder.

There's a passage in Conan Doyle's great science-fiction novel *The Lost World,* where Lord John Roxton, one of the adventurers, tells a companion: "South America is a place I love, and I think, if you take it right through from Darien to Fuego, it's the grandest, richest, most wonderful bit of earth upon this planet." He was right.

I still return to Chile every now and then, because I'm a science writer these days, and the pure air of the country's mountaintops has attracted some of the world's greatest astronomical observatories.

But on one recent trip I strolled through Santiago's gigantic General Cemetery, the resting place of both high and low. I looked at the graves of people I had known—at the modest, rose-colored marker of the late President Frei, and at the enormous white monument honoring the late President Allende. I looked at hundreds of unmarked graves, many of them freshly disinterred by forensic experts, where some of the *desaparecidos,* the victims of Pinochet's death squads, had been hidden.

Most of the Christian Democrats survived the terror, and I found that Gabriel Valdez, my expeller, was back in business as president of the Chilean Senate. A new Eduardo Frei, the son of the late president, was himself preparing to run for high office.

The biggest change was in the character of Santiago's streets, which I found had been transformed by years of military dictatorship. Hundreds of new stores bountifully stocked with all kinds of goods at reasonable prices lined the new shopping malls, and modern buildings had sprung up like mushrooms. There were some beggars and quite a few muggers, but Santiago was no longer the threadbare, drab, impoverished capital it had been under democracy. Without question, brutal dictatorship had restored the nation's economy to the bloom of health, had ended the bloody street battles and had even permitted the restoration of a limited Latin American–style democracy. The thousands who died as Pinochet's sacrifices to the god of order are still dead, but so are millions of other victims of repression throughout the world, and the world keeps turning.

It's enough to make a man a cynic.

SCHISM IN PAKISTAN

IN THE SPRING OF 1971, simmering religious, ethnic and political conflicts in the Indian subcontinent reached one of their periodic flashpoints, and a bloodbath began. Since nothing nearly as dramatic was going on in Latin America at the time, *The New York Times* asked me to pack up, leave Buenos Aires and fly to Pakistan as soon as possible.

This was not as much fun as it might sound. Packing an apartment full of belongings into crates that will be placed in storage for years takes careful planning and soul-searching. Bitter experience had taught me that anything stored in a New York warehouse is invariably plundered, so decisions as to what to store are really choices of which possessions will have to be abandoned to the thieves. Since a war correspondent cannot lug along more than a suitcase or two even on an indefinite assignment, pack rats like my wife and me have lost a lot of things over the years.

Why did we acquire so much stuff in the first place? I suppose it stems from psychopathic quirks shared by many in our line of work. Foreign correspondents without roots, anchors or real homes sometimes crave surrogates, odd bits of furniture, antique firearms, pottery, all kinds of costly impedimenta better off in museums than in hotel rooms or warehouses. Thus, we bring prosperity to thieves all around the world, and we never learn to quit buying things.

Le Lieu and I didn't quite realize when we gave up our spacious apartment in Buenos Aires that we were about to spend two years with no home at all, always jumping from one hotel room or field bunk to another.

The only item Le Lieu and I never considered leaving behind was our dog, Nif-Naf, even though we were heading for a fundamentalist Muslim country where dogs are despised as pariahs. Nif-Naf, already a veteran of war in Viet Nam and Cambodia and a tear gas victim in Argentina, was to have his share of alarming adventures in Pakistan, including bombardment by the Indian Air Force.

It was about three A.M. when Le Lieu, Nif-Naf and I staggered off a Pan Am flight in Karachi, where we were met by some of the meanest cops in the world. As usual, a sand haze from the Sind desert was blowing, and the hot air looked dirty and yellow wherever an airport searchlight pierced it.

Pakistan was in crisis at that point, and all Western newsmen were regarded as enemies. The trouble had started earlier in the year when a charismatic Bengali politician, Sheikh Mujib-ur Rahman, was elected as leader of East Pakistan, the region that is now Bangla Desh. When he later sought to lead East Pakistan into secession from West Pakistan, which lies nine hundred miles across India to the west, Pakistani troops moved into Dacca, the Bengali capital. They arrested Sheikh Mujib and shot everyone who looked like trouble.

Pakistan's dictator, General Agha Mohammad Yahya Khan, announced that he would not halt the bloody repression in East Pakistan until his troops had completely wiped out rebel Bengali forces (which included the famous old East Bengal Regiment, a relic of centuries of British rule) and the guerrillas who supported them. To make his point, he put the province under a particularly nasty viceroy, General Tikka (meaning "red hot") Khan.

The East Pakistan slaughter, coming on the heels of a devastating cyclone that had killed about a half million people, caught the attention of the Western press, and news reports of atrocities caused a howl of indignation from human-rights supporters around the world. Those news articles stung Pakistan's leaders painfully, and they itched for revenge. I really believe that Yahya's hard-line officers, left to themselves, would have slaughtered all the foreign newsmen in the country. The correspondents, it seemed to them, were enemy provocateurs and spies, whose lives should have been forfeit.

But Pakistan was heavily dependent on foreign aid, particularly from the United States, and even Islamabad's generals realized that the killing of American and European newsmen would have undesirable economic effects.

Short of executions, however, there were many other ways to deal with the press. When a move to bar foreign newsmen from Pakistan altogether resulted in a warning from the West that vital foreign aid would be curtailed, the regime relented. But newsmen who had been in East Pakistan when West Pakistan's expeditionary army arrived were quickly expelled. Back in West Pakistan, they were placed under strict surveillance and forbidden from that time on to visit East Pakistan. Authorities censored news dispatches and kept close watch over the hated newsmen.

I was not surprised, therefore, that my wife and I were not greeted with flower leis at Karachi Airport. The hard-eyed security troops searched us as we had never been searched before, confiscating magazines, a newspaper, my clippings and notes, a tape recorder, film, and many other things. Our cash was counted and recounted, I signed a dozen sworn statements of various kinds, and I was questioned for nearly an hour about any contacts I might have in Pakistan or India.

The sun and the thermometer were both rising by the time we got into a ramshackle airport taxi and sped toward town through the sand haze, passing incurious camels and their drivers.

The owner of our taxi glanced back at Nif-Naf with an expression of revulsion but said nothing, since he needed the fare and probably didn't want to risk losing a customer. But he expressed his feelings in another way. As we roared past a row of shanties along the straight, dusty highway, the driver spotted a yellow dog scratching itself by the roadside, and flicking the wheel, he swerved and hit the dog head-on. Looking back, I could see a pool of blood spreading from the mangled remains.

Luckily, the chambermaids at the Intercontinental Hotel had no such hatred of dogs, possibly because they themselves were pariahs in a fundamentalist Muslim society. Working women in Pakistan, including doctors, scholars and office secretaries as well as hotel chambermaids, are widely regarded as whores.

Pakistan's medieval attitudes toward women pleased the rulers of other fundamentalist societies, who liked the way Pakistanis whipped their women into shape. I well remember the annual mango-juice-and-caviar receptions given in Karachi by the sheikh of one of the Persian Gulf principalities, who used to fly over every year to buy Pakistani women for his harem. The women themselves were never invited to his receptions, of course.

I'm no psychologist, but it has sometimes seemed to me that Islamic attitudes toward women may reflect a widespread and deeply rooted male sense of sexual inadequacy. The classified advertisements in Pakistani newspapers contain pages of notices from doctors, quacks and nostrum salesmen guaranteeing to cure impotence and other male sexual disorders. Some offer instruction in the technique of withdrawing one's semen after intercourse to avoid losing precious body fluid, a skill the late Iranian leader, the Ayatollah Khomeini, believed was important to his well-being. To infidels like me this stuff seems a bit peculiar.

I spoke not a word of Urdu when I arrived in Karachi (although I picked up a little later on), and the first few days were spent feeling my way around what must be one of the ten most ugly cities in the world. There were miles of red tape to be sorted out, money to be changed and other housekeeping chores, besides getting up to speed on Pakistani politics as fast as possible. The main thing my employer wanted me to do was to get to East Pakistan as fast as possible.

Thanks to a lot of pressure from Washington and other capitals, Yahya Khan gave in on his press quarantine and he formed a six-man group of foreign correspondents that would be permitted to make a closely supervised visit to East Pakistan. Barely a week after leaving Buenos Aires I was again headed for a war.

Although the distance between Karachi and Dacca is only about nine hundred miles, India was ready to shoot down any Pakistani-flag carrier entering its airspace, so our flight took us far to the south of the horn of India and consumedmore than eight hours.

While the scenery around Karachi resembled the Arabian desert, I discovered that Bengal, which borders on Burma, looks more like Southeast Asia. Approaching Dacca, we flew over a flat, watery countryside covered with rice and jute paddies strikingly reminiscent of those of Indochina. For me, it almost seemed like going home.

But on the ground the illusion evaporated. Emaciated men, women and children with sun-blackened, leathery skin and eyes bulging from hollow sockets gazed listlessly at our group and our uniformed guides. A few approached us, moaning and reaching out for alms, but most just stared. The people looked neither hostile nor friendly, just dead.

After the usual baggage and body searches by the security men (in which more magazines and newspapers were confiscated) we boarded military cars and headed for Dacca. Approaching the city center we noticed that new bamboo fencing had been put up on both sides of the road, completely blocking the view; it was apparent that we were supposed to see only officially sanctioned sights. Dacca had become a Potemkin village with a spruced-up facade covering the horrors within.

At General Tikka Khan's palace, a white stucco building that reflected the glare of the hot sun on passersby, we were duly briefed on the atrocious conduct of the rebel "miscreants," who had been punished by the laws that covered all other lawbreakers. Tikka had little to say that we had not already heard, but when we demanded a chance to go out and inspect the city, he surprised us by agreeing.

Before joining our uniformed escorts and getting into the cars assigned to us, we six newsmen conferred and agreed to try to escape from our minders and split up if a chance arose. Our Chinese colleague, a correspondent from Hsinhua News Agency, was uneasy about joining in what might be construed as a provocation, because Peking was actively wooing Pakistan's friendship at the time. But in the end he agreed, and so did Harvey Stockwin of the *Financial Times* of London, despite the debilitating attack of diarrhea he endured throughout our trip.

So at the first halt our convoy made, we all dismounted and ran in separate directions, our anguished escorts yelling at us to stop. We were free, for the moment, to do our jobs.

During the next few hours we saw plenty of the havoc and carnage behind the bamboo fences, and as we went our separate ways, we talked to scores of Bengalis eager to tell us what the Pakistani military occupation was like. Little of what they told us was news, but it was important for us to report their accounts as well as those of the authorities to maintain some kind of journalistic balance. We knew that all our dispatches from Dacca were being ruthlessly censored, but we also knew that the Pakistani authorities would not be able to hold back uncensored reports forever.

In the week that followed I saw horrors in the countryside that made even Indochina's worst excesses seem mild. Across the fields were scattered the corpses of human beings and cattle, and vultures and kites were fattening themselves on eyeballs and entrails. I was reminded of *The Triumph of Death*, that ghastly allegorical painting by the Flemish master Pieter Brueghel.

In one village the houses were all wrecked, the fruit trees burned and pitiful piles of clothing had been collected from the bodies. Corpses had been hastily buried under piles of red bricks, some of them along the streets, and some stacked up on the porches of abandoned homes. A dozen corpses had been stuffed down the village well, the community's only source of water. The air reeked of corruption.

At a town near the Brahmaputra, a branch of the Ganges River, a Pakistani commander told me, "You don't go around counting the bodies of your enemies. You throw them in the river and be done with it."

The Pakistani Army was not the only culprit. When the bloodletting began, many different groups had seen a chance to even old scores; Hindus and Muslims hacked each other to bits, Bengalis and Biharis beheaded or roasted each other over slow fires, and Pathans and Punjabis from West Pakistan killed everyone who got in their way. I've rarely seen the primal blood-lust so epidemic.

But one thing was clear: that Tikka Khan's men had Bengal buttoned down tightly, and that, at least for the moment, there was little chance of a comeback by the secessionists. After our allotted week in the East, the six of us news correspondents were flown back to West Pakistan, where I got into the swing of general news coverage.

I decided to change my base from Karachi, the largest and most inefficient city in Pakistan, to Rawalpindi in the north, which was only eight miles from Islamabad, the nation's capital. Islamabad is a sleepy little town, but as the seat of government, it seemed to me to be an important place to be near. Rawalpindi, a sprawling, relaxed town with lots of trees, was molded by the British Raj and seemed more habitable than Karachi, in a threadbare sort of way.

Rawalpindi was also the gateway to the Northwest Frontier, and it still seemed like an outpost of the British Empire. Outside the Pakistani Army's regimental messes one could hear the skirl of bagpipes at evening tattoos, and at the downtown shops, one could buy Indian Army solar topi hats and even the proper ribbons to be worn with old Indian Army campaign medals, some of which, bearing the image of Queen Victoria as a young girl, had been awarded a century earlier. I bought a few of them, mostly from tribal descendants of old soldiers, and I even acquired a Kandahar Cross, complete with its rainbow-colored ribbon, a rare medal cast from ammunition casings after General Roberts's heroic relief of the British garrison at Kandahar, Afghanistan, in 1880. I also bought a flintlock jezail rifle, recalling that Dr. Watson began his association with Sherlock Holmes after being wounded by just such a weapon "at the fatal battle of Maiwand."

Among its other advantages over Karachi, Rawalpindi was much cooler, the spectacular mountains of the Hindu Kush and Karakoram ranges were not far away, and Rawalpindi's

Intercontinental Hotel had a great swimming pool. Rawalpindi would also prove to be a very convenient base for covering the forthcoming war, during which the town became a target of India's jet bombers.

After a few weeks Yahya lifted the ban against correspondents in East Pakistan, and I began commuting between the two parts of the country. Sometimes Le Lieu came with me, and besides making Bengali friends, she sometimes had time to explore the curio shops and to window-shop at the herbal medicine and *bangh* shops that sold the local version of hashish, legally available to all registered addicts. (An Urdu phrase we often heard in Bengal was *"Charsi heng!"*—"They're junkies!") We roamed the highlands tea plantations around Sylhet, we drove through the jungles to Comilla and Mymensingh, and we learned that guerrilla resistance had been merely stunned, not destroyed, by Yahya's invasion of the province.

Commercial airline flights in East Pakistan remained on a war footing, despite the government's claims to having wiped out the "miscreants." Before boarding a Pakistan International Airlines plane, passengers were thoroughly searched, and all sharp implements, matches, lighters, hair spray and other potential weapons were confiscated. After passengers were seated, a Pakistani soldier with an assault rifle would take station at the cockpit door and inform the customers that if they tried to leave their seats before landing they would be shot.

During that summer the bombings began. At first the Mukti Bahini guerrillas used homemade pipe bombs that caused relatively little damage, but when India began smuggling heavy weapons and explosives to them, the blasts became more serious. Power stations were destroyed, railroad lines severed, Pakistani officials and soldiers ambushed. The war was on, and it began to look a lot like Viet Nam.

Like the Indochina War, the Bengal campaign showed

signs of dragging on, so I interspersed coverage of Pakistan with trips to some of the countries in the region that Western news organizations generally neglected—Iran, Afghanistan, Nepal, Burma and even Indonesia. It was a globe-trotter's paradise.

The sun of history was setting over Iran's Peacock Throne, but the Shah was rebuilding the ancient city of Persepolis to celebrate the 2,500th anniversary of the Persian monarchy, and a lot of people were enjoying the good times. The fanatic mullahs sulked and bided their time, waiting to avenge themselves on the shamelessly bare-faced women who waded along the black sand beaches of the Caspian for recreation. North of Tehran, endless camel caravans carrying the nation's commerce clogged the roads meandering through the Alborz Mountains toward the Salang Pass and the Soviet border. Iran was peaceful and prosperous, the queen's politically powerful gynecologist was preparing to ban polluting diesel buses, and the biggest national problem seemed to a casual visitor to be the decline of sturgeon caviar. The Russians had diverted so much water from the Volga into irrigation projects that the Caspian Sea was slowly drying up, killing off the caviar gold mine. The Caspian is still dying.

At one point during my stay in those lands I learned of an ingenious Soviet plan for repairing the Caspian. Experts had concluded that a lot of waterways could quickly be diverted by a string of nuclear explosions. New channels created by the blasts would pour water into the Volga and thence into the Caspian, bringing the sturgeon population back.

Those big fish, after all, are precious. A female sturgeon does not begin producing eggs until about the age of thirty-five, at which point the caviar poachers call her a "Cadillac," because a single gravid fish will fetch more than enough money to buy a new Cadillac car.

But the nuclear solution to the caviar problem had a flaw.

Soviet hydrologists and planetary experts did some calculations and reported that the proposed nuclear excavations would dump so much water so rapidly into the Caspian that the center of the earth's gravitational field would shift, possibly inducing an axial wobble or a change in the inclination of the earth's axis. There was the possibility, the experts said, that saving the Caspian's caviar could bring on a new ice age. So the nuclear plan was dropped.

Coverage of Iran's fisheries and caviar industry was a high point of my career. Good fresh beluga nestling in the folds of delicate, buttery blini made by Tehran's best restaurants was a feast for the gods.

As Tehran prospered, fat, sweating, half-naked men belonging to the city's gymkhana athletic clubs paraded around with Indian clubs, beat themselves with chains, and ruled the nation from behind the scenes, helping the CIA keep the fundamentalist wolves and the communists from the Shah's door. Washington was well served by Iran in those golden days before the mullahs took over.

The monarchy in Afghanistan was also nearing extinction, but few realized it. When I learned that two-thirds of the members of the National Assembly were functionally illiterate, it looked to me as if the royal family, which could at least read and write, if little else, was on pretty solid ground.

But I discovered that in the mud forts and mountain redoubts of the Ghazi zealots, power has nothing to do with literacy. Pathan fighters, skillful and merciless in combat, destroyed a British army in 1843, and went on to win two more wars against the British, finally throwing out the feringhees altogether in 1919. The Russians under Gorbachev had a similar experience, this time at the hands of Ghazis with heat-seeking missiles and automatic cannons in place of sabers and muzzle-loading jezails.

The Pathan sport of kings and sheikhs is *buskashi,* a kind
of no-holds-barred polo played on horseback and using a calf's
head as a puck. (In the old days riders used human heads, but the
practice died out.) The only inflexible rule in *buskashi* is that no
rider can use his whip to lash the eyes of an opposing horse or
horseman, but aside from that, the game is pure cavalry warfare.
Le Lieu and I went to a *buskashi* match outside Kabul one time,
but the action was fairly mild that day; only one player and two
members of the audience were killed.

The blue-eyed Pathans believe they are descended from
the army of Alexander the Great, and some archaeologists agree.
But whatever their ancestry, war is in the Pathans' blood, and the
land has been stained for millennia with the blood of their
enemies. In one of the Northwest Frontier valleys in Pakistan
near the Afghan border stands a gigantic concrete monument in
the form of a rifle cartridge, a fitting symbol of the region.

Some of the Pathan tribes so despise national authority
that they resist any form of assimilation and live in a no-man's-
land called the Autonomous Tribal Territory, which lies astride
the Pakistani-Afghan border. It is a region where travelers risking robbery and death are still sometimes kidnapped for ransom.

I became rather fond of one village in the territory, called
Darra Adam Khel. The village's three or four thousand inhabitants, all good Muslims, make guns and high-quality hashish for
a living, only occasionally kidnapping a rich traveler to supple-
ment their income. Outsiders give them a wide berth, as a rule.

Tucked into a mountain valley skirted by treeless khaki
hills, the people of Darra led an ordered and tranquil existence
at the time I knew them. It worked like this: the Adam Khel tribe
was divided into five subtribes, which in turn were divided into
clans and families. Four *maliks,* or elders, all of them wealthy
landowners, administered the town and its industries.

To get started on a new product—say, an Uzi submachine gun—an agent of the town would travel to some foreign land where one of the guns could be purchased or stolen, and would smuggle it back to Darra. The gun was then taken apart, measured, cast in wax, tested and thoroughly studied.

The next step was to acquire from Pakistani businesses such things as steel tubing, rods, wire, girders and ingots, and then to set up the necessary lathes, reamers, furnaces and machine tools, some of them homemade and run by pedal power. Then each family would be assigned to mass-produce one complex part or several simple ones.

It was strange to see a dozen boys, none more than about ten years old, seated at a row of handmade vises, each little worker filing a revolver trigger guard or some other piece of hardware.

As parts were finished they were delivered to clan leaders who supervised their fitting and assembly, finally taking each new weapon out into the dusty street and test-firing it with Darra-made ammunition. These copied guns, very difficult to tell from the originals, blew up less often than one might expect, and many a guerrilla, terrorist or assassin swears by Darra arms.

The village also made sword canes, shotgun umbrellas, ballpoint-pen pistols, folding battle axes, many kinds of spring-loaded daggers and other assassination specialties, as well as traditional mortars, machine guns and pistols.

During outbreaks of peace, the global demand for Darra's weapons fell off, but the industrious villagers kept busy with their stamping mills, turning out smooth black sheets of hashish divided into segments, each one proudly imprinted with the maker's hallmark.

No one in Darra smoked hashish, since the people were moral and upstanding. Murder, robbery and other crimes were very rare, possibly because of the nature of the punishments meted out to miscreants. All the men and most of the young boys packed automatic pistols (some of them genuine foreign-made guns), but despite the constant racket of gunfire, accidents were rare and deliberate shootings (among the villagers themselves, at least) were practically unknown. The town produced crack rifle and pistol marksmen, whose skills the Russians, like the English before them, encountered to their cost.

The dope grown all over South Asia was a powerful attractant to swarms of young Americans in the 1970s, and to this day, many a tribesman regards Americans as a race of amiable junkies. The "Green Door" street in Kabul (so called by American flower children because of the green doors of its shops) was filled with hash houses supplying visitors from the States. Under intense and unwelcome pressure from U.S. diplomats and agents, Afghan customs men reluctantly took to body-searching all Americans with long hair and backpacks before permitting them to board flights leaving Afghanistan.

A lot of young Americans drifted to Nepal, also a Mecca for good dope. So many penniless American kids drifted around Katmandu in those days that the wife of an American diplomat opened a restaurant for them. She sold delicious, nourishing meals (including ice-cream sodas and chocolate cake) to her young customers for almost nothing, frequently feeding them on lenient credit. A good many kids were saved from starvation by Aunt Jane, as they called her.

The lotus-eaters of Nepal were mostly confined to picturesque Katmandu, because much of the country's Himalayan interior was accessible only by long, arduous treks or by plane. Le Lieu and I had somewhat more ample resources than these young Americans, however, so we bought two seats on a missionary group's Cessna and flew to the high Himalayas.

The vicinity of Mount Everest is the most spectacular place in the world. After trekking over alpine trails for a couple of days from the sloping, snow-dusted airstrip hacked out of a mountainside at Lukla, we arrived at a rustic inn that had about fifteen beds. This place, built by a Japanese businessman, commanded a view that included the towering white peaks of Ama Dablam, Lhotse, Nuptse and the citadel of Everest itself, with its streamer of spindrift. There was no heat at the inn, water was brought up on yaks to flush the toilets and brush teeth, and the air at 13,000 feet was so thin that walking uphill was exhausting.

But if the gods ever did look for a place for Valhalla, the base of Everest would be very suitable. A short hike upward toward Everest Base Camp brought us to the Kunde camp, where a Buddhist prayer flag snapping in the fierce wind proclaimed the presence of a New Zealand clinic for Sherpas and injured climbers.

At night the moaning of the wind had a human sound, and Sherpas energetically spun their prayer wheels, warning us that the dreaded yeti was probably afoot. In thin mountain air nightmares and hallucinations commonly afflict even sensible nonbelievers in the supernatural.

A *New York Times* colleague of mine, Christopher Wren, is an expert climber and has accompanied many world-class expeditions, including one in the late 1970s to the summit of Mount Lenin in the Soviet Pamirs. One of the climbing parties on that ascent was a team of five Russian girls, all of whom were killed by exposure to a sudden vicious storm that blasted the ledge where they were trying to shelter. Chris's group found and buried the bodies, but for several nights afterward, Chris and his companions heard the girls' voices calling to them just outside their tents. Sometimes the climbers even thought they heard someone scratching the canvas of their shelters. But there was never anyone there.

Sorely afflicted by tuberculosis and by goiter problems arising from the lack of iodine in their diets, the Sherpas around Mount Everest often received house calls from the mountaineering doctor from New Zealand. Ministering to Himalayan families the best he could, this brave doctor reduced fetal abnormalities with injections of iodized oil into the mothers, and he helped to squelch the venereal diseases occasionally brought back by Sherpas after visits to Katmandu.

Climbing expeditions could count on help from quite a few colorful feringhees living near the Himalayas and their mountain spurs. One of them was Colonel Eric "Buster" Goodwin, retired from the Indian Army, who had fought Britain's wars in the Northwest Frontier ever since his youth, learning to speak fluent Pushtu and assimilating himself into the Khattaks, the leading Pathan tribe of the area. For twenty-three years before he retired in the late 1940s, Buster led local sepoy troops in endless raids against outlaw redoubts, salt-smuggling caravans and bands of kidnappers, trying to provide a semblance of law and order to the region. He had loved his work and missed the days of the Raj.

Buster devoted part of his time in retirement to helping mountain-climbing expeditions prepare their assaults on K-2 and the other famous peaks of the region. On his back lawn, Buster and his Pathan orderly carefully checked the equipment of every passing climbing party, counting its stock of carabiners and pitons, checking ropes and dropping bits of climbing wisdom. He would offer friends like me some refreshment inside his house, and when they admired the huge tiger skin hanging over the foyer wall, he would remark, "Ah, yes. I bagged that chap with a Bland's .577. He'd eaten my father, d'you know?"

English survivors of the Raj lived in all kinds of unlikely places, even in the remote valleys of the former princely state of Swat. Once, after I had been covering a shooting incident sparked by the reopening of Swat's emerald mines, Le Lieu, Lou Kraar of *Fortune* magazine and I spent a pleasant Christmas at a cozy English inn tucked between glacier-laced peaks. The landlord, a retired Indian Army major from Yorkshire, invited us to help ourselves from his well-stocked bar and stretch out in front of a crackling log fire. A longtime resident of Swat, he reminisced for a couple of hours about frontier wars, his long-dead wife and his army friends, shadows from a past that seemed as romantic and distant as ancient Egypt. I've met British colonials coasting through old age in the mountains of Kenya, the Indian subcontinent and wherever else the sun shone on the Union Jack, and all of them were lonely men but great storytellers.

But my main job was to keep an eye on the war clouds gathering over Pakistan, and I spent more and more of my time in Bengal. The bombings got worse, and one blast at the Intercontinental Hotel in Dacca wrecked three floors and sent twenty people to the hospital. Most of the hotel staff, it became apparent, were sympathizers or agents of the Mukti Bahini. Hotel guests these hotel employees considered to be friendly, including, fortunately, all the foreign correspondents, were usually discreetly warned to stay away when something noisy was planned.

I strongly suspected one of the porters to be a Mukti agent, and one day I intimated to him that I would very much like to meet some of the guerrilla leaders. That evening he told me to pack anything I needed in a small waterproof bag and to be ready for an early start in the morning.

Outside the air-conditioned hotel's newly repaired glass doors, two scrawny young men in baggy white clothing approached me. "Mr. Browne?" one asked. "Yes." "*Joy Bangla*, Mr. Browne." "Right. *Joy Bangla*." ("Long live Bengal" was our agreed sign and countersign.) With no further words between us I followed them to a crowded river jetty where about half the people standing around were tall, well-nourished Punjabis in army uniform. "Better not talk," one of my guides said. "The soldiers don't understand Bengali, but some might understand English."

We crammed ourselves into a motor sampan loaded with women, children and livestock, and headed off across the sluggish water. The trip was a long one because we frequently stopped at some banana grove or clearing to let off or take on passengers. Finally, we ourselves disembarked and boarded a much smaller boat with an outboard motor, on which we were the only occupants. "We'll be in liberated territory from here on, so we can talk as much as you like. But sometimes Pak airplanes or helicopters look for us, and if they do, we must hide," one of my guides remarked.

Sure enough, about fifteen minutes later we heard the *pop-pop-pop* of an approaching helicopter. My companions swiftly nosed the prow of our boat into some rushes, handed me a hollow reed and jumped overboard. The idea was that we should remain hidden under water while breathing through our reeds until the danger passed, a trick used in lots of adventure movies, but which is much harder to do than it looks on the screen. The main difficulty is that people tend to float, and staying down is really hard. You need something to hang on to, and even then, you feel your legs getting away from you and floating upward. What's more, you have only one hand free to hold on, because the other is pinching your nose to keep out the water. I guess it takes practice.

After about five very disagreeable minutes, my guides decided we could come up and continue our trip. Once, we caught sight of a pair of Pakistani F-86 fighters, but they were too distant to spot us. I was beginning to see how easy it is for guerrillas to evade regular soldiers, provided the soldiers (like the Americans in Viet Nam) are foreigners who cannot understand the guerrillas' language. I hadn't been able to cover Viet Cong military operations in Viet Nam, but in Bengal I got a pretty good substitute for the experience.

We arrived at a hamlet where the houses were almost

concealed by fruit and palm trees, and I was taken to a wooden house, offered refreshments, and shown to a room containing a large bed. Neither my guides nor the villagers were willing to talk about the war, the Mukti Bahini, or any of the subjects that had brought me there, and it was evident that my hosts were waiting to see whether I had been followed by Pakistani government troops. I had an uneasy feeling that if any Pakistani boats or aircraft did show up, I would quickly land in a shallow grave. But my hosts seemed friendly, for the moment.

Some hours after I had been served dinner and the sun had set I was encouraged to go to bed. I did so, sweating, swatting mosquitoes and sleeping fitfully. But at about three A.M. a glaring light came on, and with a start, I saw that the room was full of men, all carrying submachine guns. "Welcome to Bangla Desh," said the smiling leader. "We are the Mukti Bahini, and I understand you wanted to see us. We regret the delay, but certain precautions had to be taken. What would you like to know?"

Until nearly sunrise I was given one of the most informative and detailed military briefings I had ever had, in which the guerrillas frankly acknowledged their weaknesses while explaining their strengths. One weakness was that they were so distant in that district from the Indian border that fresh ammunition supplies were slow in coming. A strength, they said, was that like the guerrilla armies of Mao Tse-tung and Vo Nguyen Giap, they had learned to swim like fish among the people, everywhere counting on help and support against the hated Pakistani occupiers.

I spent some time with the guerrillas and joined one of their combat patrols for an operation, but we never saw any sign of government ground forces, who were always spread very thinly in the Bengali countryside. When I got back to Dacca's Intercontinental Hotel, filthy, unshaved and with my clothing torn to rags, the porter gave me a wink and Le Lieu gave me a long, juicy kiss.

Le Lieu and I were in Rawalpindi when the big war broke out at the end of November, and Nif-Naf was in Karachi under the care of the hotel chambermaids, who had promised to take him to the shelter when the air raids began. They were as good as their word, and Nif-Naf was never scratched by the hail of Indian bombs that fell on the city and its port.

My *New York Times* colleague Sydney Schanberg (now with New York *Newsday*) was accompanying the Indian units advancing swiftly into East Pakistan, and Jim Sterba (now with *The Wall Street Journal*) was holding the *New York Times* fort in Dacca.

In northern Pakistan, coverage of the two-week war consisted for me of desperate (and mostly vain) attempts to drive to the fighting on the Sialkot front, sitting through mendacious press briefings each evening, and filing reams of cable copy that never went anywhere. It was a while before we correspondents realized that the censors had imposed a total news blackout, so that none of our employers had any idea whether we were alive or dead.

Some in our group spent most of the war playing poker for huge stakes in the hotel dining room between raids, a diversion that had no appeal for me. Instead, I kept moving, and I took my turns ferrying news copy across the Khyber Pass to Kabul, where we could file telegraphic copy freely, thereby getting at least some news out of embattled Pakistan, better late than never.

The hundred or so of us newspeople gathered in Rawalpindi also got bombed pretty regularly. We squawked when the army installed an antiaircraft gun on the hotel roof, marking our home as a target, but to no avail. Luckily for us, the Indian Sukhois, Hunters and MiGs were less interested in the Intercontinental Hotel than in the nearby airport and the arterial roads leading to the front.

The Indian bomber pilots loved to hit Rawalpindi just after sunrise, and few things are more disagreeable than being bounced out of a warm bed by the shuddering nearby blast of a 1,000-pound bomb. The hotel fire alarm, which was supposed to warn us, usually started up only after the raid was over.

Driving to Afghanistan, a beautiful trip through majestic passes and gorges, was no picnic, because the trip could never be completed entirely in daylight, and driving at night was nearly suicidal. Under the regulations, cars could drive with parking lights on or with slits in the tape over their headlights, but Pakistanis aflame with patriotic and religious fervor considered any light shown by a vehicle to be treasonable. Diplomats' cars that shed even a spark of light were routinely overturned by angry crowds, which manhandled and even detained occupants. Pakistanis camouflaged their own cars with brown and green paint, but often spoiled the effect by adding anti-Indian slogans in conspicuous white paint. One popular slogan intended as a sexual slur against the Indian prime minister read (in English): "Indira kisses."

Returning to Pakistan one night after a long drive from Kabul, I nearly slammed into a pyramid of wreckage on the main road, where a dozen cars had plowed into a halted bus. None had displayed lights of any kind, and even with blood running over the road and the dying moaning for help, no one dared to turn on a light. It was just the sort of nutty behavior jihads always encourage.

But I understand that zealous Indians were sometimes just as foolish during the war. Their own hotheads smeared mud and paint all over the white marble Taj Mahal, for example, to keep Pakistani bombers from using it as a landmark. Pak fighter pilots laughed scornfully as they told me this.

One afternoon Le Lieu and I were chased by Indian planes. Driving along the Grand Trunk Road with the windows open (there being no air-conditioning), we heard the screech of distant jets just in time to pull over and jump into a ditch.

Seconds later a fighter swept over and peppered the road with bullets, happily missing us and our car.

The air war was much more accessible than the ground action, and Pakistani Air Force leaders, most of them trained in Britain or the United States, were far more friendly than their army counterparts toward foreign correspondents. The air force chief himself, Air Marshal Abdul Rahim Khan, befriended a couple of us and brought us to Pakistan's main fighter base at Sargodha. (My companion on this expedition was a young woman named Hillary Brown, no relation of mine, whose pluck in both Pakistan and during the final debacle in Viet Nam made for some memorable television.)

We had a hair-raising trip to and from Sargodha, which began before dawn in a military car whose driver believed he could outrace the Indian Air Force by flooring the accelerator around hairpin turns. But worse was to come. Returning to Rawalpindi at the end of the day, Marshal Rahim Khan invited Hillary and me to join him in a twin-engine utility plane, which hedge-hopped at tree level the whole way. We were less than one hundred miles from the nearest Indian fighter base, the Indians enjoyed air superiority, and we were almost certainly visible on their radar. Our pilot intercepted a couple of very unnerving conversations between Indian fighters patrolling near us off to the east, but we made it.

I've always been fascinated by airplanes, and I had a very happy day watching Pakistan's Soviet- and Chinese-built fighters sortieing against nearby enemy bases and coming back with exciting tales of dogfights and narrow squeaks.

But there weren't many days left for the Pakistani side. In less time than it takes to tell, the Indians triumphed in both East Pakistan and on their western front, the war ended (ignominiously for Pakistan), Bangla Desh became a nation, and Air Marshal Rahim Khan overthrew President Yahya. Rahim Khan then summoned another acquaintance of mine, Zulfikar Ali Bhutto, to return from residence abroad and become Pakistan's interim president. (Bhutto had won a free election in 1970 but had been barred from the presidency when the generals voided the election, one of the acts that ignited the civil war.)

After Yahya was removed, the would-be military junta was forced back into the woodwork, although it would reemerge a few years later to sweep aside civilian government.

With the new year of 1972, Air Marshal Rahim quietly restored democracy to Pakistan, setting aside any temptation he might have had to seize power himself. I liked Rahim and wished that all third-world generals were as democratically minded as he proved to be.

I'd gotten to know Bhutto sometime earlier and we had become friendly, partly because he considered New York City his second home. An avid reader, he haunted Brentano's bookstore, enjoyed the New York theater, and enrolled his daughter Benazir (Pakistan's future prime minister) in an American college. Bhutto himself spoke unaccented English, and although he was the head of the socialist Pakistan People's Party, he was no enemy of the West.

That may have been Bhutto's undoing, because Pakistanis, by and large, dislike the customs and social structure of Western countries. Many particularly disliked Bhutto's Western-style agenda of restoring civil rights; Pakistanis, after all, are Third World Muslims, not secular democrats.

In 1977 General Muhammad Zia ul-Haq overthrew Bhutto and had him hanged. After Zia died a new election in 1988 brought Bhutto's daughter Benazir to power as the first woman prime minister of an Islamic nation, a real landmark, but she lasted only until 1990, when she, like her father, was charged with corruption and abuse of power, and deposed.

Meanwhile, Pakistan's military rulers have worked diligently to build a nuclear bomb so their country will be better prepared for its next confrontation with India.

When Bhutto was prime minister I once spent a while at his home at Larkana, which lies in the historic Indus Valley of Sind Province, thought by many archaeologists to have been the true cradle of civilization. We had a Pakistani-American barbecue, and two of Bhutto's kids were there, wearing jeans and U.S. Army fatigue jackets covered with emblems and patches. In conversation and interests they seemed like full-blooded American teenagers, if perhaps a tad less bratty.

With the Bhuttos I visited Mohenjo-daro, the ruined capital of the Indus civilization, which flourished in an era that predated the Egyptians and even the Sumerians. I've looked at many of the great archaeological sites in Egypt and elsewhere, and though they are tremendously impressive, it's hard to understand why so few Westerners have even heard of the Indus civilization. Its ruins bespeak architectural genius and an astonishing gift for making all kinds of mechanical gadgets. The ingenious and beautifully wrought artifacts dug up from the ruins of Indus cities are prized by archaeologists, because few other clues are available to the character of a civilization that was already going strong 3,500 years before Christ. One thing is certain: the Indus people were using flush toilets while the rest of the world was still squatting over ditches.

With all its warts, there are few countries in the world that can match the romance of Pakistan.

In the spring of 1972 I had to move on, this time because of North Vietnam's invasion of South Viet Nam, an episode described in an earlier chapter. I was also due for a radical change in venue, politics, climate and comfort—a posting to Eastern Europe.

BEWARE THE THIRD WORLD

I HAVE SEEN THE future and it doesn't work. It's the Third World, and it's coming our way, as inexorably as the Africanized killer bees from Brazil.

When I lived in South Asia I discovered that a Bengali or Indian or Sri Lankan could fetch more money chopped into pieces and sold as laboratory specimens than he or she could as a live person. The reason for this horrible reality is that medical specimens are always in demand, while there is always a surplus of people in places like the Indian subcontinent.

In just a few months in 1971, war and monsoon floods combined to kill about one million people in East Pakistan, and the Bengali landscape in 1971 looked like a medieval allegory of the Apocalypse. But though death seemed to reign supreme, birth swiftly overtook it. United Nations demographers I knew, whose detailed census produced the first really reliable estimate of population growth in Bengal, computed that another one million people were being created every eighty-four days. Put another way: in less than three months, Bangla Desh replaced all the million human beings whose corpses choked its rivers, floodplains, villages and wells. And since then, the time needed to grow a million Bengalis has been cut in half.

The brutal fact is that most of the people of Bangla

Desh—indeed, most of the people living in the Third World—
are unneeded and unwanted by the rest of the human race, and
living in lands that simply cannot sustain them. Chronic opti-
mists cluck and say, well, all we need do is teach the benighted
people of South Asia, Africa and Latin America to produce more
and to limit their consumption.

Produce what? And limit what consumption? Hordes are
starving already. And are we to tell the Indians and Bengalis and
Chinese and Somalis and Andean peoples that they must curb
their appetites for refrigerators, cars and television? Have we the
right?

To me, Bengal is the Ghost of Christmas Yet to Come,
for it shows what can happen anywhere in the creeping Third
World.

Bengal once supplied the world's jute market, but today's
producers of grain ship their products in bags made mostly of
synthetic fibers, and the market for Bengali jute has largely dried
up. The country sells its only other major crop, Basmati rice, to
China. This brings in some badly needed foreign exchange, but
in return, Bengal often imports inferior Chinese rice to feed its
own people. Bangla Desh and China, in effect, trade rice for rice.

With neither any industry worthy of the name nor a
profitable agricultural base, Bangla Desh has few jobs, and the
poverty of its people is beyond belief. The average person is a
liability to his or her community, not an asset. The only consola-
tion is that most people die young.

But there has long been a brisk market for human skele-
tons, skulls, brains, livers and other odds and ends. Human parts
are used in the West by medical schools, laboratories and phar-
maceutical manufacturers for a variety of purposes, and the
cadaver trade has been largely supplied by India, Sri Lanka and
Bengal. (These countries have all outlawed the export of human
remains and reduced the flow—unwisely, in my opinion—but a
living can still be made from the human flesh market.)

It's hardly surprising, then, that a lot of poor people have come to value the contents of their nation's graves and rivers more than their own living kin. The price of a human skull in America can feed a Bengali family for a year!

When I speak of the Third World, I mean something more than a range of latitudes or distinctive colors on a map, something that goes beyond the numbers describing gross national product, literacy, infant mortality and the other indices of good fortune. I mean a collective state of mind.

The label "Third World" is a euphemism for a domain embracing the urine-drenched sidewalks of New York City and Los Angeles slums, as well as the villages of the Nile Delta, the festering hamlets of Africa, Latin America and Asia, and all the other places where cruelty, intolerance and superstition rule. The Third World is not a "developing" culture. It is a putrefying state of existence perpetually in the grip of a plague deadlier than anthrax: the burgeoning human race.

For the last dozen years I have devoted most of my reporting to science, including the sciences applied to environmental problems. I have become convinced that until population growth can be controlled, all other environmental problems will remain insoluble.

We hear and read quite a lot about these problems—acid rain, depletion of the ozone layer, "greenhouse" planetary warming, the fouling of the seas and the proliferation of waste of all kinds.

Meanwhile, biologists tell us that as we chop away at the wilderness we are killing thousands of species a year simply by depriving them of habitat, and that the greatest mass extinction in the planet's history is now taking place, not because of the impact of an asteroid or the drying up of inland seas, but because of unchecked human reproduction. We are destroying the global gene pool, a resource that might not only have made our planet more interesting but which has given us some potent defenses against disease and starvation.

Some world leaders have begun to worry particularly about the torrent of carbon dioxide we pour into the atmosphere, which may end up warming the whole earth, with devastating effects on agriculture and life.

But rarely do the politicians mention that all human beings exhale carbon dioxide from their own lungs, not just from their chimneys and the tail pipes of their cars. We each foul the global nest merely by breathing.

Moreover, every human being consumes energy, resources and food. We all also produce vast amounts of waste, and something physicists call entropy, an entity that reflects the disorder of systems. Scientists who study environmental problems are in wide agreement that until we do something about unchecked human reproduction, piecemeal attacks on chlorofluorocarbons and carbon dioxide and desertification and all the other man-made scourges will always be inadequate. Our biggest problem is people.

That simple and seemingly obvious fact is indigestible. News directors don't like it much more than does the Vatican, or the mullahs of Saudi Arabia, or any who believe that more is better when it comes to population.

The Third World, like AIDS and killer-bee swarms, gropes outward with persistent tendrils, like the tender roots of plants that pierce even concrete sewer pipes. The branch of medicine called epidemiology has turned up evidence that the Third World has something in common with bacterial cultures and cancerous tumors.

In a bacterial culture, organisms propagate exponentially and without limit, as long as they have food and room to dump their wastes. Given the chance, they will consume every last molecule of the nutrient medium in which they live. But when the nutrients are exhausted and waste products increase without limit, a population crash in the colony inevitably occurs, as every freshman bacteriology student knows.

Less well known is the fact that expanding cities at the close of the twentieth century have come to resemble bacterial colonies that are on the verge of depleting their nutrient media to extinction.

Scientists have noticed similarities, for instance, between the changing shape of Los Angeles as seen by space satellites, and the changes visible in petri-dish cultures inoculated with *E. coli* bacteria, organisms that live in animal guts. Both the bacterial and human colonies expand in intricate fractal patterns, gradually filling the spaces surrounding them. Judging from satellite pictures, human beings in Los Angeles exhibit no more ability to control their own collective growth than do the *E. coli* germs.

Human reproduction also has some disturbing similarities to cancer. In an analysis he published in 1990 in the journal *Population and Environment,* Warren M. Hern, an anthropologist at the University of Colorado, noted some striking clinical parallels between a typical urban community and a malignant neoplasm, a cancerous tumor. They share rapid, uncontrolled growth, they invade and destroy adjacent tissues, and cells (or people) lose their differentiation, the concerted specialties and skills needed to sustain a society or a multicelled animal.

In his monograph, Dr. Hern included photographs taken from space satellites showing the growth of Baltimore and the colonization of the Amazon basin, side by side with photomicrographs of cancers of the lung and brain. They were hard to tell apart.

"The human species," Dr. Hern wrote, "is a rapacious, predatory, omniecophagic [devouring its entire environment] species" that exhibits all the pathological features of cancerous tissue. He grimly concluded that the human "cancer" will most likely destroy its planetary host before dying out itself.

Many would disagree with that assessment, but for what it's worth, my own experience as a journalist bears it out.

And as we contemplate the social, political and economic needs of, say, Somalia, it may be well to remember that kindly instincts may do more harm than good when the real ogre is overpopulation.

In 1990 *The Lancet,* Britain's leading medical journal, included a paper and an accompanying editorial that shocked some readers by saying what public health experts have long acknowledged: there are things worse than merciful death.

The author of the *Lancet* paper, Dr. Maurice King of the department of public health medicine at the University of Leeds, England, has devoted his career to saving lives, and he is no callous crank. But he has observed how excess population inflicts famine and other curses on many parts of the Third World—and how the population plague is engulfing more countries every year. Dr. King believes that for people caught in the demographic trap, there are only four possibilities:

They can stay where they are and die of starvation and disease; they can flee their homelands to seek salvation in more prosperous countries; they can kill themselves off by war or genocide; or, finally, they can live on foreign aid, "first as emergency relief and then, perhaps, indefinitely."

In countries racked by cholera and dysentery, many of the infants who in the past would have been doomed to die of dehydration can now be saved by oral rehydration, Dr. King noted. But when a nation afflicted by cholera is also dying of hunger, a thoughtful public health official must make Solomonic decisions. "Such . . . measures as oral rehydration should not be introduced on a public health scale," Dr. King wrote, "since they increase the man-years of human misery, ultimately from starvation."

In other words, millions of the world's people today would be better off dead, in Dr. King's opinion. Another British scientist, A. V. Hill, asked the following question in an address before the British Association for the Advancement of Science: "If ethical principles deny our right to do evil in order that good may come, are we justified in doing good when the foreseeable consequence is evil?"

The conservative editors of *The Lancet* endorsed Dr. King's shocking conclusions.

"Global population grows by a remarkable 1 million more births than deaths every four days," the journal said. "If a bomb as destructive as the one that destroyed Hiroshima had been dropped every day since Aug. 6, 1945, it would not have stabilized human numbers. . . .

"Through an unhappy combination of indecision, political cowardice, scientific illiteracy and bureaucratic myopia, will human numbers simply drift toward 15 billion?" *The Lancet* asked.

Among the answers proposed for the population bomb are an intensive campaign to educate and emancipate Third World women; a crash program to reduce the economic gulf between the rich and poor nations; and a bounty to any man or woman willing to undergo sterilization.

But many scientists believe such measures will inevitably be too little and too late. One ingenious alternative that some experts are pondering would exploit a harmless virus to spread an epidemic of human sterility for a few years—long enough, perhaps, for the planet to catch its breath.

The scheme would depend on the meshing of two biological techniques, both of which are under investigation. The first is the development of an antifertility vaccine that would immunize a man or woman against conception for a few years, just as people are protected by vaccines against tetanus, smallpox and many other diseases.

The other prong of the new therapy would be the development of a bacterial or viral carrier that would make the antifertility factor infectious—capable, that is, of spreading through-out the human race on its own. Infection of a few individuals with the sterility bug might produce an epidemic that might spread widely enough to reduce the global birthrate for a while, until human beings became immune and resumed breeding.

One of the pioneers in this little-known but potentially important field of research is Dr. Cecil Hugh Tyndale-Biscoe of the Australian government's Commonwealth Scientific and In-dustrial Research Organization. He and other scientists are cur-rently looking into the feasibility of springing something like this on Australia's overabundant rabbits. But the scientists involved are very much aware that the technique might work for humans as well, although, as Dr. Tyndale-Biscoe put it, "I can't imagine the government of Australia or any other nation authorizing such an approach to human population control."

I suppose journalists should be grateful to the Third World for supplying us with much of the dramatic misery we are able to pass on to our readers and viewers. But since most sensible people would want to avoid personal contact with the Third World, here are some of the warning symptoms I have observed that can tell us when the Third World is nigh:

- *People refuse to stand in line for anything—buses, bread, railroad tickets, economic recovery, lifeboats—anything. Altruism toward strangers disappears, and devil-take-the-hindmost public behavior eclipses common decency.*
- *The clan takes precedence over collective society in all matters, even while strolling the sidewalks. Friends or relatives fan out as they walk along, obstructing the way to strangers.*

- *Unenforced laws and edicts proliferate as rapidly as worthless money.*
- *Police take to carrying automatic weapons.*
- *Locally made products break, and the busiest and most prosperous artisans are the handymen and fixers.*
- *Range wars, wars for water rights and wars for simple living space become endemic.*
- *A pervasive religious hierarchy—priests, mullahs or witch doctors—dominates society and suppresses dissent.*

One reason the Third World illness is so hard to treat is that people persist in kidding themselves with euphemisms like "Third World" and "developing." Argentina, for instance, is classified today as a "developing" country despite its retrograde progress over the past half century. In the 1930s, economists ranked Argentina as "developed," because of the riches it earned from its pampas, the vast grasslands that once produced enough cattle to feed a large part of the world. But because of the hemorrhaging of Argentine capital into foreign investments—and because of the country's backward social and political practices—Argentina has declined, and bankers now call it a "developing" country.

Why do otherwise reasonable people tolerate such distortions of language?

Now we have another misnomer called the "North-South Dialogue," a shouting match between the underprivileged nations of the Southern Hemisphere (a.k.a. "The Group of 77") and the alleged economic exploiters of the Northern Hemisphere, especially the United States. The North-South Dialogue has no more chance of a friendly resolution than the Hundred Years War, but it does, at least, provide work for diplomats and journalists.

Elusive though a good definition of the Third World may be, I think it boils down to an overall lack of commonweal, a collective unwillingness to work for anything larger than a family or clan.

Like Pleistocene society, the Third World is violent. It offers constant work for people like my friend Clyde Collins Snow, a forensic anthropologist and defender of human rights, who travels far and wide searching for bones of the victims of Third World pogroms. Snow and his colleagues even sometimes manage to finger the state-sanctioned murderers themselves, for all the good it does them.

Experts like Dr. Snow have some interesting insights into human behavior. For many years Snow was employed by the Federal Aviation Agency as an expert in the identification of bodies from airplane crashes. He examined the pitiful bones of thousands of crash victims, and from them, he came to an appalling conclusion: in virtually all airliner crashes that leave any survivors, the passengers who pull through tend to be sturdy, active men—frequent-flyer business travelers, for the most part. Women and children don't survive crashes very often. The clear evidence, which the FAA tried at one time to suppress, is that in a crash, it's every man for himself, even if this means putting a heel in some child's face to get through the exit door.

That, to my mind, is the essence of the Third World.

THE WRONG SIDE OF
EUROPE'S TRACKS

ONE SPRING DAY IN 1976 a letter arrived in my shabby little Belgrade office inviting me to attend the Bulgarian Communist Party Congress in Sofia, a real wingding, at which Todor Zhivkov would be elected to another five years as dictator, and the visiting Soviet party leader, Leonid Brezhnev, would deliver a stirring pep talk. I knew the occasion would probably warrant no more than a few paragraphs in *The New York Times,* but spring in Bulgaria is very pretty (a bit like spring in western Massachusetts), and there were some news-gathering chores I needed to take care of along the way.

So Le Lieu, our dog, Nif-Naf, and I jumped into the office Opel and headed south into Yugoslav Macedonia, a region of magnificent (but earthquake-prone) mountains, political unrest and excellent goat-cheese salads. After sweeping up some crumbs of news and political gossip in Skopje, Macedonia's capital, we headed east to the Bulgarian border.

The border between Yugoslavia and Bulgaria lies in a lovely mountain pass guarded by a Bulgarian checkpoint and customs office. We stopped for the usual formalities.

To our astonishment, Bulgarian soldiers snatched our passports and ordered us out of the car while customs officials took the vehicle apart, examining the engine, the transmission, the spaces under the interior lining and every other nook and cranny. But it was in my suitcase that they hit pay dirt—a dozen file folders of news clippings, notes and other journalistic material. To the guards' delight, my files contained some news articles distributed by Tanjug, the Yugoslav government-controlled news agency, presenting the Yugoslav viewpoint in the row with Bulgaria over territorial and other claims to Macedonia. Bringing such "propaganda" into Bulgaria, it turned out, was so illegal that I could have faced years in the slammer.

I was led off to a detention cell, Le Lieu was taken to another room, and Nif-Naf was placed in a closet. For the next three hours I underwent an intense interrogation (in German), with insistent questions about my attitude toward the Macedonian question (I didn't give a damn about it), my contacts in Bulgaria (I had precious few) and my affiliations with Yugoslavia's UDBA (secret police) or the CIA or the Mossad. I told my inquisitors that I was coming at the invitation of the Communist Party to report on its clambake, and that if the frontier guards didn't believe me they could phone the protocol chief in Sofia. But the grilling went on and on, and when I demanded our passports back to return to Yugoslavia, the response was humorless laughter.

But as the sun was setting my hosts got bored and someone did phone Sofia. I was released with an apology, Le Lieu was released with a kiss on the hand, and Nif-Naf was released with a piece of chocolate. When we reached Sofia in darkness, our first task was to get our party congress photo identity badges, without which we could not enter our hotel, since maximum security prevailed during the conclave. This meant missing dinner, but at last, two full-size badges were issued to Le Lieu and me, and a small identity card was given to Nif-Naf. After tying it to his harness we took him out for a badly needed walk, and spotting a billboard with a gigantic picture of Brezhnev just outside the door, Nif-Naf trotted over to it and lifted his leg. It was the greatest political act I witnessed all that week.

Perhaps the most significant revolution of our time was brewing in Eastern Europe during my four years there, but superficially the political scene was remarkably calm and stable. For journalists, it was rather nice not having to learn a lot of new names after each election or coup; there was Enver Hoxha in Albania, Todor Zhivkov in Bulgaria, Gustav Husák in Czechoslovakia, Erich Honecker in East Germany, János Kádár in Hungary, Edward Gierek in Poland, Nicolae Ceauşescu in Romania, Josip Broz Tito in Yugoslavia and Leonid Ilyich Brezhnev in the USSR—and none of them changed during my four years in the region. Happily, they're all out of office and mostly dead now. With the possible exception of Hungary's Kádár, they were a gang of despots the world will not miss.

Still, I have strangely mixed feelings about the postcommunist era in Eastern Europe.

In 1993 I revisited the region, mainly to do some articles for *The New York Times* on potentially dangerous Soviet-built nuclear reactors, but also for a look around at places I had known in the bad old days. I was appalled.

The sweet air of political freedom had begun to lose its savor, it seemed to me, and I was conscious of a yearning everywhere I traveled for the economic and political security of totalitarianism.

Crowds of jobless men and homeless beggars lounging around the town squares attested to staggering unemployment rates, and, ironically, some of the injustices that befell Eastern European farmers when the communists first collectivized the area were recurring. With the privatization of lands in former Soviet republics and satellites, families that had worked on collective farms and state cooperatives for several generations suddenly faced eviction under laws intended to restore land to the descendants of the original owners.

A palpable gloom has settled over the Eastern European countryside. Collective farmers who had once conscientiously tended the tiny plots of land the communists had allowed them to farm for themselves no longer seemed to care. Fuel was too expensive to use for heating the makeshift plastic-covered greenhouses they once used to supply the free markets with fresh vegetables, and everything seemed in a state of decay.

In Lithuania, the first popular election since the country's independence was held while I was there, and the main winners were former high communist officials; the people were simply fed up with the chaos of what passed for democracy.

In Czechoslovakia, a formerly prosperous nation now split in two, freedom had brought a drug-dealing underclass of pimps and racketeers, along with high unemployment and a sinister resonance with the strident neo-Nazi movement of Germany. The principal targets of the new Czech and Slovak racism were Gypsies, who were barred from many shops and restaurants, beaten up by thugs and sometimes murdered.

In Bulgaria, the border police no longer seemed to care who entered the country, but neither did police seem unduly concerned by a wave of car thefts, burglaries, assaults and acts of vandalism sweeping even downtown Sofia.

Meanwhile, the mutually hostile ministates that once were bonded within the Yugoslav Republic have reverted to warfare more barbaric than any seen since the Nazi occupation. Mass graves are filling day by day and atrocities have become commonplace. My former Belgrade secretary tells me that one of her acquaintances, a young man, was recently castrated by his captors and forced to eat his own testes.

Ethnic strife smolders in Romania, Hungary and many former Soviet states, and in Bulgaria a lot of people fear the possibility of a confrontation with Turkey, the traditional enemy of many Balkan nations.

The collapse of European communism has left an astonishing and disquieting paradox. People enjoy their new freedom to shout their displeasure with politicians, but when it comes to caring for their families, many people are not so sure about Western "free enterprise." Communism for most Eastern Europeans was brutal, unfair, inefficient and corrupt; but it also guaranteed nearly everyone some minimal level of employment, food, clothing, accommodation, medical care, education and personal safety, the very things many Americans are yearning for these days.

Never have the respective merits of laissez-faire capitalism and state socialism seemed so difficult to gauge. With the cold war over, it's tempting to wonder what it was all about, aside from the territorial shoving match between Moscow and Washington.

But these reflections come long after my first protracted exposure to Marxism-Leninism.

In 1974 the Browne family settled into a large flat on Lole Ribara Street in Belgrade, began studying Serbo-Croatian, and adjusted itself to life in communist Eastern Europe. Before we completed our stay there I was to be arrested three times and thrown out of half the countries I was supposed to cover. Still, I wouldn't have missed the chance to know the fascinating places and people I encountered in a region extending from the Baltic to the Black Sea.

All Western journalists in the USSR and Eastern Europe were considered spies, of course, but we also enjoyed many of the privileges of diplomats: we could shop in the hard-currency supermarkets and curio shops of Moscow and Prague, we could go to the head of the line when applying for a local driver's license, and we were entitled to the same medical care extended to high party officials and foreign diplomats.

But even for the elite class—party officials, diplomats and foreign journalists—there were some problems never encountered in the West. Take dentistry.

Once, when I needed attention for a bad tooth, I went to the dental clinic in Belgrade reserved for diplomats and foreign journalists. The clinic's polite and kindly staff, consisting of two oral surgeons and three nurses, all examined my tooth, excused themselves, and returned ten minutes later with their verdict: the vote was three to two against the tooth, so it had to be pulled.

The prospect did not fill me with confidence because I had heard many a horror story about Belgrade dentistry, and I sighed with relief when I had a last-minute reprieve occasioned by one of the city's frequent power failures. With the lights out I walked away from the clinic to freedom, and the following day I drove to Bonn, where an expensive German dentist fixed my tooth in twenty minutes.

The ferment that eventually destroyed Yugoslavia was already brewing during my four-year residence there. The Tito government, moreover, feared every neighboring nation, where enemies were thought to be waiting their chance to strike. Among Belgrade's nightmares were Italian "irredentism" (the seizure of territory claimed by Italy) from the direction of Trieste; an extension of Austrian influence into Slovenia; an invasion from Hungary by Soviet forces; Albanian infiltration of the province of Kosovo; and Bulgarian nationalism in Macedonia. Alone of Yugoslavia's neighbors, Romania seemed fairly inoffensive, although, even there, tank traps and barricades bristled along the border.

Tito and company had worries at home, too. Within the Yugoslav federation, the Serbs and Croats were always on the verge of fighting, Serbs and Macedonians detested each other, constant friction between Serbia and Kosovo led to shooting incidents and violence, and the Serbs and the Muslims of Bosnia-Herzegovina were scarcely friendlier than they had been when Yugoslavia was patched together in 1918.

As Tito and his hard-line lieutenants became more repressive of any kind of criticism, supporters of human rights in Yugoslavia became more determined than ever to loosen the grip of dictatorship. There was little they could do at home, but since Yugoslavia (unlike the Soviet bloc) allowed its citizens to travel abroad, exile bases of opposition to Tito sprang up in Canada, Italy, the United States and many other parts of the world. As Yugoslav intellectuals and Belgrade's secret service traded blows, assassinations claimed ambassadors on one side and critics of the regime on the other.

But one figure in the human-rights struggle, Milovan Djilas, stood alone. Viewed by Tito as a Lucifer and by dissidents as a heroic Prodigal Son, Djilas had been one of the commanders of the communist partisans resisting the Nazi occupation, and he was anointed as a top national leader after the war. Djilas was a key engineer of Yugoslavia's break with the Soviet Union in 1948.

But Djilas also loathed the local brand of totalitarianism, and in 1954 he was expelled from the government for demanding greater popular freedom of expression. In 1956 Tito jailed his former comrade, but the following year Djilas retaliated with a blast at the communists in a book he published abroad, *The New Class*. He charged that the communists had created an oppressive state capitalism, the beneficiaries of which were mainly the privileged bureaucrats. Djilas, a onetime leader of world communism who had stood at Stalin's side, had betrayed the cause, and Tito was incensed.

Djilas spent many years in jail, but in 1966 the regime realized it was only hurting itself by martyring him, so he was released.

Djilas was our neighbor in Belgrade, and we became friends. Like many Eastern European army officers, he played chess at the master level, and neither Le Lieu (who's pretty good) nor I (who am not) could ever stay with him for more than twenty moves.

Djilas's wit and political vision awed all who knew him, and Amnesty International listened when he pointed out that proportionate to their populations, Yugoslavia had more prisoners of conscience in its jails than did even the Soviet Union.

I spent a lot of time attending and reporting on Yugoslavia's endless political trials, and lawyers from Amnesty International were at some of them, too. One of the best-publicized trials concluded with a six-year prison sentence for Mihajlo Mihajlov, a political analyst and critic of the regime. Mihajlov's sin was a series of articles (including one published in *The New York Times*) that pointed out striking similarities between the Yugoslav communist constitution and the 1933 constitution of Fascist Italy. Tito didn't like being called a fascist.

The UDBA (Yugoslav secret police) terror was ubiquitous, even outside the country. I recall a Yugoslav tourist in Czechoslovakia who made some slurring remarks about Tito while drinking at a café in Bratislava. When this indiscreet tourist returned to Yugoslavia, police confronted him with a transcript of his treasonous conversation and he was sentenced to seven years for disseminating "hostile propaganda."

One of the most disgraceful episodes I reported for *The New York Times* foreshadowed the blood-lusting violence that racks the Balkans today. In 1976, the Yugoslav secret police arrested Franz Miklavcic, a federal judge and wartime hero of the anti-Nazi resistance, in his own courtroom. The arrest rekindled all the ethnic bitterness left by the horrors of World War II—a heritage that is driving Serbs, Montenegrans, Croats, Bosnian Muslims, Macedonians and Kosovo Albanians to kill each other, even as this is written.

In 1945, Miklavcic and a comrade, Edvard Kocbek, were

high-ranking partisans in Tito's guerrilla army, an army that offered little mercy to its opponents.

To understand the brutality that prevailed in those days, as it does today, one must remember that Serbs were butchered on a staggering scale by the Nazi occupation. Croatia escaped the Nazi horrors by joining the Axis, but invoked the lasting hatred of Serbia for sometimes assisting the Germans in mass executions of Serbs. Postwar Serbian hatred also extended to Yugoslav Slovenes, who, by being drafted into the occupying Italian Army, also became soldiers of the Axis.

Miklavcic, the judge, was a victim of this web of atrocities.

After World War II his partisan comrade Kocbek served for a time as a cabinet minister under Tito, and Miklavcic, who never joined the Communist Party, became a judge. But both men broke with the regime, and in 1976 they published shocking articles in a Slovene-language magazine, *Zaliv,* published in the Italian border city of Trieste.

In Kocbek's article he revealed that Tito had ordered a massacre at the end of the war comparable to some of the outrages the Nazis themselves had perpetrated. At the war's end some twelve thousand Slovene troops who had been forced to serve in the Italian Army found themselves prisoners of the British Army and awaiting repatriation to Yugoslavia. The British turned them over to Tito's partisans.

According to Kocbek, a witness of what followed, partisan executioners slaughtered the entire group of Slovene captives and buried them in mass graves. His 1976 article revealed this ugly partisan secret, and many Yugoslavs were stunned.

Kocbek was living safely in exile in 1976, but Judge Miklavcic, who published a scathing commentary on Kocbek's revelation, was not. Secret police raided his home in Ljubljana and confiscated his private diary, which he had been keeping ever since the war years. And on May 17, 1976, the police stormed into his courtroom in the midst of a trial and arrested Judge Miklavcic. He and Viktor Blazic, a journalist working for the local Communist Party newspaper, were tried, convicted of treason, and sentenced to six years in prison.

I attended Miklavcic's Ljubljana trial as a *Times* correspondent. During the tribunal's hasty proceedings, evidence for the defendant was suppressed and he never stood a chance. But human-rights supporters throughout Europe took up the cry against Tito's kangaroo courts, and within Yugoslavia, the Miklavcic trial nourished the seeds of dissolution that eventually tore the country apart.

I think the power of the press really did make a difference to some of the judicial victims of Tito's regime. Miklavcic was released, and he and his family have told me they believe my articles were responsible. I must say that one of the major satisfactions I had from international reporting was in helping to bring pressure on some of the world's political jailers.

But this sometimes brought me up against the U.S. State Department, believe it or not.

The scandals involving Tito's conduct during and after the war disturbed the State Department because American postwar foreign policy was based on the simpleminded premise that any enemy of Moscow was a friend of the United States. For three decades Tito had been our ally in the crusade against Moscow, and the portrayal of Tito as a bad guy was seen in Foggy Bottom as antithetical to U.S. interests.

One official who did not share this reaction was U.S. Ambassador Laurence H. Silberman, a Ford appointee, who arrived in Belgrade in time to create a scandal of his own.

Tito and his "self-managing Socialists" had been stung by the press coverage their political trials were getting abroad. During an official celebration to which I was inadvertently invited, Tito, who looked in his later years like a pugnacious toad, recognized me as I approached the reception line. He might have ignored me, but instead he spat an unintelligible insult at me and turned his back.

Tito's government never arrested or expelled me, but it found other ways of expressing its exasperation with Americans. On July 31, 1976, the police spotted a golden opportunity.

A naturalized American of Yugoslav birth, Laszlo Toth of Loveland, Colorado, had been sent by his employer, an American sugar refinery, to inspect a refinery in the Yugoslav province of Vojvodina. He had brought a camera along, and naturally took some pictures of the Yugoslav plant. To Toth's amazement, he was arrested on the spot as a spy, tried and sentenced to seven years' imprisonment.

I began writing about the Toth case, and my reports were read in Washington. But whatever the perspective there, Ambassador Silberman in Belgrade saw Toth's imprisonment for what it was, a deliberate anti-American provocation. Disgusted, he told me that the Yugoslavs had offered him a deal: freedom for Toth in exchange for an intelligence channel to Washington that would help Belgrade's spies keep tabs on anti-Tito émigrés in the United States.

Silberman naturally refused, and launched a campaign of his own, openly blasting Tito at meetings of the Belgrade chamber of commerce and other public forums. When Tito responded in a speech by denouncing American meddling and naming Silberman as the culprit, the U.S. ambassador began getting warnings and flak from his own home front, Washington. The ambassador was indulging in grossly undiplomatic behavior, which must stop, he was warned.

Larry, a political appointee with no illusions about the permanence of his diplomatic posting, shot back with some flak of his own. At a Belgrade press conference, he announced that the State Department's Eastern Europe desk had tried to get him reprimanded, but that despite Washington's disapproval, he intended to stick by his guns in defense of Toth. Apart from the Foggy Bottom bureaucrats out to get him, Silberman said, he still enjoyed the confidence of Secretary of State Henry Kissinger and President Gerald Ford, and he intended to go on trying to help all fellow citizens in trouble abroad.

As it turned out, Silberman, a Republican, stayed in Belgrade until the election of Jimmy Carter, a Democrat. Before his appointment ran out, Silberman had the satisfaction of seeing Toth freed.

Driving between political trials and the many other news developments I covered in Yugoslavia was fun but dangerous, because of the country's abominable roads. During my residence in the country, there were more accidental deaths per mile on Yugoslavia's roads than anywhere else in the world, although Morocco ran a close second. Narrow and usually without shoulders, Yugoslavia's roads were jammed with trucks traveling in long convoys that could be passed only by accelerating to about 110 miles an hour and getting past a dozen or so trucks at a time, slipping back in lane inches ahead of an oncoming truck. The hazards were heightened by horse and ox carts that moved at night without lights, and by streams of exhausted, half-asleep Turkish and Yugoslav "guest workers" driving to and from their jobs in West Germany. Every few hundred feet black wreaths placed along roadsides marked places where accidents had claimed lives. I had many a close shave, myself.

But the beauty of some of these roads was breathtaking. The mountains of Montenegro and the deep Bosnian gorges where the green Neretva River foamed toward the Adriatic are among my vivid memories. Dubrovnik, the target of Serbian artillery fire in recent years, had some of the most picturesque medieval architecture in Europe.

Sarajevo, also ripped up by Serbian artillery these days, looked when I knew it like a setting for a historical movie, with its old-fashioned trolley cars, fin-de-siècle coffee shops and Turkish minarets. Footsteps cast in concrete marked the street corner from which the Serbian schoolboy Gavrilo Princip shot the Archduke Franz Ferdinand in 1914, starting the World War that carved Yugoslavia out of the defunct Austro-Hungarian Empire. Sarajevo had hardly changed in the late 1970s, and engineers repairing the city water and sewer systems discovered lead and wooden pipes laid down by the Romans. Now war is demolishing that wonderful old city, and a new generation of visitors will never know what it was like.

Yugoslavia was not the only country jailing critics of communist governments. I found myself constantly on the move keeping up with human-rights cases throughout Eastern Europe. Strikes had begun at the shipyards and in the coal mines of Poland, and dissidents everywhere had begun to speak out, becoming targets for arrest.

From Belgrade, Bucharest was a twelve-hour drive across the beautiful but incredibly dangerous roads of Transylvania, and I visited the Romanian capital regularly. At first, Romanian government officials treated me with elaborate courtesy, even conducting my wife and me through the spectacularly beautiful Byzantine monasteries of the mountainous district of Moldavia.

But the regime was one of the most oppressive of the entire communist bloc, a fact that my reporting could hardly ignore. I must add that Washington rather liked Romania, despite the excesses of the Ceaușescu family, because of Romania's refusal to integrate its army with the Warsaw Pact.

Antiregime resistance was stirring. Among the Romanian troublemakers was the writer Paul Goma, whose family was under constant surveillance and harassment. Goma's novels, published in France but banned in Romania, were hostile to the communist regime, and Ceaușescu acted to muzzle the writer. Plainclothes police barred visitors from entering his modest Bucharest apartment, and I had to meet Goma at other places. We knew he would be arrested sooner or later, probably when I was out of the country, so his wife and I agreed that when it happened, she would send me a coded telegram saying *"Bonne anniversaire"*—"Happy birthday."

The cable arrived in 1977. Goma as well as scores of other Romanian dissidents had been rounded up, and I hopped a plane. But when I arrived at Bucharest airport, instead of sailing through immigration as usual, I was grabbed by the cops and taken to a back room. My passport, they said, was a forgery. When I argued, the chief shrugged and said, "Well, you can take it up with our consulate when you get back to Belgrade." I thus achieved the distinction of becoming the first American news correspondent to be barred from Romania since the end of World War II.

I got plenty of practice in being expelled while I was in Eastern Europe, and I have to say that the Hungarians were the nicest ones in kicking me out.

Hungary's tasty soups and stuffed peppers, and the delicious pastry and *Schlagsahne* sold at Budapest's Vörösmarty Café were not the only reasons I liked visiting the country. Although János Kádár had been installed by the Russians in 1956 after they crushed the Hungarian revolution, Kádár turned out to be a moderate who tolerated even political barbs aimed at him in cabaret skits. The regime rarely arrested dissidents, and the yearly anticommunist processions to the monument of the patriot-poet Sandor Petöfi rarely led to trouble. Two prominent writers I saw fairly regularly, Gyorgy Konrad, author of *The Case Worker*, and Ivan Szelenyi, were prevented from leaving Hungary for a while, but both eventually got exit visas.

Hungary's senior officials were far more candid and

friendly toward Western correspondents than were the leaders of any of the other communist countries, and this fact produced both news and trouble. One evening in 1975 an official close to the ruling Politburo invited me to supper at one of the noisiest restaurants on the Pest side of the Danube. The meeting was anything but social.

It seemed that a team from Gosplan, Moscow's planning agency for trade and commerce within the Soviet bloc, had arrived in Budapest and had just laid down the economic law for the next five years. The Russians, I was told, had decided to double the cut-rate price they had been charging Hungary for petroleum, even making the price increase retroactive for several years. In return, the Hungarians were not to get a ruble more for their exports to the Soviet Union—for uranium ore and leather, in particular.

Budapest's Politburo was furious at the high-handed Russians, my informant told me, but the Hungarian government was impotent. As a gesture of defiance to Moscow, it had decided to let me in on its woes.

Carefully concealing the identity of my informant, I filed a story on the Soviet squeeze, which the *Times* duly published. Moscow was so angry about the leak that it forwarded a threatening complaint to Budapest, which was forced to retort upon me. "We're sorry to have to do this to you," said the official who notified me of my expulsion, "but the Russians are angry, and you know how things are here," he said with a wink. "Just apply for another visa a month or so from now, and I'm sure we'll be able to accommodate you." He was as good as his word.

Hungary was a full-fledged member of the Warsaw Pact, its army was integrated with that of the Russians, and Soviet divisions were stationed in the country. The State Department therefore considered Hungary as much an enemy as Romania was a potential friend, ignoring the vast difference between

Romanian repression and Hungary's relative freedom of political activity. An Eastern European nation's relations with Moscow was virtually the only criterion Washington considered in formulating its own relations with that country.

Czechoslovakia posed no dilemmas for anyone, however: it was a staunch ally of Moscow, and it was as repressive as any country in the world.

Physically, the country is very beautiful, particularly the gentle farmlands, forests and streams of the northwestern region known as Sudetenland. Prague, to me, is the most beautiful city in the world. Its cobbled streets, Gothic churches and castle, its antiquarian bookshops and its faint aura of medieval mystery are simply enchanting.

The city's New-Old Synagogue, built in 1270, still functions, and though Czechoslovakia's Jewish population has dwindled to almost nothing, a few Jewish mothers still tell their children about the golem who lives in the synagogue's attic, the monster created in the sixteenth century by Rabbi Judah Löw Ben Bazelel out of animated mud to protect the Jews of the world from their oppressors.

Across town from the golem the Tyl Theater, where Mozart first conducted *Don Giovanni,* is still an architectural gem where great music is still performed.

Until the fall of Husák and communism, however, Czechoslovakia was a sinister and dangerous place. I was followed whenever I drove out of Prague, and I was occasionally stopped and questioned. The Czech police never had any compunction about squeezing American newsmen hard; Bill Otis of the Associated Press rotted in a Czech jail for years.

Czech police surveillance extended even to model kits of airplanes. As I have mentioned, one of my hobbies was building model airplanes, and there was a state enterprise in Czechoslovakia that manufactured by far the most accurate model kits in

Eastern Europe, particularly kits of Soviet warplanes. I wanted to visit this plant, so I asked the government press office to make the necessary arrangements. After six months I received my reply: I had been turned down.

This was not so much of a surprise to me as it might have been to someone unfamiliar with Moscow-line thinking. Communist governments regarded model kits as potential intelligence sources, and to some extent, they were right.

In 1960, the U.S.S. *George Washington*, the first of the Polaris missile submarines, successfully fired a dummy nuclear missile from under water, a landmark that changed the global balance of power. The Revell model kit company, always alert to new kit possibilities, quickly asked the Electric Boat Company of Groton, Connecticut, for drawings detailed enough for Revell to work up a scale model kit of the boat.

Admiral Hyman Rickover, who directed the development of U.S. nuclear submarines, told me years later that the Revell kit had been a disaster for the navy. "Probably the first twenty or so of those *George Washington* kits were snapped up by the Soviet military attaché, and for good reason," he said. "The model included a perfectly detailed reactor plant, complete with fuel core, steam generators, turbine and so forth—all of it top secret. That model kit showed the Russians how a Polaris submarine worked."

At about the same time the *George Washington* kit was issued, another American model company came out with a kit purportedly representing the Soviet MiG-19—a new fighter at the time. Almost everything was wrong with this kit, even the general outline of the plane, and the Russians were delighted with the errors, because they suggested that American intelligence was completely off the track. In 1975, more than a decade later, Dyetsky Mir, Moscow's main toy store, itself began selling Soviet-made MiG-19 kits. The Russian kits proved to be exact copies of the American kits, with all the American errors faithfully reproduced. No Soviet kit manufacturer was going to include anything that might feed Washington's intelligence mill.

The Czechoslovak authorities did let me visit the Skoda automobile works, where I was given company brochures and a tasty lunch with good Pilsen beer, but no opportunity to see any of the production lines. But I had a feeling that embarrassment rather than state security might have been the reason for keeping me out. Talking to Skoda workers elsewhere, I was told that the famous auto plant had been brought almost to its knees by lax management. Workers would clock in when their shifts began, sneak out through a hole in the perimeter fence, and spend the day working somewhere else for a second salary. Just before quitting time they would return to Skoda to clock out. "They pretend to pay us and we pretend to work," one of them told me.

Today, of course, Skoda is surviving largely because of its postcommunist affiliation with Volkswagen, and there is a new worry for the company's workers: the Germans, they say, are taking over everything.

In 1977 some seven hundred Czech intellectuals and human-rights supporters drafted a manifesto that came to be known as Charter 77. It demanded a return to free speech and other concessions to the human-rights movement, and from the moment Charter 77 became public, the fat was in the fire, not only in Czechoslovakia but throughout Eastern Europe. Husák, the Czech party boss, responded with thunder and lightning, ordering arrests and other persecutions for all the troublemakers. Among them was the playwright Václav Havel, destined to be Czechoslovakia's first postcommunist president (and the first president of the newly founded Czech Republic) and Ludvik Vaculik and Frantisek Kriegel, also playwrights.

At the time, however, Pavel Kohout was the Czech playwright best known in America, and one of his plays on Broadway,

Poor Murderer, had just closed after a respectable run; the play was about an actor detained in a mental hospital.

Communist authorities treated Kohout and his wife as privileged citizens until they began criticizing the regime, up to which time they occupied a charming apartment in the same building as the Swiss Embassy, overlooking the picturesque square facing Prague Castle.

Le Lieu and I happened to be in Prague when Charter 77 was coming to a boil, and one night we had dinner with the Kohouts, at which the writer detailed the wave of dissident arrests that had hit Prague. The following afternoon Kohout phoned me at my hotel, his voice hoarse with excitement. "Well," he said, "you're in Prague at a good time. Why don't you come over the river and visit me? The police are outside my apartment getting ready to break down the door."

Le Lieu and I jumped into our rented car, arrived at the Kohout flat in five minutes, and sure enough, a score of uniformed and plainclothes police stood outside the building, with four more inside at Kohout's door. They told us in halting German to go away. No, I told them, I had come to visit my friend and was entitled to be there. We argued for a while, and then Kohout called out, "Wait a minute, Malcolm, I'm coming out to interpret for you. They've already got my wife when she drove up, so I might as well join her."

Kohout opened the door and the police seized him, shoving Le Lieu and me out of the way. The playwright begged permission to leave his dog with a neighbor, and the cops agreed. As they led Kohout to a police car he yelled to me, "Tell Arthur Miller."

After Kohout was driven off as a prisoner, the police demanded our passports, copied down everything in them, and ordered Le Lieu and me to be gone. As we were leaving the building the Swiss ambassador, who had witnessed the incident, reached out, pulled us into his office, offered us drinks and asked if he could do anything to help. I wondered if an American ambassador would have stuck out his neck with such kindness under the same circumstances.

In the story I filed that night I reported Kohout's request to inform Arthur Miller, and the *Times* did so. The American playwright expressed shock.

When the Kohouts were released, the government moved them to a dingy, cramped apartment far from the center of Prague, a strong inducement to leave the country, which they eventually did.

A wave of arrests swept Poland at about that time, which coincided with a visit to Warsaw by Leonid Brezhnev. I was covering Brezhnev's activities, and one day I picked up a story from a usually reliable quarter that an assassination attempt had been made on the Soviet leader. I told the Warsaw press chief what I had heard: that during a reception at the former Royal Palace, one of the waiters had threatened Brezhnev with a grenade, but was subdued by police. The unhappy press chief said he would ask the authorities.

Two days later he told me that just asking about the alleged incident could easily get a newsman jailed, and that I should forget it. I continued my efforts, but never did get a positive confirmation that someone had tried to kill the Soviet leader.

I spent summers in the Soviet Union when the regular Moscow staffers were on vacation, and despite all, I enjoyed working at the heart of the Red Menace. Russia has many attractions if one overlooks its traditionally wretched politics.

Many of the Russians who fell afoul of the Soviet system were initially indifferent to communist politics, but stumbled into trouble unintentionally. One such victim was a chemical engineer named Svetlana Shramko, who phoned me late one night from her home in Ryazan, a city that was off limits to foreigners. This poor woman, who worked for a plant making synthetic fiber for textiles, had complained to the plant manager about the toxic smoke the factory produced, which was choking the city and causing an epidemic of respiratory diseases. When Ms. Shramko realized that her pleas were falling on deaf ears she complained to higher levels of the government and party, finally sending a letter to the Central Committee with a copy to the United Nations. That was too much.

The next thing that happened, she told me, was that she was seized by the plant's security police and dragged off to a mental institution. She was released after a couple of days, but only after promising to write no more letters. Ms. Shramko, of course, was furious, and willing to risk her freedom by telephoning an American journalist. Thus, an ordinary citizen, initially interested only in cleaning up the environment of her community, was converted by a malignant state bureaucracy into an enemy of the communists. I thought her case was rather illuminating.

Meeting such people in Moscow involved a certain amount of tradecraft, as the spies call it. Correspondents often used to meet dissidents across the street from the Sadova Samotechnaya compound, where many foreign correspondents and diplomats lived. Facing the compound was Moscow's famous Puppet Theater, outside which there is a huge clock with animated figures of animals. The clock makes a terrific racket every hour when the mechanical animals perform, and with a crowd of spectators always present, it was difficult for the ubiquitous KGB snoops to eavesdrop on private conversations. So newsmen and dissidents frequently visited the Puppet Theater.

As a former chemist, I was especially interested in Soviet scientists who had been targeted by the regime's displeasure— the great Andrei Sakharov, of course, as well as Anatoly Scharansky, Valentin Turchin, Yuri Orlov and many others. The scientist dissidents who were not in prison touched my heart with their hospitality. Living in cramped poverty as most of them did, they were invariably kindly, always offering a visitor tea and vodka with some fancy, expensive bit of fruitcake.

One of the few scientists allowed to keep his nice (by Moscow standards) apartment after applying unsuccessfully for an exit visa was Veniamin ("Ben") G. Levich, one of the world's renowned theoretical physicists, and a former protégé of Lev Landau, the "Soviet Einstein." Politically disgraced, Levich nevertheless remained a member of the Soviet Academy of Sciences, in which he had an impressive office. But the Academy's library and other facilities were closed to him, and his fellow scientists were forbidden to have any personal or professional contacts with him. It was five years before he finally emigrated, and I like to think that my articles may have helped a little in getting his exit visa. Alas, after arriving in the United States, Tanya Levich, his wife, died of a heart attack, and Ben died soon afterward.

Moscow is at its best in winter when the snow is heavy, the thermometer drops below zero and a thimble of vodka tastes especially restorative. Le Lieu and I first got to know the city during a vacation (from Buenos Aires!) during the winter of 1970–71. We rode in tourist troikas, we went to the Bolshoi, we looked at Lenin's mummy and we ogled the Kremlin treasury.

On one night I particularly remember, we went dancing with a quarter million Muscovites in Red Square. It was New Year's Eve, and everyone within reach exchanged kisses as a blizzard dusted us all with snow. We danced the night away to loudspeakers blaring a medley of balalaika tunes and Russian rock, and people sang drunken hymns to the brotherhood of man. The gassy Soviet champagne Le Lieu and I consumed left us with excruciating hangovers.

The Kremlin's crenellated walls and corner spires tipped

with red stars, St. Basil's onion-domed church, and the black-faced Spassky clock tower—these are true wonders of the Eastern world, with or without the communists.

Even the Kremlin's master, mighty Leonid Brezhnev, had his friendly side. Brezhnev's bushy-browed, grim public demeanor softened when one met him face to face, and he seemed almost avuncular. On one of my visits to the Kremlin inner sanctum I was with Senator Hubert Humphrey and some other American luminaries and correspondents when Brezhnev received us in the conference room adjoining his office. In front of the Party First Secretary's chair at the U-shaped table was a perfectly scaled model of a warship gun turret—just the kind of gadget Brezhnev loved. As we took our places Brezhnev leaped behind the table and swiveled the little turret around, aiming its gun at the American visitors. "See?" he said. "This is our new secret weapon. It really shoots, too, so watch out," he added with a bearish laugh. Later, he insisted on showing his photo album, with pictures of himself as a young political commissar during World War II. "You and we were good friends in those days," he said.

During the long days of summer when the sun never got far below the horizon, Moscow was usually rather short of news, and Novosti, the government press agency, would sometimes arrange for correspondents to visit parts of the country that were normally inaccessible to them. One summer Le Lieu and I, in the company of Peter and Susan Osnos of *The Washington Post* and a few other foreign journalists, were taken through the Ukraine to the Black Sea. We were shown the spas and night spots of Sochi, Krasnodar, Novorossisk and other resorts, and we made the usual mandatory trips to several collective farms.

During that tour of the Ukraine we actually saw a bit more of Soviet agriculture than our hosts might have wished. The wheat crop had been excellent, for a change, catching farm managers woefully unprepared. At every farm we visited we found the silos filled to overflowing, with mountains of freshly harvested wheat lying on the ground, some covered by plastic sheeting, but most open to the rain and beginning to rot. It was an appalling sight, typifying the wasteful management that afflicted Soviet agriculture; as Lester Brown, director of the World Watch Institute, observed, "Karl Marx was a city boy."

Any Moscow resident knew that the country grew plenty of food, but that the managers lacked the least idea of how to get it to market. This led to a thriving black market for fruit and vegetables brought to Moscow by a variety of illegal scams.

History permeates Eastern Europe, and few journalists, even those who must concentrate on hard-boiled politics, can escape the lure of its mysteries and traditions.

In Yugoslavia near the Hungarian border, Le Lieu and I joined an archaeological expedition hunting for the tomb of Attila the Hun, who, fittingly enough, was born, spent much of his life and died in the Balkans. The old Hunnish rat is supposed to have been buried in a triple-layered casket of iron, silver and gold, and if we had found it, it would have been the archaeological sensation of the century.

We didn't find any Huns, but the Yugoslav archaeologists were delighted to find ruins of a large Sarmatian settlement. The Sarmatians were a trans-Ural people who spent most of their history in unsuccessful flight from the Huns, who exploited them as parasites.

There were plenty of old villains besides Attila to interest Eastern European archaeologists and ourselves. One was Prince Vlad Tepes (pronounced "Tsepesh"), the Impaler of Walachia, notorious in the West as the Son of Dracul, or Dracula. Vlad wasn't really a vampire, but he had the habit of driving stakes through the dissidents of his day and planting them upright so he could watch them die as he ate lunch.

But to many Romanians of the 1970s, Vlad Tepes was a national hero. He may have been crude in his methods (exaggerated, many Romanians believe, by German anti-Dracula propaganda of his day), but he steadfastly resisted the Turks. In the iconography often used by Romania's communist leaders, the Turks of the sixteenth century served as metaphors for the twentieth-century Soviet colossus, and Turk-killers like Dracula supposedly prefigured such Romanian patriots as the Ceauşescus.

Romanian tour agencies, however, preferred to leave Dracula as a monster and vampire, an image more likely to attract American tourists with deep pockets.

Hero or monster, the real Dracula founded the city of Bucharest and built a chain of spooky castles around the country that were fun to visit. He also left a mysterious grave under the floor of a monastery chapel on Snagov Island, fifteen miles north of Bucharest. There, Dracula's beheaded corpse supposedly lay for five hundred years, not far from where archaeologists disinterred some of Dracula's victims, buried upright and still pierced by the stakes on which they were impaled long ago. But when scientists dug under the slab in the chapel where Dracula was supposed to be, they found only scraps of a red cloak and some jewelry bearing the dragon crest of Dracula's clan. No body. Take that, you skeptics!

I had to cover a lot of catastrophes in Eastern Europe— train and plane crashes, but worst of all, earthquakes. The first, on May 6, 1976, was centered in the northern Italian province of Friuli near the city of Udine. About one thousand people were killed in this tremor, and the red-brick Renaissance campaniles and churches, along with most of the homes, were left in ruins. Hundreds of pine coffins lined village streets, and people shivered outdoors through the chilly nights, fearful of aftershocks.

One such shock came while Le Lieu and I were asleep in

our fifth-floor room in Udine's main hotel, and it literally knocked us out of bed. As the quake rumbled past with a sound like a speeding train, we had visions of falling five floors and landing under a pile of rubble. But Udine's modern buildings, like the digital departure-and-arrival clocks it supplies to the world's airports, are built to last.

The worst quake I've ever experienced came on March 4, 1977, interrupting a dinner party at our Belgrade home with a crunch and a jolt that set our chandeliers swinging. An American newsman at the party and I made some phone calls and found that the epicenter had been somewhere near Bucharest, so he, Le Lieu and I jumped into a car and drove through the night.

I suspect that the Romanian quake of 1977 helped to harden popular hatred of the Ceauşescu couple, a resentment that led to the ghastly firing-squad execution of the president and his wife on Christmas Day, 1989.

After the earthquake Bucharest's Magheru Boulevard, the city's main downtown thoroughfare, was a shambles. Apartment buildings had telescoped like accordions, taking a particularly heavy toll on the musicians and artists concentrated in the neighborhood. On another downtown street, Alexandru Sahia, the quake had eradicated even the general shapes of buildings and the rubble was piled into a huge pyramid. As the days passed, the bodies buried in this rubble cast a stench over the city that was hard to bear.

Although people could find no good reason to blame the government for the quake, they found plenty of reason to complain about slow government efforts to find survivors, dig out the dead and provide shelter for the homeless. It was one more score to settle with the Ceauşescus.

During my Balkan years I traveled more than I ever had in my life. Belgrade was a convenient hub from which I made extended trips to Portugal for a coup, to Spain for the tense period following Franco's death, to the Sahara for a guerrilla war in the desert, to Egypt and Kenya and even the South Pole.

I also went back to Viet Nam for a while, to witness Saigon's final tragedy.

SAIGON'S LAST GASP

On March 14, 1975, I was gassing up the Belgrade bureau's Opel to drive to Budapest when I received a cable from Jim Greenfield, *The Times*'s foreign editor, asking me to drop everything and fly to Saigon. The situation in Viet Nam had begun to fall apart and he wanted an old hand there to help out.

I was still blacklisted by the Saigon government and I expected trouble getting into the country, but the harried cops at Tan Son Nhut Airport hardly glanced at my passport before stamping it with a tourist visa. While I was driving into town, however, Jim Markham, *The Times*'s Saigon bureau chief, had a phone call from an exasperated official at the Information Ministry saying that the government had just learned of my arrival and was issuing an arrest warrant. I was to turn myself in at the central police station as soon as I got into town, Markham was told.

The French journalist Paul Leandri had just been shot and killed by Saigon cops after turning his back on them, so arrest warrants were being taken seriously.

It would never have done to turn myself in, of course, so Markham met me outside the *Times* office on Tu Do Street, bundled me into a car and drove me to the home of the U.S.

Embassy's press chief, who offered me hospitality and diplomatic sanctuary until my status could be straightened out. It was a ridiculous situation.

However, I still had some influential friends in the Saigon government, and in a few hours I managed to get two of them to put their necks on the line by countermanding my expulsion and arrest order. I was free.

The episode had an ironic aftermath six weeks later, when the same Information Ministry official who had been intent on keeping me out of Viet Nam came to visit the *Times* office. Knowing that I was one of the newsmen helping endangered Vietnamese families get out of the country, this official came with hat in hand to ask for forgiveness and help in getting out of Viet Nam. I may have made a wry face, but I did as he asked.

Saigon was becoming more jittery by the day, and reliable information was scarce. The communists were on the move in the northern and central parts of the country, but reports from Vietnamese commanders and foreign observers (including the various U.S. missions) had become sketchy and contradictory. Markham, who was getting information from an acquaintance in one of the American intelligence agencies, believed that government forces would hold, serious though the situation seemed to be. By contrast, my own information convinced me that the end could be no more than a few weeks away.

The United States had refused to step up assistance to the Saigon government, and President Nguyen Van Thieu, believing he would be better off with less territory to defend, pulled his hard-pressed forces out of Ban Me Thuot, the jungle town once used by Vietnamese emperors as a tiger-hunting resort. Thieu's decision was a fatal mistake that was followed by the panic-stricken rout of Saigon's forces throughout the region. Overnight, South Viet Nam was cut in two, and the effect on national morale was devastating.

Differences between Markham's and my assessments of military prospects led to an argument. When I filed a story on March 20 reporting that the South Vietnamese armed forces were in the process of abandoning two-thirds of the country, Jim bitterly objected, insisting that his own informants were much more sanguine about short-term prospects. Some warm words passed between us, and I suggested we break off the conversation for lunch and talk things over later.

That was the last I ever saw of Jim. When I returned from lunch, Nguyen Ngoc Luong, our chief Vietnamese newsman, told me that Jim and his family had boarded a flight to Hong Kong.

The years passed as Jim and I went our separate ways, and in 1989, I was stunned to hear that he had shot himself in his Paris apartment, for reasons that may never be known.

Normal civilian and military transportation around Viet Nam in the spring of 1975 had almost ceased to exist, so our bureau chartered a twin-engine Beechcraft Baron with a free-lance pilot named Rocky. Rocky and the Baron stayed with me almost to the end.

Rocky would fly almost anywhere, even inside territory occupied by the North Vietnamese. One day one of our Viet-namese staffers had a phone call from his brother in the coastal town of Nha Trang, to report that Nha Trang and the nearby naval base at Cam Ranh Bay had just fallen. The brother said he was hiding from the communists (who had not yet severed tele-phone links to Saigon), and if the *Times* could send an airplane to a secondary airstrip near Nha Trang, he would meet it there.

It sounded like a long shot, but I wanted a look at Nha Trang anyway, so Rocky and I took off, hugging the ground to avoid fire. When we reached Cam Ranh Bay we could see the North Vietnamese all over what had been the largest U.S. naval base in Indochina. The green-uniformed North Vietnamese were setting up gun positions and blocking all runways at the huge Cam Ranh Bay airfield, so we turned northward, circled for a while, and finally spotted the airstrip outside Nha Trang. Rocky touched down at the deserted field, taxied to the perimeter fence and shut down both engines to avoid attracting attention.

We waited and waited and waited, and as the precious minutes passed we could hear the crackle of gunfire from a nearby hill. It looked as though we were going to have to abandon our rescue attempt.

But just as we were climbing back into the plane, our man and his wife appeared at the fence, scuttled through an opening in it, and jumped aboard. Rocky started the engines, rammed the throttle forward, and as we lifted off I could see the twinkle of muzzle bursts just below us.

One of my first trips after returning to Viet Nam was to the north of the republic, where the initially orderly evacuation of Hue had turned into a full-scale rout. The coastal road through the Hai Van Pass south of Hue was a river of agony, through which military vehicles were ramming their way past tens of thousands of civilian cars, bicycles and pedestrians lugging belongings slung from their balance poles, all fleeing the North Vietnamese tide.

The North Vietnamese themselves seemed to be in no hurry. Their artillery would occasionally prod rear units of the retreating ARVN, but the communists seemed to want to avoid causing panic. On March 25, however, Saigon forces completely abandoned Hue, the ancient capital of central Viet Nam, and the panic was on.

In Da Nang, the town to the south of Hue that had been the military anchor of the whole northern region, chaos was also spreading, so I got hold of a Honda motorcycle at the airfield and joined the traffic jam. A colonel who commanded Da Nang's

airport hitched a ride on the back of my bike, and I let him off
at his family's house. "I've got to get them out," he said. "That's
all that matters. The Americans have abandoned us and the war's
over."

The Americans seemed as demoralized and incapable of
purposeful action as the Vietnamese. At the U.S. Consulate in Da
Nang a blizzard of papers were scattering in the wind, blowing
through open windows and doors. A handful of Americans aimlessly wandered around, ignoring the incessant ringing of tele-
phones.

Newsmen learned later that the American officials in Da
Nang had promised to evacuate their Vietnamese staff, but when
the end came, the Americans sneaked out the back and abandoned their colleagues.

Washington's official representatives in Viet Nam were
so distraught they sometimes neglected even to help each other.
The big U.S. administrative hub at Cantho in the Mekong Delta
was never told by the American mission in Saigon that the
evacuation was on. When the Cantho group finally got the word,
officials commandeered some landing craft and sailed down the
Mekong past enemy gunners to the South China Sea. I talked to
some of them later, and they vented seething bitterness.

One of the organizations that did try to get people out of
Viet Nam was World Airways, a charter airline owned by the
flamboyant Richard J. Daly, who had won the money to buy the
line in a poker game. Daly called a press conference when he
arrived in Saigon, slammed a revolver down on a table, and
announced that he was going to evacuate every American news
correspondent. To his apparent chagrin, none of us wanted to
leave.

Rebuffed by reporters, Daly then announced that he
would fly as many Vietnamese orphans out of the country as his
DC-8s could carry. Soon afterward, the orphan lift began, with

weeping Vietnamese natural parents at one end of the line and happy American foster parents at the other end.

None of the correspondents liked the orphan lift, which most of us considered a cruel public relations stunt, causing more grief than happiness. One newsman, however, put the orphan lift to use in getting some of his priceless antique statues out of the country. Wrapping one of the most valuable (and heaviest) pieces of his collection in diapers, he hitched a ride on one of Daly's orphan flights, and when he arrived at Travis Air Force Base, California, a kindly representative of a foster parents group tried to relieve him of his precious baby, only to discover that the rocky infant weighed about forty pounds. The correspondent put his statue into storage and took the next Daly flight back to Saigon.

Another orphan lift, set up by the United States Air Force, had a more tragic outcome. One of the air force's C-5A Galaxies, which were the largest planes in the world at the time, was packed with 243 America-bound Vietnamese "orphans" (many of whom were really just refugees) and 61 adults when it took off from Saigon airport. Something went wrong, and the huge plane plowed into the ground, killing most of the people aboard.

A Vietnamese Air Force officer I knew, one of many who regarded the orphan airlift as a disgrace to both Viet Nam and the United States, remarked: "Too bad. A load of nice souvenirs for American parents, and they're all broken. But never mind, Viet Nam has plenty more to send you."

By then many Americans as well as the throngs of Vietnamese who had worked for them were near panic, and there was talk about the need for some kind of large-scale evacuation plan. Washington did very little at first, except to move the Seventh Fleet a little closer to Viet Nam and to pass the word that if the bugout should come, Armed Forces Radio in Saigon would notify Americans by broadcasting "I'm Dreaming of a White Christmas," a tune so incongruous to the season and events that it would be noticed by all listeners.

American news organizations, by and large, were very reluctant to initiate an evacuation of their own. Except for those at CBS, news executives decided to sit tight and hope that the U.S. government would take care of things when the time came. But it looked for many weeks as if Washington also had no intention of preparing for evacuation.

In Saigon, angry correspondents began discussing possible ways of getting their Vietnamese staffs and staff families out of the country on their own. One proposal was that we pool our resources to charter a DC-6 in Hong Kong and recruit a platoon of Vietnamese rangers to work with us. The idea was that the rangers would overpower the perimeter guards at Cantho Airport long enough for the charter plane to take a few loads of refugees out to Thailand or some other nearby country. As payment, the rangers would get transportation out of the country themselves, a reward we knew would be a powerful incentive.

But in conference after angry conference, the CBS planners finally succeeded in getting the cooperation of the other media in supporting an airlift and bringing pressure on Washington to get on with the show.

The CIA, I'm bound to say, responded heroically, even at the cost of ruffling a lot of feathers in both Washington and Saigon. When the time came, the CIA's spook airline, Air America, carried out a "black" airlift that was as successful as it was unpublicized, and countless people alive today owe their survival to that operation. The news community was just one of many beneficiaries; thousands of others, including Vietnamese military, police and government officials and their families were also taken to safety. I remember noticing that even the French proprietress of one of Saigon's most fashionable bordellos was helped aboard a helicopter and seated next to a fleeing Vietnamese general.

Very few Vietnamese left their country enthusiastically, and many families were torn apart by personal decisions to stay or leave. The decisions were agonizing even in our own office, and realizing that I needed help from an expert in resolving moral and practical questions in the Vietnamese context, I asked *The Times* to send Le Lieu out from Belgrade. She began the trip all right, but before she reached her destination, *The Times* heard (erroneously) that Saigon was about to fall, and that Le Lieu should be stopped and taken off the plane when it landed in Beirut. Our correspondent in Beirut did as he was asked, which landed Le Lieu right in the middle of Lebanon's civil war for a couple of days until she could get another flight to Saigon.

Meanwhile, *The Times* asked me to trim down our bureau as much as possible, getting as many Americans out of the country as I could spare. I believe Bernie Weinraub was the last to depart, leaving Fox Butterfield and myself as the only Americans.

But important though evacuations seemed to all of us, our main job was to cover the news, and we worked long days, sometimes two or three at a stretch with no sleep at all.

I was in the field driving our office Mazda a lot of the time, and sometimes Le Lieu came with me, doing her usual job of picture-taking for *The Times*.

Our worst day together was the time a landing craft docked at Vung Tau, forty miles east of Saigon. The big steel boat had traveled for nine days with a load of refugees from Da Nang, and without food, water or shelter from the blistering sun, more than fifty of the passengers had died. Some of the decomposing bodies of children still clutched dolls as the landing craft limped into port. A survivor said that as the boat passed Cam Ranh Bay, some traders had come out in sampans offering water at two dollars a glass. "But we had almost no money," the survivor said, "so we bought just a few glasses and shared the water. It wasn't enough," he added, nodding toward a pitiful clump of bodies.

At that moment, I'm ashamed to recall, American sailors were enjoying their Cokes and high-calorie dinners aboard the ships of the Seventh Fleet, not far away. But no American came to offer water or comfort to the doomed passengers aboard Vietnamese Navy Barge An 2801. And far worse was to come; the landing-craft incident was merely a prelude to the tide of tragedy that befell countless "boat people" fleeing Viet Nam, most of whom ended up as victims of Thai and Malaysian pirates, or in the concentration camps of Thailand and Hong Kong.

Viet Nam was not our country's finest hour.

During those last weeks and days I was naturally supposed to keep track of the military and political situation for our readers, and one of the things I did was to get in touch with both the CIA station chief and his Viet Cong opposite number.

CIA Station Chief Tom Polgar shared with Henry Kissinger a deep voice, courtly manners and a Middle European accent. A Hungarian by birth, he hardly fit the stereotypical Fordham University–hardball image of CIA field men. Polgar struck me as a man motivated at least partly by strong humanitarian instincts, whose main goals at the close of the war were to avoid bloodshed, to get the Americans and a lot of Vietnamese refugees safely out of the country, and—if possible—to persuade the North Vietnamese to participate in an interim coalition government.

Following the Kissinger–Le Duc Tho agreement in 1973 that got American combatants out of Viet Nam (and won Kissinger and Tho the Nobel Peace Prize), a liaison office of the Viet Cong and North Vietnamese forces was set up in a compound inside Saigon's Tan Son Nhut Airport. There, the communist officers lived as virtual prisoners in the heart of the enemy's country, in a camp named for Specialist-4 James T.

Davis, the first American killed at the beginning of the Viet Nam War, in 1961.

The Viet Cong boss, Colonel Vo Dong Giang, and his press chief, Captain Phuong Nam, held regular Saturday press conferences, attended by scores of foreign correspondents. These press conferences were discontinued toward the end of the war, but the liaison office still received newsmen and took their phone calls. Such contacts were often more informative than the nightly news broadcasts from Radio Hanoi.

During the last month of the war I phoned both Polgar and Phuong Nam at least once a day to listen to anything they might want to impart, and it wasn't long before both sides began using me as a communications link for floating trial balloons. Polgar would ask me how the communists would react to some idea, I would ask them, and they would reply. I harbored no secrets, relaying everything I heard from both sides to *The New York Times,* which printed it all; I was therefore serving the legitimate needs of journalism, and only incidentally acting as an intermediary.

This caused a rather abrasive flap within the official U.S. community. *The New York Times* had published some articles by one of my predecessors that had so annoyed U.S. Ambassador Graham Martin that he refused ever to see me. This was why, although I knew the CIA chief quite well (we had been contemporaries in Buenos Aires back in the 1960s), I never even met Martin.

Ambassador Martin was infuriated by my conversations with Polgar. In a statement published in Kim Willenson's *The Bad War: An Oral History of the Viet Nam War,* Martin described his anger at Station Chief Polgar's back-channel contacts with Hungarian diplomats—and Polgar's contacts with me:

"I didn't even know he [Polgar] was doing that. It was one of the few times that things kind of got away. He was passing

it on to Washington, and Kissinger came back and says, 'You
know what's going on here?' He wanted to know what in the
goddamn hell am I doing letting this go on. He [Polgar] was
using Malcolm Browne of *The New York Times* as a conduit to the
people in the North Vietnamese delegation out at Tan Son
Nhut. I called him [Polgar] in and I told him that if I had any
more trouble I'd cut off his balls and stuff one in each ear."

The gist of the CIA–Viet Cong dialogue communicated
through me was simply this: Polgar wanted a peaceful end to the
war with guarantees for the safety of departing Americans and a
shot at a coalition government. The Viet Cong kept hinting that
maybe such conditions were feasible, but they never committed
themselves to anything, and when the end came, the conquerors
arrived in force, without compromising an inch. Martin, Polgar
and I, among many thousands of others, ended up as refugees on
ships of the Seventh Fleet as Hanoi's tanks rolled into Saigon.

Proof that the war was closing in on Saigon came on
April 7, when two Vietnamese Air Force F-5 fighters whose
pilots had defected to the Viet Cong swooped down on Saigon.
Bombs fell not only at the airport but on the presidential palace
a few blocks from our office, giving all of us quite a scare. From
then on, the push by hundreds of thousands of Vietnamese to get
out of the country became acute, and the CIA's humanitarian
airlift got under way.

All the foreign news organizations had people they
wanted evacuated, about thirty from *The New York Times* alone.
(Included in that number were two of Le Lieu's brothers with
their wives and children. Two other brothers and their families,
as well as Le Lieu's widowed mother, elected to stay in Viet
Nam, and Le Lieu's mother died two years later without seeing
her children again.) Le Lieu counseled prospective refugees,
mentioning the language problems and touches of racism they
might encounter in the United States, along with America's

political and social greatness. The decisions made by the potential refugees were always painful, because all knew that an iron curtain was descending between their homeland and a safe but unfamiliar foreign land.

Everyone involved in the evacuation, "big noses" included, suffered through a hell of doubt, anxiety and guilt. There were times when even Le Lieu and I were at each other's throats as we tried to sort problems out.

But despite President Thieu's refusal to allow any Vietnamese to leave the country (reinforced by the Viet Cong's announcement that it would also prohibit emigration), the CIA's planes started flying people to the processing camps in Guam and to new lives.

Once approved as a passenger eligible to leave on the airlift, a refugee had to find a way to get to his or her flight without being arrested by the police. David Greenway of *The Washington Post* and I were among the newsmen who ran a kind of underground railroad. David and I had neighboring offices, so we could cooperate closely.

Several times a day he and I would don ties and jackets with airline tickets protruding prominently from our jacket pockets. Using our two cars, we would load up as many refugees as we could carry, drive to the airport, and explain to the cops at the gate that some of our Vietnamese friends were seeing us off as we departed for America. The weary police would usually wave us through, and we would proceed to the passenger terminal, park, and go to the cafeteria for a soda. Finally, when we had made certain that the airport MPs and civilian police were not watching us, we would lead our little flocks outside and sprint the last few hundred yards to the entrance of Air America's sprawling compound. Once inside, our charges were safe, and it only remained for us to wave goodbye and drive back downtown.

The trials, tragedies and triumphs of the Vietnamese who made the United States their country is beyond the scope of this chronicle, but it needs to be said they had a mixed reception. Some American organizations that helped them leave Viet Nam simply abandoned them when they arrived in the United States.

But American news organizations, by and large, extended a lot of help to their Saigon people. *The New York Times,* in particular, was magnificent, as one would expect of a great and humanitarian newspaper. The paper made sure every single member of the *Times* Saigon family found jobs and places to live. Many of us owe a special debt to the selfless efforts of Andrew Malcolm, who until recently was a distinguished *New York Times* columnist; Andy personally took care of the *Times* refugees arriving in California, in ways that went far beyond the call of duty.

Those who decided not to leave Viet Nam regretted their decisions. Luong, our Saigon bureau's perceptive political reporter, has been regarded with suspicion ever since the Americans left Saigon, and has led a wretched life under the communists. Life has also been terrible for those of Le Lieu's family who stayed, as it was for millions of Vietnamese.

Spending as much time as we did around Tan Son Nhut Airport in those hectic days, we correspondents witnessed constant intermingled misery, fury, sacrifice, love, corruption, betrayal and selfless nobility. The scene was profoundly ugly. Wealthy police and military officers crowded around Americans like panhandlers, offering newsmen and other foreigners huge cash bribes to get them on an Air America flight. The newsmen I knew scorned these offers, but many American contractors and entrepreneurs certainly sold Vietnamese seats on Air America that they had no way of delivering. These swine would promise rides in exchange for money or gold, or the sexual favors of women. After being paid they would disappear. The weeping of abandoned Vietnamese filled Tan Son Nhut's passenger terminal day and night. Would-be refugees grabbed any American in sight to show him the slips of paper on which bogus benefactors had scrawled promises of Air America rides or offers of sponsorship in the United States.

And there were other Vietnamese with valid papers of their own, who decided at the last moment to trade places with people they considered more worthy, thereby sacrificing their own chances for freedom.

As the final battle crept closer to the capital we newsmen had to drive out of the city every day to see for ourselves where the front was and how things were going. One day Ron Moreau of *Newsweek* and I took a drive toward the besieged government bastion at Xuan Loc. As we neared our destination something about the countryside looked wrong, so I pulled over and stopped. We got out, strolled into a roadside grove that offered some shade, and scanned the surroundings with binoculars. Seconds later a barrage of well-aimed mortar shells began bursting all around us.

Flat on our bellies, we endured several minutes of bombardment as steel splinters from the shells whined past our bodies. With the war nearly over, it was one of the closest shaves I'd ever had.

Things were coming to a head in Cambodia, too, where Sydney Schanberg and his redoubtable assistant, Dith Pran, were covering the collapse of the Lon Nol regime and the victorious advance of the Khmer Rouge. The entire *Times* family was worried about Syd and Pran, and the foreign desk sent me a telex asking that I do what I could to get them out.

That posed a problem. Rocky, my pilot, was eager to fly to Phnom Penh, but was forbidden by the airplane's owner to make the flight unless *The Times* bought an "extraordinary war risk" insurance policy, one that cost vastly more than the ordinary war risk policy that covered our less hazardous flights.

Phnom Penh Airport was under Khmer Rouge fire by then, and insurers did not consider us a good risk.

I knew of one airplane, a tough old C-46, which was covered by the necessary policy. But the plane was chartered jointly by the three American TV networks, who used it for carrying camera crews around and evacuating people from places that were being overrun. I asked the three network producers in Saigon to trade my Baron for their C-46 for just one day, so that we could try to get our people out of Phnom Penh. CBS, ever helpful, and NBC, agreed, but ABC turned me down.

I was angry at ABC, my erstwhile employer, but as it turned out, the rescue mission would have failed anyway. I didn't know it at the time, but Syd had no intention of leaving Phnom Penh, and Pran had agreed to stay with him. Syd did leave some weeks later, and years later, Pran got out too, but only after an unbelievable ordeal of horror and privation under Pol Pot's murderous regime. Pran's odyssey was vividly recounted in the movie *The Killing Fields*.

April 17 was my forty-fourth birthday, and our *Times* bureau family made me a cake, but as we joked and toasted each other the news came that Phnom Penh had fallen, and the office fell silent.

Our own turn in Saigon was not long in coming. Four days later, President Thieu denounced the United States as untrustworthy, and he resigned after ten years in office, bequeathing the presidency to seventy-one-year-old Tran Van Huong. Any who might have hoped that Thieu's resignation might halt Hanoi's relentless drive toward Saigon were quickly disabused; the rumble of distant guns became audible even along Tu Do Street, and Radio Hanoi said Huong was no more acceptable to the communists than Thieu had been.

South Vietnam's frantic National Assembly then passed an act empowering Huong to pick a successor, General Duong

Van ("Big") Minh, the man who led the 1963 coup against Ngo Dinh Diem. Minh was a neutralist who favored a coalition government, and many hoped that the communists would buy him, at least for a while.

On the morning of April 28 communist forces were less than a mile from our office, and we could hear the rumble of their artillery. I decided it was time for Le Lieu to leave, knowing that even a U.S. passport might not keep her out of trouble. There were still a few seats left on an Air Viet Nam 727 leaving for Hong Kong, and as an American, she was able to buy one. (Vietnamese refugees could not use commercial flights without exit visas, which Thieu had banned.)

Around noon Le Lieu phoned me at the office to say her flight had been delayed for some technical reason, so I told her to retrieve her suitcase and get a taxi back to town before it was too late, since North Vietnamese tanks, I knew, were already moving into a former GI recreation compound on the outskirts of the city. While I stayed on the phone Le Lieu passed this piece of news along to the crew of the airliner, and it had the expected effect: they took off five minutes later. The Vietnamese flight crew never even had time to say goodbye to the families they were leaving, some of them forever.

Late that afternoon I joined a mob of newsmen in the presidential palace to hear a little speech by Huong, saying he was immediately turning over the presidency to Big Minh. Huong faltered and coughed as he spoke, and just then a storm that had been gathering all afternoon broke. A torrent of rain swept through the open windows of the hall, drenching all present. As Huong concluded, a thunderclap as violent as a nearby bomb shook the hall, and it occurred to me that Shakespeare might have added just such a touch of atmospherics if he had been around to write about the fall of Saigon.

That night volleys of communist rockets began hitting

the city, each with a whoosh and a roar, and I rose from my bed at the Caravelle Hotel to get to work. It was the fiercest bombardment Saigon had ever felt, and the sky, pierced with yellow tracers and the exhausts of the incoming rockets, grew orange as fires spread. Large sections of the city were in flames as the sun rose, and several thousand wooden shanties had already burned to the ground.

With the coming of daylight, we watched American and Vietnamese gunships pouring streams of tracers at the enemy rocket positions across the river, but enemy tracers were rising toward the friendly aircraft, and from the roof of the Caravelle, we saw at least one plane shot down in flames.

That morning I filed lengthy descriptions of the night's activity to New York, and then went driving for a look around, leaving Fox Butterfield in the office to man the phones and answer the inevitable flood of questions from our editors.

Saigon was sorely wounded, and it wrenched my heart to see the damage to landmarks that had been so much a part of my life for so many years. The woman who sold cigarettes outside our office building smiled and offered me a free pack.

When I got back to the office in the early afternoon, Fox breathlessly awaited me on the street outside with two pieces of news: our publisher, Arthur Ochs Sulzberger, had ordered both of us to leave Saigon, and the evacuation had actually begun early that morning. There was no "I'm Dreaming of a White Christmas," but the word was getting around anyway.

I was sorely torn. On the one hand I wanted to stay to see the beginning of the new era, but on the other, I felt obliged to follow orders. I knew that *The Times* was not happy that Syd Schanberg had insisted on remaining in Phnom Penh, and I could see the publisher's point.

So Fox and I left. We bade tearful farewells to Luong and the other bureau people who had opted to stay, we strapped on our backpacks and walked to the street corner where hundreds of other American refugees were lined up for buses to the airport.

The airport itself was under sporadic fire despite the cover provided by F-4s from Seventh Fleet carriers offshore. The night before, the gymnasium being used by refugees awaiting transportation had been hit by a rocket, and there had been casualties.

It was late in the afternoon when the military bus Fox and I were riding in reached the evacuation compound where Chinook helicopters were landing and taking off at intervals of about two minutes with fresh loads of evacuees. By the time I arrived the airlift was almost finished, and we hadn't long to wait as we squatted in the hallway of a bombproof bunker with other latecomers. Everyone was ordered to abandon their luggage— everyone, that is, except the television crews; the Marines in charge wanted to make sure the evacuation was duly televised.

The rear loading ramp of our chopper stayed open to provide a field of fire for the Chinook's Gatling machine gun, and I had a good view of the capital as we spiraled upward and then turned southeast. Tears were rolling down my cheeks.

We landed on a supply ship called the *Mobile,* where crewmen searched us for weapons and dope before ushering us to the bowels of the crew's quarters. Officers warned us to tape our money to our chests when we showered, because otherwise it would be stolen. The predominantly black crew below decks cursed the honkies on the bridge, cursed the navy and cursed the Vietnamese. But they were generally friendly to the American newsmen who joined them for a while.

On deck, the setting sun illuminated a hellish scene. In all directions were the warships of the Seventh Fleet, and swarms of Vietnamese Air Force helicopters were hovering over many of them, waiting to land. Each time one of these machines landed, a few seconds would elapse while its crew and passengers got out, and then the American sailors would heave the Huey overboard to make room for the next one. We watched hundreds of millions of dollars' worth of choppers thrown into the South China Sea that evening, but we refugees were thinking mostly of the people we had left behind.

The sea was also strewn with fires and columns of smoke from scores of sampans, junks and work boats that had put to sea seeking refuge. As navy ships picked people up from the little vessels, the Vietnamese fishermen were setting fire to their own boats, partly to keep them out of the hands of the communists, and partly as a gesture of faith that the Seventh Fleet would not abandon them. Before long the *Mobile* and most of the other ships were filled to overflowing with refugee families, but the fleet stayed where it was for several days, and the sampans kept coming.

It seemed like the end of the world.

Only after Fox and I arrived in Manila did we fully realize that the war was over and Viet Nam was gone. I took years to come to terms with the trauma those last days of the war left me, and even now I try not to think about that cruel April.

In 1979 I was based in New York, temporarily covering the United Nations, when Kurt Waldheim, the U.N. Secretary General (who was later fingered as a former Wehrmacht intelligence officer), invited several reporters to join him on a trip to Asia. His goal was to help end the short but very destructive war that had broken out between China and Viet Nam, and to work on a rapprochement between the two Koreas.

Our U.N. group was in Saigon (or Ho Chi Minh City, as the victors call it) for a few days, very sad days for me. Locked inside the walls of a former diplomatic compound, our delegation could go nowhere without escorts, but the communists let us see the deserted shell of Cholon, the formerly thriving Chinese quarter of Saigon, as well as a heart-wrenching orphan school for abandoned Eurasian offspring of departed GIs. I went to a dinner at the former presidential palace given by the Ho Chi Minh City Central Committee—all ethnic northerners. One said he didn't like the food or lazy habits of the *nam ky* (southern people) and would be glad to return to Hanoi when his assignment was finished.

I had brought a little package for the families of Le Lieu's brothers, containing soap, aspirin and other items that I knew were in short supply, and our official minders assigned a car to take me to the family apartment in the Dakau district. But the family itself had been moved out for the day, and they later wrote to my wife to say that they never received the package.

I have not visited Viet Nam since then. Saigon was home to me for a long time, and it's probably true, as Thomas Wolfe observed, that you can't go home again.

WHAT WOULD WE DO
WITHOUT WARS?

LE LIEU AND I resettled in America in 1977, mainly because wars and international confrontations have a certain sameness that palls after a while. My primary interest in journalism has always been the variety of experience it affords the reporter, and in 1977 I was hungering for something different: the intellectual experiences that come with science reporting. I haven't been disappointed.

A science beat has not confined me to offices and laboratories, however, nor has it kept me away from wars. Although science is chiefly about universal realities, the handmaiden of science, applied technology, encompasses poison gas, smart bombs, stealth fighters and germ warfare, so that there's always use for a science writer on the battlefield.

When Iraq invaded Kuwait in 1990 I was nearly sixty years old, but my indulgent editors still reckoned I could be useful. I landed in Dhahran a few days before Desert Storm began, and was duly issued my helmet, a poison gas suit and an antidote kit. But when it came to settling in with the U.S. military, I was in for some surprises.

For nearly four decades after World War II the United States had been unable to win a single war, and one conflict, Viet

Nam, had been an unmitigated disaster. But in 1983 we broke our losing streak with a massive invasion of the communist-governed island nation of Grenada, the first American campaign from which the Defense Department succeeded in excluding all newsmen. United States forces crushed Grenada in short order, but no civilian journalists were there to observe.

I may be unduly suspicious, but I can't escape the feeling that in the Pentagon's eyes, the absence of newsmen in Grenada helped to achieve America's victory there. Whatever the case, the Pentagon certainly organized its press relations in Saudi Arabia with Grenada in mind. It was impossible to altogether bar the Persian Gulf to the thousands of correspondents from many countries who poured in, but by confining newsmen to officially licensed tour groups called pools, the U.S. commanders achieved much the same thing.

The pool to which I was assigned was ferried to one air base after another to interview pilots returning from their raids, but never did I get to cover American ground units in the field. Only after I joined a Saudi army pool was I able to witness a land battle, at Khafji, an abandoned border town in northern Saudi Arabia that had been occupied by the Iraqis. When I got there Khafji was in the process of being retaken by a mixed force of Saudis and U.S. Marines.

As battles go Khafji wasn't much, but at least I saw something of the land fighting—rockets and tracers sparkling under a full desert moon, the stench of burning rubber and flesh, crumpled bodies and pools of molten aluminum from burned-out personnel carriers.

The Gulf War did offer some novelties, including the experience of being bombarded by ballistic missiles. Nearly every night for a while, the big Iraqi Scuds came floating over my hotel room in Khobar, and when the U.S. Patriot missiles went up to meet them, onlookers were treated to an impressive sound-

and-light show. Of course, the Scuds occasionally killed people, including a building full of American servicemen and -women.

One night I happened to be in Riyadh, the Saudi capital, and after finishing my day's budget of news stories I was taking a shower when the municipal Klaxons warning of an imminent missile attack went off. Covered with lather and bored with missile alerts, I ignored the warning bleeping, but a horrendous crash a few seconds later shattered my composure. A Scud had landed just down the street and the windows of my hotel bathroom erupted in a spray of splinters. The shock wave knocked me off my feet, and the hotel lights flickered, went out, and came on again.

Recovering from my astonishment I dabbed at some cuts, threw on my clothes and ran out to the missile's impact site, where I found buildings razed to the ground, a parking lot full of cars half buried in rubble and a pall of dust settling over some bodies. Scuds, I realized for the first time, were somewhat more formidable than harmless fireworks.

But for most journalists most of the time, the Gulf War was safe, hygienic and untainted with the doubts that clouded Viet Nam. Americans were elated by our quick victory over the forces of evil, and General Norman Schwarzkopf, I believe, could have taken over the White House without a shot, if he had fancied a coup d'état.

At war's end I realized that despite a lot of hard work I had really learned very little. I was profoundly uneasy about the whole news-gathering exercise.

On the positive side, we had been able to report that America and its European allies had assured themselves of access to the great oil fields, assuming that we could put out the fires Saddam Hussein had ignited in Kuwait. (Which we did, some months after the war.) Oil, it could be argued, was ample justification for our intervention in the Gulf, even though our forces were used to sustain the brutal and corrupt family dynasties that rule Saudi Arabia and Kuwait. (Luckily for American planners, the ruling sheikhs had the good sense to interrupt the public mutilation and beheading of prisoners for the duration of the war. Such displays make for bad press.)

Another felicitous outcome of the war was the reassurance that sophisticated American military technology could, after all, crush peasant armies, notwithstanding our defeat in Viet Nam.

The Gulf War was dominated by American technology, and our side won. But the glory of victory was a bit dimmed for some of us who had watched the show.

One night in the desert I stood watching the slow progress of a convoy of old Saudi school buses loaded with freshly surrendered Iraqi troops being taken to a prison camp. The soldiers in those buses all wore brand-new, pressed green fatigues that looked as unseasoned and unwarlike as the terrified faces of the boys themselves.

I thought of those young Iraqi conscripts a month or so later when thousands just like them died while running away in full retreat. Our B-52s blew them to bits.

On television we Americans saw precious little of the war's ugly side, and I was left with the feeling that our coverage, while well intentioned, had been fundamentally flawed and misleading.

After the war I was one of the journalists asked by a Senate subcommittee to describe our impressions of military-press interactions, and I testified that news coverage had been so heavily constrained and controlled by the Pentagon that American news consumers had been shortchanged.

Little did I imagine the uproar my remarks would produce. In the months that followed, my Senate testimony and my television appearances and articles brought down on my head an avalanche of angry letters. Who were journalists to intrude them-selves on our nation's military operations? they asked. Which matters more, selling papers or winning victories? The sensation-alist journalist-traitors who undermine the security and morale of our forces deserve any punishment they get!

It was no use pointing out that even the Pentagon never accused us of disclosing military secrets. It was equally futile to remind the authors of these hate letters that democracy depends on a free people informed by honest journalists.

It's slowly dawning on me that honest reporting is the last thing most people want when the subject is war. Ben Franklin wrote that "there never was a good war or a bad peace," but in the eyes of millions of enthusiasts, there may never have been a bad war. War is thundering good theater, in which cheering the home team is half the fun.

When I was a kid one of the best wars of the twentieth century was in full swing, the Spanish Civil War. A lot of Ameri-cans who thought they hated war—Ernest Hemingway, among others—saw Spain as a true contest between good and evil: the satanic fascists on one side and the defenders of liberty on the other. Even in my pacifist family's home, my parents hung on the radio as it broadcast the latest from the Ebro front or the bomb-ing of Barcelona.

Tragically doomed though they were, the Spanish Loy-alists were dying in the good fight, many Americans believed, and if only freedom-loving people had clipped the fascists' wings in Spain, the world might have checked the Nazis without hav-ing to fight World War II.

But the Spanish Civil War had no happy ending. More than a million people died in that good war, and in the end, the bad guys won and shot all their opponents. The freedom-loving nations grieved.

And yet, what did the fascists win in the long run? I got

to know some of the doddering old veterans of the opposing armies—International Brigade fighters exiled to Chile, and Falangists eking out their pensions in Madrid. They ended their days playing dominoes and reminiscing, not so much about the Spanish Civil War as about old girlfriends.

Franco, the archvillain, died peacefully of old age, and with virtually no transitional strife, Spain became a liberal constitutional democracy, as if the bloody passions of civil and world war had never been kindled. So why did all those people have to die?

The answer, I suppose, has to do with some fundamental human need to kill and die for exalted causes, causes that become exalted precisely because we wage war for them. When one looks at war in terms of circular reasoning like that, it doesn't seem to make much sense. Perhaps my mother's pacifist views were wiser than I thought them while she lived.

On the other hand, war has always been popular theater, and I suppose it will always find eager audiences. For me, however, there are better things to claim my attention these days.

There's Antarctica, a gleaming white continent that seems the more beautiful for its resistance to human colonization. I return there every few years to recharge my spiritual batteries, such as they are.

And there are remote mountaintops in Hawaii and the Canary Islands and Chile where thoughtful men and women point mighty telescopes at the origins of our existence.

In 1987 a blazing supernova appeared over the Southern Hemisphere, the nearest such stellar explosion in four hundred years, and Cory Dean, my kind and intelligent editor at *The New York Times* science department, dispatched me to the Chilean Andes.

At the Cerro Tololo Inter-American Observatory, I watched as a platoon of scientists from many countries manipulated their big telescopes, spectroscopes and photometers, hastily gathering and analyzing light from the supernova before it faded out. Night after night, the astronomers were pinned to their video screens and arrays of instruments in crowded control rooms, sweating like racing-car drivers rounding a series of tough curves.

I was not obliged to do anything but watch, so I sometimes stepped outside into the darkness to look up at the stars, something astronomers rarely have time to do. It was chilly on the mountaintop, but there was not a breath of wind. The only sound was the occasional soft whir of machinery as one of the observatory domes rotated, and the sky was so dark and clear one could easily imagine oneself floating in space.

High above the horizon were the Tarantula Nebula, the inky Coalsack Nebula, and the Large Magellanic Cloud, within whose luminous boundaries I could discern the tiny point of light that marked the supernova.

I stared at it, transfixed, as fascinated as a child watching a fireworks show. I was seeing only the ghost of the exploding star, of course, since the supernova had long ceased to exist during the quarter of a million years its light had taken to reach me. But the light itself seemed special. For four centuries no human being had witnessed a supernova so close it could be seen by the unaided eye, yet we inhabitants of 1987 had been chosen for a special celestial vision.

Supernovas are the givers of life. It is the monstrous furnace of the supernova that works the alchemy needed to stock the universe with heavy elements—the carbon from which living beings are created, the iron from which we fashion our guns, the gold that adorns the fingers of our brides.

Supernova 1987A glinted at me with rainbow-tinted sparks. Perhaps, I thought, I was looking at the cradle of a new breed of intelligent beings: an explosion that would provide the material substance to make new Darwins and Einsteins and Mozarts, beings to replace us long after our own solar system flickers out.

I considered, then, whether we humans might at least contrive to leave something by way of a monument, so that any who visited our ancient tomb from the precincts of Supernova 1987A might know that we had been here, that we had thought and created and suffered. But then I thought of Shelley's vision of the statue of Ozymandias, a crumbling remnant in the desert where "boundless and bare, /The lone and level sands stretch far away."

The ultimate tragedy, perhaps, is that at the universe's last gasp, none will be left to behold it. Whatever traces may once have been left by geniuses and fools, by saints and sinners, will all be reduced to precisely zero.

I gloomily pondered this, but then I looked up again and thought: What the hell, that sure is a beautiful supernova! Whatever damn fool blunders we're doomed to make—and whatever horrors may be in store for us, the supernovas of our minds are treasure to sustain us for a long time to come.

Index

About the Author

MALCOLM W. BROWNE spent two decades as a foreign correspondent for wire services, newspapers, magazines and television, covering wars and general news in most parts of the world. His many awards include a 1964 Pulitzer Prize for coverage of Viet Nam, a World Press Photo Award for his famous photograph of a burning monk, and the 1992 gold medal of the American Chemical Society for interpreting chemistry to the public. He is a senior writer for *The New York Times*, and lives with his wife, Le Lieu, in New York City.